The TWO WITNESSES

THE HOLY-GRAM OF BIBLICAL PHYSICS

by Dwayne Sheffield

The Two Witnesses

© 1996 Dwayne Sheffield

all rights reserved. Published in the United States by
The Magni Group, Inc., P.O. Box 849
McKinney, TX 75069

Cover design by Joe Ann and Dwayne Sheffield
Printed in U.S.A.

ISBN 1-882330-29-3

PREFACE

I was born asking why. Why? How come? How does that work? Who told you? Where did you get that? How do you know? It just didn't make any sense: why so many questions, and then answers that left you asking more questions?

On top of that, my dad entered the ministry when I was around eleven or twelve years old and I immediately landed on that proverbial merry-go-round. I spent the next four years under the domineering finger of guilt and scorn. I loved my parents, and now I know they meant well, their intentions were good, considering the way they were raised and how they believed.

Little did I know at the time, the religious input was going to be the catapult for a life of contradiction and, a type of hell. The more I tried to find the truth in the system, the more conflict I ran into. I kept reading "we are without excuse for not having the mind of God." And that we should "be perfect, even as our Father which is in heaven is perfect." And, "Let this mind be in you, which is also in Christ Jesus." There's more.

Needless to say, it wasn't long till I passed from them, "the system." then I found him whom my soul loveth, and that is, the keys to find the answers that I have searched for all my life. These keys, I have included in this book. My intentions for the way I deliver these hidden mysteries are to stir up the pure conscience of the inquirer.

All Biblical references are from the King James version. Reason being, it still contains most of the words that are used for multilevel allegorical interpretation, which is explained in the text.

For those of you who have not read the Bible, you may need to read this book more than once.

Dwayne Sheffield

CONTENTS

	Page
Bob	1
The Meeting	09
The Change	17
The Anger	27
The Baptism	47
The Barbecue	60
The Barbecue-Part Two	90
The Weekend	111
The Next Day	146
The Levels	193

DEDICATION

I sincerely dedicate this work to all who seek, hunger, and thirst after righteousness. May this book help guide you to find that which is your universal birthright: freedom, happiness, joy, and above all - love.

ACKNOWLEDGEMENTS

I dearly thank all the people I have met, and those whom I have befriended, and those who have or have not befriended me. Either way, everyone has been instrumental in my life one way or another and my love reaches out to them all.

There are no words to express my gratitude and love for those who have and do love me, and have tried to understand me throughout my tribulations. It seems I could not have endured, without my wife, Joe Ann, my children and immediate family, that helped me through my tribulation periods. There were years.

It is to you, O life, that I give my thanks. It is to all, I give my universal love.

THE TWO WITNESSES

Chapter 1.
Bob

Bob answered the door expecting Deena to be there for the party they had planned to go to that evening. The guy at the door looked surprised and said, "*Excuse* me, I must have the wrong apartment. I'm looking for Cindy, I thought she said apartment number 302. Do you know a Cindy on this floor?"

"Not really," said Bob. "Are you sure you have the right building?"

"This is 2500 West Wilmer Drive isn't it?"

"Yeah, *that's* the correct address. Would you like to call her and see if you might have gotten the apartment number wrong?"

"Great, thanks. By the way my name is Tony."

"Mine's Bob. Nice meeting you, Tony. The phone's over by the couch."

As Tony was using the phone, Bob felt as though he knew him somehow, even though he was sure he'd never met him. As Tony hung up he said;

"Man, I was a hundred and eighty degrees out of phase. She lives in 203; somehow I had it backwards. Sorry for the hassle though."

"Oh no hassle. Glad to be of help."

"Well thanks anyway Bob. Good night."

"Good night Tony."

About that time Deena arrived and Bob thought no more about it. However, that kinship feeling was still in the back of his mind. It seemed like a couple of weeks had past, when one afternoon Bob arrived home from work, he noticed Tony getting out of his car.

"Hey guy, how's it going'?"

"Great! So far so good. Bob *wasn't* it?"

"Right! Good memory. Can I give you a hand with those books? Looks like you gotta load there."

"Sure if you don't mind, a little help wouldn't hurt at all."

"Say, you got some neat books here. Are *you* into physics?"

THE TWO WITNESSES

Chapter 1.
Bob

"Well, in one sense of the word, I guess you could say that. A good friend of mine is sort of a philosopher. He's working on the synthesis of world religions and theoretical physics. These are just a couple of the books he let me borrow to review a few things we discussed last night at his house. But as far as knowing *physics*, I have no idea what it's about. The *only thing* I understand is its application in the universal order, and I'm just *now* getting into that with James, the guy I'm studying with."

"Wow, that's mind boggling! Does he believe in God or Jesus, or *any type* of religion?"

"At one time he was I guess what you'd call a preacher or teacher, but through many years of research he has been led into *unifying* world religion, philosophy, and theoretical physics. Yes, he believes in a Jesus and a God alright. That's basically *the root* of his whole message."

By this time they had reached the apartment and were setting the books on the table when Bob noticed a Bible.

"You study the Bible too, Tony?"

"Yeah, it goes along *with it*. It's really beautiful seeing how it all merges together into a unified story. The way he explains it, it really fits, without *any* contradiction. Are you into any type of religion, Bob?"

"No, not now. I went through all of that when I was a kid. I haven't found anything that makes any sense. Seems like all they want is your money, and they say the same thing over and over. You know what I mean?"

"Yeah, I sure do. I went through that too. They mean well but they just don't understand the *true meaning* of *money* yet; what I mean is, the *esoteric sense* of the word."

"What does esoteric mean?"

"Well, let's take the word 'money'. Money has a literal meaning such as currency: dollar bills, quarters, dimes and so on. On the other side, it implies *knowledge*, or wealth, riches,

THE TWO WITNESSES

Chapter 1.
Bob

understanding, power, etc. In the Bible, they use the word 'spiritual'. It means the same as esoteric: *hidden* or invisible message. I guess from what I can see at this point, the equations in physics have what they call a ghost theory, or esoteric or spiritual side to them. That's what I'm getting into now. So then, what money really means in the Bible is knowledge, understanding, and wisdom."

"Wow, I hadn't thought about it like that. That's some interesting stuff. Does James have a church or something?"

"Nah', he just shows those truly interested in learning the universal laws what he's discovered and how to find it for *themselves*. Once you can grasp the keys for interpreting the terminology and stories in the Bible, you can understand *all* of the ancient religions, if you understand their terminology.

All I can tell or show you right now, is what I've seen from studying with James. If you're *really* sincere and would like to know more about it, you're *certainly* welcome to go with me sometime and talk with him."

"Sounds neat! I'd really like to hear what he has to say. I learn something new every day."

"I do too Bob. So does James. He'll tell you that himself."

"I hear that! By the way, are you moving in with Cindy? I don't mean to be nosy, but..?"

"No no! No problem. Cindy and I see each other a lot. She has a key to my place and I *now have* a key to hers. She just moved out from her roommates to here, well - *nearly* all moved out. That's one of the reasons I had her number mixed up with yours the other night. I hadn't been over since she got the apartment. We still have a few things to move, but with the way her schedule is, it's tough getting together at times. She sells insurance. Tonight she's supposed to be here around 6 or 6:30, and I was gonna try and show her a few things she was interested in about allegory, woven throughout the Bible."

THE TWO WITNESSES

Chapter 1.
Bob

"I guess one of the reasons I was curious is...well, if you were *going to be* living here, I could drop by and see you occasionally. You see, the other night after you left, I felt like I should know you somehow. I guess there's a reason for everything."

"You bet! I believe *there is*, Bob."

"Well, I won't keep you any longer, Tony, give me a shout when you hear something from James. Here's my number, just whenever is fine."

"No problem, have a good evening. I'll holler at you pretty soon."

On the way up to his apartment Bob couldn't help but wonder how things work out in life. He had almost given up even trying to search for answers. But *this* concept really intrigued him, and in a strange way, he was somewhat excited. It felt good to think there might be hope again.

The next day, fighting traffic going to work was not as frustrating as before; it was almost a breeze. "I *really do* feel better," he thought. His whole day was filled with anticipation mixed with a little anxiety. After parking the car and walking toward the apartment, he felt himself hoping Tony might have called. Then reservations struck. "Am I really going to get into something this time? After all, I don't really know Tony, at all. Who is this James guy?"

This went on for about thirty minutes: "What am I doing! What can Tony and James say that I more or less haven't heard before? Besides, am I really curious to see if *there is* any connection between world religions, the Bible, and science? Oh well, I shouldn't worry about it; everything's gonna be fine. I worry too much! But there's nothing wrong with being a little skeptical. Besides, that's what's kept me from swallowing all this other stuff on religion."

After checking his answering machine and finding that

THE TWO WITNESSES

Chapter 1.
Bob

Tony had not called, he decided instead of going out to eat or cooking, he'd just "nuke" a TV dinner, lie back, maybe browse through the Bible a little, and brush up on some of it's *stories*, even though he had read them in the past a couple of times off and on.

While reading, he kept hearing the words Tony had mentioned about physics and world religions. "I don't see any correlation! How in the world can anybody see natural science in this? There has got to be a..." The phone rang out like a school bell and broke his concentration.

"Hi Deena! My gosh, is it 9:15 already? I had just sat down about 7:30 or so to do a little reading. Looks like time got away from me, glad you called."

After explaining what had been going on, Deena reminded him about the Branch Davidians in Waco, Texas, and other strong cult activity prevalent on the religious market. After convincing her he knew what he was doing, she was a little more comfortable with the situation.

Before going to bed there was a pulling to go back and read -- as if he hadn't finished something, but he couldn't figure out what. After tossing around for what seemed to be an hour, he finally slipped off into a deep sleep.

Bob had made up his mind by the time he got off work he was going to call and check with Tony, just to see how things were going. The hours drug by, but finally the time came to go. Still, no message. He decided to take a shower, unwind and then go out to eat. If he hadn't heard from him by then, he would probably give *him* a jingle.

By now it was seven o'clock and since he hadn't noticed Tony's car around the complex anywhere, he couldn't hold off any longer. The phone rang a few times, Tony's recorder came on requesting the caller to leave a message.

"Hello, Tony, thought I'd call and see how things are

THE TWO WITNESSES

Chapter 1.
Bob

going. Give me a call when you have time. No biggie; just wanna touch base. Thanks."

"Well, since Tony isn't in, now would be a good time to open up the book again, I'm sure I'll hear from him when it's time." Bob thought.

Tumbling out of bed to get the ol' coffee brewing, he cocked one eye toward the answering machine to see if perhaps there was a message, since he had gone to bed before 9:30. "Nope, not yet. Oh well, tomorrow's Saturday; he's probably waiting till then when he has the time to spare."

Without wondering if Tony was going to call or not, Bob's last day of the week went smoothly, and he was ready for the weekend. Nothing was really planned; maybe he and Deena would get together and do something. About the time he had the water adjusted for the shower, he thought he heard the phone ring, but by the time he had reached the bathroom door, if it had been ringing at all, it had stopped. As he was drying off, he checked the recorder to see if it was blinking. *It was!* Wrapping the towel around him, he played back the message. It was Deena. From the message she left, it didn't take long to figure out what his plans were for Friday night. Deena hadn't seen him in a few days, and she was in the mood to be with him. After calling her back they decided to go out for dinner, maybe a show, or just rent a video. They'd figure it out later. As he was leaving his apartment to pick her up, he saw Tony and his girlfriend headed toward *his* place.

"Hey, Tony, what a surprise! Did you get the message on the recorder?"

"No, not yet Bob, I haven't been home for a couple of days. I've been with Cindy. Her brother graduated from school, and we all went to her mom and dad's for the celebration. It's about two hundred miles from here. Oh, I'm sorry; Cindy this is Bob- Bob, Cindy. This is the guy I was telling you about the night I

THE TWO WITNESSES

Chapter 1.
Bob

came over trying to find your apartment."

"Hello, Cindy, my pleasure."

"Thank you, Bob, nice meeting you too."

"Cindy and I noticed you coming out of the apartment, and I thought I'd bring you up to date just in case you *had* tried to reach me."

"Good, I was wondering if you had talked to James."

"As a matter of fact, Bob, I talked with him later on that day, when you helped me with the books, but then Cindy called and reminded me of her brother's graduation. I had to scramble around and get things ready for the trip and totally forgot about calling and letting you know. Anyway, *he* said, as soon as I returned and settled in, to give him a call and we'd try to get together. What are you doing tomorrow?"

"Nothing planned. I was just on my way to pick up Deena. We're going out for dinner and maybe a movie or something. But tomorrow, nothing planned at all."

"Great! Why don't you give me a call after you get up and start moving around. I'll call James and we'll go from there."

Needless to say, Bob's blood was pumping again, and after a couple of nights of reading he was really anxious to see what this was all about. "Looks like tomorrow will be the day." The meeting was all he could think about for the evening, which really got Deena curious to know what he would find out. Dinner was inhaled, and it appeared that a video was more appropriate than the theater. So, off to the video store and to Deena's they went.

The next morning Bob was up early compared to his normal Saturday risings. After coffee and breakfast, he decided to call. Tony answered and said he was on the line with James at that moment and would call Bob right back. Since he was still at Deena's, he gave Tony her number. It wasn't five minutes until he returned the call.

THE TWO WITNESSES

Chapter 1.
Bob

"Today will be fine with James, Bob, but he has some errands to run first and it will most likely be around 4 or 4:30 before he gets through. Why don't you and I tentatively plan on getting together around 3:45 or so and you can ride with me. He only lives about 30 minutes from where you do."

"Okay man, I'll be home by then. Give me a call."

"Sounds like you two have known each other a lot longer than you have," Deena said.

"I know. When I first met him I felt that way. You know, when you first meet
someone and there's some kind of connection."

"Yeah, I know. That's the way it was when I met you, Bobbie baby," she chuckled.

"Flattery will get you everywhere, little girl."

Bob and Deena spent the next few hours together before he decided to go on home and change clothes. Deena chided him about leaving her for another man. They kissed goodbye and Bob headed for home. On the way, he was wondering what to wear-slacks, suit, casual, or what. "Oh well, I'll just wait till I get back then call."

Tony answered, "Yeah Bob, you about ready?"

"That's why I'm calling. What should I wear?"

"I'm wearing cut-offs and a tee-shirt."

"Alright, I guess I'll wear jeans, see ya when you get here."

THE TWO WITNESSES

Chapter 2
The meeting.

It didn't seem like five minutes had gone by till Tony was at the door.

"Hey, Tony, come on in. I can't believe we're finally getting together. It seems like a long time but I'm sure it's only my anticipation that makes me feel this way. It's just that it's so astounding to conceive a concept such as this, if it is true."

"Relax, Bob. Eventually what you're going to see is nothing more than a scientific approach to the Scriptures, using theoretical physics. It may appear a little scary at first, because it challenges everything you've been taught. Don't worry about it; just keep an open mind. It's okay to be skeptical; as a matter of fact, *it's good* to be skeptical. Remember what the Scriptures said? I think it was in Paul's writings, he said, 'to weigh all things, prove all things, hold fast to that which *is* good'? It went something like that. It doesn't bother James if you don't believe what *he* sees. He's *not trying* to convince anyone. Say, we'd better get moving. I called him just before I left; he's expecting us within the hour. I need to make one stop on the way."

"Sure, I'm ready. Let's go.

As Tony was about to pull into a quick-stop store, he asked if it bothered Bob if he smoked. It caught Bob off guard. It was no big deal to Bob either way; it's just that everybody he'd ever met that read or studied the Bible never smoked or drank.

"Of course not. Go right ahead. It's never bothered me, even though they do say it's bad for your health. And I'm sure it is, to a degree. Sometimes I like the smell, but I personally have never smoked. I tried it once; that was enough."

"I know what you mean Bob. I'm *really* trying to quit. I'm down to about three or four cigarettes a day now. I've gone from regular to the lights, now ultra lights. It's been tough, but everyone needs to stop. Maybe through education and help it might be possible. We certainly don't need some form of government or religion *making* us do it, at least that's the way I see it."

"Makes sense to me," Bob replied.

As they pulled up to James's house, Bob was surprised. For some reason he thought James would live in some sort of mansion or

THE TWO WITNESSES

Chapter 2
The meeting.

something, rather than a modest partial brick and frame house. However, it was a nice little home. By the time they got out of the car, James was at the door waiting for them.

"Hello, Tony, good to see you again."

He *seemed* very pleasant.

"Hello, James. James, this is Bob Allbright; Bob this is James Martin."

"Come on in guys."

As they walked in he led them toward the kitchen where he had some books stacked around what James called the "round table". He was dressed in jeans and loafers so Bob felt right at home.

"Tony, if you or Bob would like anything to drink, you know the rules: help yourself."

Tony fixed them a glass of water and they sat down at the table. James and Tony visited a few minutes, talking about someone that James had met in the past and had gotten involved in a discussion about religion. Eventually James asked Bob if he was of any religious faith or belief.

"No, not at this time," Bob said. "I did at one time visit several different faiths, when I was searching for answers."

"Are you still searching?"

"Well, I am now that Tony here has roused my curiosity up again. He sure speaks highly of you."

"Ah, Tony can stir up a hornets' nest and never run. He dares them to sting. He's full of what I think you call 'zeal'. Tony tells me you have some biblical background Bob. Have you done much studying?"

"Some. Not *intense* studying; I have read the Bible a couple a times, just to get *more* confused. I guess I finally laid it down about six or seven years ago. After that, I delved into the self-help books, some new age stuff, astrology, and eventually, nothing."

"Sounds a lot like my early years," James said.

Bob couldn't help but notice all of his books.

"I see you have some books on astronomy."

"Yes, astronomy, biology, all the world religions, physics, you name it. If it has anything to do with creation, the cosmos, or natural

10

THE TWO WITNESSES

Chapter 2
The meeting.

laws; not just talking about them, but actual facts, I want them for reference. As in the Scriptures, I want to, 'make full proof of my ministry,' have the facts to back it up, you know what I mean?"

"Yeah, I do," Bob gleefully replied. "In what type of religion would you classify yourself James?"

"Well, I'm sort of like you, Bob, I don't follow any of them. You might say, 'what ever Jesus was,' I am."

"Whatta you mean, 'whatever Jesus was'? Wasn't he a Christian?"

"Not *exactly*. His followers are Christians. He did the will of *His* Father, remember?"

"Yeah, that's right, how could He be a Christian? He *established* Christianity. Never thought about it really. That's true though, when you think about it."

"Oh, there is *no end* to the beauty that's hidden in the Scriptures, Bob. I personally prefer the Bible, since I'm in one of the countries that uses *it*. If I were in some other country I would use the Bible appropriate for *that* country. It really doesn't matter which one you use, once you get past the *veil*, they all say the *same thing*."

"Man, that's heavy. What does the *veil* mean ?"

"It means the *cloak*, or *flesh*, which is nothing more than allegory or parables, and, well, here's one of my little sayings that I have stuck here on the book shelf. I think it'll paint a pretty good picture of the veil, It reads: 'Have you ever pondered the paradoxical metaphors of allegorical parables'?"

"Wow! That'll take a little while for me to put together."

James chuckled and said,

"That's what I mean by the 'veil.' These are the type things that are *wrapped around* the *hidden truth*. These are the *things* that you have to find your way through, to get to the life or blood of the inner spiritual meaning of what is being constructed in the mind by the stories or messages put forth in the wording of Scriptures."

"Whoa, whoa," Bob, sighed. "Give me a minute to absorb some of this."

"See what I was telling you, Bob?" said Tony, "It gets even

THE TWO WITNESSES

Chapter 2
The meeting.

more beautiful. Just hang in there and don't hesitate to ask questions."

"Oh, no problem, Tony, I just had a few million of them dancing around in my head, all wanting to be *first* at the same time. I'm sure they'll get sorted out - I think." As he chuckled under his breath.

"I'm sorry, Bob." James said heartily. "If you come around much, ask Tony, you'll learn to slow me down. I get on a roll and it sometimes gets moving *too* fast. So don't feel shy, please do like you just did: 'whoa' will work fine. It is something I have been working on and need to keep practicing. My friends help remind me, but you do get an idea of what I'm trying to say don't, you?"

"Yeah, I see what you're saying." Bob couldn't keep from grinning as he said that. James noticed and was grinning too.

"You know, James, I think I'd really like coming over and studying with you and Tony if you don't mind. I've just got a good feeling about it."

"You're certainly welcome anytime we do. Or if you want to come over sometime when Tony can't, give me a call and we'll try and set it up. That's one thing I do love, and that's talking about universal laws and knowledge."

"Yeah, anytime I come over, Bob, I'll give you a call and see if you can make it. We'll just jet over and aggravate ol' James here."

"Sure," said James. "You know better than that, Tony. Throw me in the briar patch. Like I told him, I love it. There is one very important thing I must get across to you, Bob, before we go any further. There are curses written in the book of knowledge, and it warns very strongly about setting your 'hand to the plow and then looking back.' What this means is, do not make a vow and *not keep it*. I'm sure you've read in the scriptures about the 'curse of the law'?"

"Yes I have, I've read it several times." Bob replied.

"The reason for the warnings, Bob, is to make sure that the student of the Bible, or any sacred text for that matter, is extremely careful, and has made *full proof* of his or her ministry when giving an interpretation. Remember, what it said about those who said, 'The Lord saith, the Lord saith, when He did not'? And, 'the prophets

THE TWO WITNESSES

Chapter 2
The meeting.

prophesy falsely, the priests bear rule by *their* means,' and so on? The curse that's written is interwoven throughout all ancient writings. Paul is very bold in Romans, chapter three, verse seven where he says, 'For if the truth of God hath **more** abounded through **my lie** unto **His** glory; why yet am I also judged **as a sinner**'?

What he was referring to was the way that he was *writing* his epistles, about which he goes into full detail in chapter seven and eight. The..."

"Hold on James," Bob said as he shook his head. "Wow! That's deep. Let me think about that one for a minute."

"I'm sorry, Bob, I'll slow down. Did you have a question"?

"Well...yeah. I'm familiar with Romans, but I hadn't thought about what you just said that much. I...I'd like to *see that*, if you don't mind?"

"Of course not. Tony, hand Bob my Bible over there - you're closer to it."

"You bet. Here you go, Bob."

"Thanks, Tony. Where was that again, James - Roman's three and what?"

"Uh, seven, I think."

"Oh yeah, here it is."

You could hear a pin drop as Bob read and reread *that* verse and the ones *connected to it*.

"Man...! That's what it says alright. How come I never noticed *that* before? Hm. What then *is* he talking about? I thought Paul was an apostle and could not lie? I don't understand."

"I know what you mean, Bob, that's the way I was when it first hit me." James answered. "Over in second Thessalonians, Paul is talking about Satan and **all** of *his* 'power and signs *and* **lying** wonders.' That's in chapter two and verse nine. *Lying* is the point here. As you remember, *the veil* was put around the truth to protect it from the unrighteous. As he said in another place, 'Father I thank you for hiding *it* [the truth] from the wise and prudent, but revealing *it* to the babes *in* Christ.' The truth is hidden behind or in the *lie*, the allegories, parables, metaphors, and images. All of these build a

THE TWO WITNESSES

Chapter 2
The meeting.

picture story in the mind which is called the *graven image*, and also referred to as the *idol*, and again **sinful-flesh**."

Bob just couldn't hold back. "Yes! yes! Holy cow! I get it! I think I see what you're saying. Jesus came in the *likeness* of sinful flesh. He's referred to as the 'truth,' the *hidden* truth."

"That's a great part of it Bob. Tony can tell you, once you can grasp *where* the truth is hidden, you're well on your way to understanding the rest. Let's go ahead and finish the other verses in second Thessalonians. Turn to it there and look at ten, the next verse. Remember we were talking about the 'lie.' And in verse ten he's talking about the non-spiritual people, teachers, preachers that say the Lord saith and so on, and ends *that* verse by implying they had not received the love of the truth or Christ that they *might* be saved from the 'lie,' as he says in verse eleven. Notice it says, '*God* shall send them strong delusion, that they *should believe* a **lie**,' this *lie* is the one Paul said, once it was seen for what it was, would reveal the truth because once the lie has been seen, that leaves nothing but the truth. That was referring to verse six. The lie is the same thing as the *letter*. Can you recall the scripture where it says, 'the *letter killeth*, **but** the *spirit giveth life*'? The *letter* and the *law* are one, which brings us back to the *curse* of the law."

"Golly, James, *this* is awesome. Tony, you were right, when you said it would challenge *everything* I'd ever been taught. Not so much by what we've been reading, but the ramifications of where it's leading, that's what I think I'm *beginning* to see. This concept opens up a whole new way of looking at things doesn't it?"

"Yes, Bob, a complete whole and *new* way. As a matter of fact **all things become new.** You might say, the **renewing** of the mind, or the mind of *understanding*. The word 'understanding' and the word 'Christ' are synonymous. So to have the mind of Christ, is to have the mind of understanding."

"That makes sense, but how did you come up with it? Does it work all through the Bible?" Bob asked.

"Yes. The word Christos, or Kristos means illumined, enlightened, anointed or understanding. Hand me the Bible, Bob, I

THE TWO WITNESSES

Chapter 2
The meeting.

want to read you a verse here in Proverbs four and seven, listen closely. 'Wisdom *is* the *principle* thing *therefore* get wisdom **and with all thy getting** ***get understanding***.' As a matter of fact, Bob, sometime when at home, and have a little time on your hands, run reference on the word *understanding*. Do you have a concordance?"

"Yeah, there's one in the back of my Bible."

"Well, that one will be too small for *research* work. What you need to get, is a large comprehensive *analytical* one with the Hebrew and Greek lexicon in the back of it. The reason being, when you are researching a word, you want to be *like sheep* and go to the root of the word you're looking up."

"Oh, Okay. I see what you're saying. Where can I get one?"

"Tony, where did you get the one you picked up for your buddy, Larry?"

"I think I got it at Smith's or the Cosmic book store; it doesn't matter, they both have them. If you want to, Bob, we can go by tomorrow and pick one up, neither of them are not far from where you live."

"Heck yeah, I want one, as long as you and James are around to help me out. But wait a second, tomorrow's Sunday, are they open on Sunday?"

"Oh, that's right, it is." Tony said.

"Cosmic's open on Sunday now" James reminded.

"I remember *now*, said Tony. They just started staying open two weekends ago. Alright, we'll go about lunchtime, so we can grab a bite to eat while we're out. Sound okay to you Bob?"

"Shoot, I'm so wound up I'm ready to go right now!" Tony and James both laughed.

"What? Did I say something funny?"

"Oh no - Bob, it just reminds us of *us*. That's the way we are when we run across a new book we get excited and want it *right now*. However, they are closed now, it's nearly ten o'clock."

"Good gosh, already? What happened to the time. I guess we should get going Tony."

"If you want to, Bob, there's no rush on my part; I'm like

THE TWO WITNESSES

Chapter 2
The meeting.

James, I could talk all night about the *word,* especially when there's an ear to bend."

"Gee guys, I'm sure I will too, later. But right now my mind is doing flip flops. I don't know where I could put any more."

"No problem, we understand. You can only *eat* so much, then you have to digest it. But anytime you have a question, or you want to study, like I said, you can come over whenever we can get together."

"Don't worry, James, I'll definitely want to get together again. And needless to say, it has been a trip. I really enjoyed it."

"Me too, Bob. Watch out for Tony there, he'll have you wrapped up every spare minute if you're not careful."

"I dare him." Bob invited.

They all chuckled and shook hands as they walked toward the car. After leaving James's house, Bob was quiet and distant.

"Everything alright, Bob?" Tony inquired.

"Is it ever! Man, nearly everything we talked about is buzzing through my head; inside I'm asking questions, answering questions, bringing up questions, but they *all* make sense. I can't find anything that doesn't seem to fit somewhere."

"Say, Bob, would you like to stop and get a sandwich or something? I think I could eat a whole hamburger".

"Sure, I think a hamburger would be great right now."

THE TWO WITNESSES

Chapter 3
The Change

That night Bob slept like a log. Crawling out of bed was almost a chore, but after a couple of cups of coffee and a shower, the old bones were back in order.

"Wow!" he thought. "Last night was something else. For what little was discussed it sure brought up a lot of things to think about. Whoops, I didn't even notice the recorder blinking, ten to one it's Deena."   "Hi Bob, I guess you're not in yet. It's nearly eleven, give me a call when you get up. Love ya, bye."

"I know she's going to have a thousand questions, better call her and see what's up."

"Hello, this is Deena, I'm not in at the..." Deena answered. "Hello, hello. Hi Bob, I was in the shower, well, just getting out. I thought I heard the phone. So, how did it go? Was it as interesting as you thought it would be?"

"Oh yeah, plus tax. Really! It was enlightening. He talks insuch a way that it builds your curiosity to want to know more."

"What all did you talk about?"

"Part of it was the law and the curses that are written in them, and how one should not undertake the endeavors of a diligent search for the truth unless they are sincere, and seek answers with a pure conscience. What I got out of that was not to have any exterior or ulterior motives, outside of wanting truth for truth's sake and no other reason, except maybe to show others so that they may find it *for themselves*. The words are written in such a way as to protect the truth from being found by any other method. If your motives are impure, the letter tricks you into believing what is called **the lie**. Does that make sense?"

"Oh sure, Bob, let me repeat it back to you," she chuckled. "I'm kidding, honey. Why don't we wait till we get together, and we'll talk about it then. I think it'll be a lot easier."

"Okay, sugar, sounds good to me. What are we having for breakfast? Want to go out or fix?"

"Let me finish drying off and getting dressed and I'll call you right back. Love ya, bye."

"Love you, *too*, talk to you in a few. Bye bye."

THE TWO WITNESSES

Chapter 3
The Change

"What a poet!" she growled. "Bye!"

"Let's see," Bob thought, "what shall I put on? Can't wear my robe. Ha, ha, my robe. Boy, that stuff really gets in your head. But why not? I'll surprise her and fix breakfast this time and keep my robe on. Nah, I need to get dressed too, then I'll whip up some sausage and eggs or whatever.

By the time he'd dressed, she called back. He told her breakfast was in the making.

"I was going to suggest that," she screeched out. You read my mind, you little rascal, you. Wonderful! I'll be right over."

Halfway stumbling around in the kitchen, he couldn't help but wonder, "What's next? I'm already wanting to go back over to James's,' and I haven't even been home ten hours yet. Oh well, play it by ear, that's all I can do for now. I guess I need to call Tony when we get through eating. Maybe I should call him for breakfast. No, that's really pushing it. Am I losing it? Need to slow down a bit. Huh, reminds me of Tony and James. Does this make everybody anxious? But I do need to call him about going to get that concordance."

As Deena walked in the toast was popping out of the toaster.

"Good morning, sunshine" she said. "It smells good in here! Where's the non-smoking section and a table for two? I see the cook but no waiter."

"Very funny. Will I do? I'm the new chief cook and bottle washer."

"You'll do just fine," she said as they hugged and gave each other a peck. "Set the table or buffet?" she asked.

"Let's save the extra dishes. I'm supposed to give Tony a call and run up to the bookstore with him after while to pick up a concordance for my studies. You want to ride with us? It shouldn't take long, it's not far from here. You know where the Cosmic book store is don't you?"

"Yeah, it's up off Strand by Hurst Street If I remember right."

"Yeah, that's it. You're certainly welcome to go or wait here, whatever."

"Sure, I'll ride with you. You don't think Ton-"

"No, Tony won't mind at all, he's real good people. You'll like him once you get to know him."

THE TWO WITNESSES

Chapter 3
The Change

"Sounds like you're really getting into this thing with he and James. Do you understand what they're talking about?"

"Very much. Do you remember right after we first met and the topic of religion came up? I think we were at your cousin's or one of her friend's house for that barbecue you bragged about for so long."

"Yeah, I still believe that was the best I've had in quite a few years."

"Anyway," Bob interjected, "someone there brought up the subject of religion and asked If we went to church."

"Yeah, I think that was Don and Linda who were talking about it. Yeah, that's who it was."

"Well, remember the part where he almost got hot because I told him I had enough religion to last me two lifetimes?"

"Yeah, Linda too. I thought she was going to yell at you there for a minute, especially when you said, 'Even then, you didn't think you could save enough money to make it *all the way* to heaven.' That was pretty shoddy of you though, Bob."

"Well, at that time I was fed up with religion, and their better-than-you *attitudes*. I just couldn't help it. I guess I wanted to attack them like I've seen them do to others when I was searching for so many years. I was just plain fed up, I guess. But to answer your question, do I understand where *they're* coming from? I think I could say, they have opened up new insights that I feel will open a bunch of doors that I couldn't quite get to open before. Maybe the timing wasn't right. Like they say, there is a time and place for everything."

"You want some more toast or juice while I'm up?"

"No thanks, Deena. I think I've reached my limit. I'll help clean up though."

"Don't be silly! Let me do it. You fixed it, I'll clean it."

"No argument here. I could lay back down again and sleep all day the way I feel now. Just kidding!"

"What makes it so different when James and Tony talk about the Bible, than when the preachers do?"

"Well, with them it's more of a discussion, you know, questions and answers. If you don't understand something, you can stop and break it down, till you do. Sorta like James said last night, 'be

THE TWO WITNESSES
Chapter 3
The Change

like sheep, get to the root of the matter'. That's another reason for getting this concordance. It has the Greek and Hebrew lexicon in it, so you can break down the words you don't understand. Which reminds me, I guess I should give him a call and see when he wants to go."

"You know, I can tell a difference in you. I just realized I *realized it*." She chuckled.

"What do you mean, a difference?"

"I don't know, it's something, maybe it'll come to me later, I think you look more content or something, I don't know, *something*."

"Yeah, I do feel a little different, I think, now that you mention it. I think maybe a little more confident. That's what it is! Deep inside, I do feel a bit more confident."

"Great! I'm happy for you, I *really am*. It's got to be wh-" The phone rang out.

"Oh shucks, I bet that's Tony. Hello? Hello, Tony! how's it going? Man, I can't get last night out of my mind. Does it do this to everyone?"

"Well, not really everyone," he said. "Of everyone we've had opportunity to talk with, very few can grasp the gist of what it's about."

"Are you serious? I would've thought anybody with knowledge of the Scriptures would see where they lead to. The concepts fall into place beautifully, and after reflecting somewhat, even simply."

"I know Bob, Not everyone wants to go to the trouble to diligently search *until* they find. So many get discouraged and fall by the wayside, you know?"

"Yeah, I sure do. I was there myself."

"Well, you were a little different, Bob. You evidently still had a flicker of spiritual life left in you or you couldn't have grasped some of the things we were talking about. Say, if you're ready, I'll pop on over and we'll go get your concordance."

"Sure, come on. Oh, Tony! I almost forgot. My girlfriend is over, and I invited her to ride with us. No problem is there?"

"Of course not. I'm on my way."

"There you go," Deena said.

THE TWO WITNESSES
Chapter 3
The Change

"There I go where?"

"That *thing* I was talking about earlier, you know, that *change,* that *confident* thing."

"Ohhh, yeah, you're right I do notice it. It's mixed with anxiety *and* curiosity. I recognize it now. Well, I can't help it. This reminds me of the good old days when I had a drive to learn about the Bible and *save the world.* This time the world I need to save is mine."

About 20 minutes went by and Bob noticed Tony out the window.

"Oh, there's Tony. Get the door for me while I shut off the lights. Hey, buddy! Come on in. Tony, this is Deena, or should I say Deena, this is Tony? Whatever. Tony this is a very dear friend of mine, Deena."

"Any friend of Bob's has got to be good people. It's my pleasure, Deena."

"Mine too, Tony, that's all I hear anymore, Tony and James, James and Tony, I'm glad to see Bob perked up again. I wish he could have met you sooner."

"It wasn't time, Deena. Bob and I weren't ready for each other yet."

They happily grinned and shook hands.

"Look, Tony, why don't we take my car. You've been doing most of the leg work lately. Besides, I might want Deena to drive after while. It's been a dream of mine to have a female chauffeur."

"Ha, ha, you're crazy Bob." Deena laughed.

"Watch what you're saying or I *will* drive! You don't want *that* do you?"

"I'm kidding, honey, If I didn't love you so much I wouldn't pick on you."

"I know, silly. I love you, too."

"What do you think, Tony - hit Marsh and go to Strand and then Hurst from there?" Bob asked.

"Yeah, that's about the best way I can think of from here. You know, Bob, maybe next weekend, we can all get together for a picnic. I think it would be nice for us to get together and do something. That way the girls could meet, and we could sit around and rap and just

21

THE TWO WITNESSES

Chapter 3
The Change

have a fun day at the lake or park, or maybe James and Martie's backyard.

They have some nice shade trees and a picnic bench - everything we need for a cook out. I'll get in touch with him and see if he's in the mood. I have to tear him away from working on his new book. He never gets out of the house, unless he has to run a service call or something."

"You know," Bob said. "I forgot all about James being married. In the back of my mind I knew it when I walked into his house last night because of the way it looked inside, you know? But after that, I forget it. I was out to lunch from then on. Ha, 'out to lunch,' boy, was I ever."

"I think I like you better this way, Bob. You're giddy! You've lost it!"

"I know it! Keep it up, I love it when you talk to me this way."

"You two sound Like Cindy and I...."

"There it is, right over there to the left, honey," Deena prompted.

"I see it! Hey, they have a pretty good business for a Sunday, the parking lot's nearly full. Oh, no wonder, look at that sign. Looks like Jeff Curtis is here to autograph his new book. I forget what it's about; I read in the paper the other day he was coming to town, but I didn't remember where. I guess I know now!"

Upon entering the store Deena said, "I think he's the guy that wrote *Two Path's Down, One Path Up*. I hear it sold fairly well. I've never read it though."

"Let's see, Bob," Tony excused himself. "This way to the Bible section. There they are. Here's the one we like. It has more in the lexicon than the others."

Bob picked it up and noticed the price.

"Wow, I was thinking it would probably be around 40 or 50 dollars."

"How much is it?" Deena asked.

"Only $19.25." Bob replied.

"That's well worth it too, Bob, believe me. James and I have practically worn ours out. You just can't do *what we do* without it."

THE TWO WITNESSES

Chapter 3
The Change

"I'm satisfied," replied Deena. "Let's pay for it and get home and check it out. You and Tony have got my curiosity going now as to what this book's about."

"We'll let Tony explain it to us when we get back. That is if he has time?"

"Oh, yeah, I have a couple of hours to kill before I meet Cindy. She had two calls to make this morning and said she might be through around three or so. I'm supposed to beep her later and get a more definite time. I'll probably just beep her from your place when we get back and give her *your* number, that way she can call me there when she's through."

"Good idea, Tony. That'll give us more time to check out the concordance."

The first thing Bob did was go straight to the table and open it up.

"It's not really that difficult to understand, I'm through, makes sense to me."

"Yeah, you wish," said Deena.

Tony grinned and encouraged him.

"You're not too far off, Bob. Once you get the hang of it, it's not that hard to use. Go ahead, think of a word in the Bible you'd like to find."

"Uh, let me think. I know: 'lie,' the word Paul used. We talked about it last night. Here *it is*. Holy cow, there's a bunch of them."

"Okay," Tony said. "Now, where was it or what book was it in?"

"It was in Romans, I think."

"Okay," Tony instructed. "Follow the entries down till you find Romans, then look for the statement where he says, 'my lie.'"

"Oh, I see, here it is - Romans three and seven: '...hath more abounded through *my lie* unto....' That's neat!" Bob exclaimed.

"When you want to find a word," Tony explained. "all you need to know is some kind of idea how it's used and if it's in the old or new testament. And it always helps to know what book. Okay, Bob, look at the word again, and you'll notice to the right of it is either a Hebrew or Greek word, depending whether it's in the old or new

23

THE TWO WITNESSES

Chapter 3
The Change

testament. Normally if you have a word you want to go to the root with, you'll get *more* information by running the Hebrew ones first. Let's take this one and I'll show you. If you'll notice, there are several listings. What we want to do is run reference in the Hebrew lexicon on each one of these so we can get an overall view of how this word fits spiritually. With the definition of 'to lie'.

"The first one is 'akzab' and beside it are two words: 'lying', and 'failing'. There's one more for it here in the lexicon and it is 'liar.' The next one is 'bad.' Ha, that's appropriate! And beside 'bad', is 'device.' Now in the lexicon under 'bad,' it lists, 'bars,' 'branches,' 'staves,' and 'strength.'

"Let's do one more, that'll be 'kazab.' Which means, 'lie,' and 'deceit.' And again in the lexicon, we have more meanings than we *already* have, including, to be in 'vain,' to be found a 'liar,' to be made a 'liar,' 'deceitful,' 'false,' and 'leasing.'

"As you can see, there are many more. The point here is, when you run into these *other* words, you know they are referring to 'the letter' or 'the lie.' You can read here in these scripture locations and get a very good idea how the word is used throughout the Bible, and you'll find it's always depicting someone who teaches *the stories* or *the images*, which is the very thing Paul said he hated, but he had to do it in order to get his message across and also hide the truth.

"We'll most likely cover all of this with James. Okay, now let's look at the *Greek* word for lie: *pseudos*. Here in the Greek lexicon it only gives *lie* and *lying*. Quite short compared to the listings in the Hebrew. Always check them both just to be thorough."

"Tony, I'm sorry - would you like something to munch on? I got all wrapped up in this and totally forgot to ask."

"No, thanks, man, Cindy and I will probably go out for something....darn it! I almost forgot to call and give her this number. See! You're not the only one that gets lost when you get *into this*. James too. I will take a glass of ice water when you have time."

"You got it! The phones by the couch."

Deena offered to get the water so Bob could continue to scan the concordance.

"Hey! Look at this, Tony. I was searching this like you said

THE TWO WITNESSES

Chapter 3
The Change

and saw this *one* reference. It's Psalms 58 and verse 3: "..astray as soon as they be born, speaking *lies*."

"Let me get my Bible, I want to look that one up," Deena remarked. "Here it is: 'The wicked are *estranged* from the womb: they go astray **as soon as they be born, speaking lies**.' "

At that moment the phone rang.

"More than likely that's for you, Tony. You want to answer it?"

"Sure, thank you Bob."

By this time Bob was looking over Deena's shoulder.

"Let me see that, honey, I didn't quite get it."

"Me either! Maybe if we start at the first of the chapter...."

"Well, guys, she's gonna meet me in 30 minutes at Lonzo's Italian Saucer. Why don't you give me a call, Bob, when you get settled tomorrow, after work? Maybe we can get together for a couple hours and rap a little more if you want to."

"You bet! You sure you don't mind?"

"Of course not. I'm like James - this is my love too and unless I'm totally beat, after a hard day at the office, I'm always eager to study. Remember where it said, 'It's more blessed to give than to receive'? One of the joys of learning, is giving. In other words give me a call. We'll see if we can get together - either my place or yours."

"I'll give you a buzz and we'll go from there."

"Sounds good to me. Deena, again, it was very nice to meet you. Keep an eye on Bob - looks like he might turn out to be a good Ox."

"A good what?" Deena quizzed.

"Think about it; I'll explain next time we meet. Bye now, have a good one."

"You too, Tony," they said.

"Nice guy, huh? I told you you'd like him, he seems to be a very sincere person. You'll like his girlfriend too, her name is Cindy. She's like him, very congenial."

"Well, good, we can finish this verse in Psalms tomorrow. It looks like it has a lot of hidden meaning in it."

"Yeah, let me know if you and Tony do get together, I want to

THE TWO WITNESSES

Chapter 3
The Change

see what all this is saying, too."

"You *know* I'd love for you to be here. As a matter of fact, why don't you just plan on it."

"Great! Well, come on, I'm buying."

"But Deena, baby, twist my arm. Ouch, you win - let's go!"

THE TWO WITNESSES

Chapter 4
The Anger

    The next day was without a doubt, the longest one he'd had in some time. All Bob could think about were the circumstances in which he met Tony and James and what was taking place in his mind regarding the scriptures. He noticed on his way home he was slipping back to his intolerance of other motorists. "I guess I'm just a little too anxious. I need to get a hold of myself."
    "Finally", he thought as he pulled into a parking spot. "Another Monday!"
    As soon as he walked into the apartment he headed toward the phone to call Tony and saw the recorder blinking.
    "Hello, Bob this is Tony I've got to work about half an hour later today. I thought I'd let you know in case you tried to call and I wasn't there. What we probably need to do if you can is meet at my place - that'll save us time. I should be there around 6:30. If you can, meet me there at seven, if not, leave me a message and we'll go from there. Later."
    "Now," Bob thought. "is when I really don't like these machines. But I wouldn't have gotten the message without it. Huh, there I go again. I guess I need another fix. I'll just have to wait till seven. Oh! I forgot about Deena, better call her now and give her the news.
    "I'm positive it's okay Deena, he doesn't mind at all. What I'll do is pick you up at 630. Let's see, that's about 45 minutes from now. Then we'll get there about seven. Okay?"
    "You're in the drivers seat. I'll be ready when you get here."
    "Good. I'll see you at 6:30."
    As he hung up he thought,
    "Well, I think I'll make a sandwich so I won't have to worry about getting hungry physically that is. No question about being mentally starved."
    Bob arrived at Deena's about 6:25, and as he started toward her apartment, she was already walking toward him.
    "Hey! Fancy meeting a good-looking girl like *you* here, of all places! What are *you* doing tonight?"
    "I'm going with you if you'll tell me your name."
    "Hi baby. Give me a kiss."

THE TWO WITNESSES

Chapter 4
The Anger

"Hi baby. Give me a kiss."

"Bob! Watch it! The cam corders might be out tonight."

"Shucks! You're right - I forgot about big brother. Here, let me open the door for you, little lady."

"Bob? You don't really want *that* on video too, do you?"

"Darn it, caught me again. Have you eaten anything?"

"Yeah, I just finished a small salad with crackers I have to watch *your* figure for you."

"That's my girl."

"Do you know where he lives?" Deena asked.

"Yes. He told me where he lived the other day, when we were going to James's. I know exactly where it is, I've been by there several times while driving around town doing different things."

Tony met them at the door.

"Hi Bob, hello Deena, come on in. Go ahead and have a seat at the table while I clean it off. I just finished a TV dinner."

"Oh the life of a bachelor." Bob groaned.

"No, not really a bachelor," said Tony, "I've been spoiled - I was married once. If I had always been a bachelor, bachin' wouldn't bother me."

They all chuckled, and agreed.

"Doggone it!" Bob cried.

"What Bob?" Deena asked.

"I was in such a hurry, I left my concordance."

"That's all right buddy, I have one, we can use it."

"Yeah, I know, but..."

"I understand, Bob," I like to have my own books with me, too. Look at it like a lesson."

"Yeah, *really*." Bob lamented.

"Oh, by the way, Tony, what did you mean by 'ox' last night? You said you would tell me the next time you saw me."

"That's right! I did, but I didn't say when." Tony teased. "We'll finish where we left off last night with *lie,* and then go to the *ox*.... I won't forget you, Deena. Here you go, Bob, look it up again, and give me that scripture reference."

THE TWO WITNESSES

Chapter 4
The Anger

"I'll get my Bible. I think you said it was in Psalms. Yeah, uh.., okay, Psalms 58 and verse 3; Deena and I read it after you left."

"Okay, let me read it." Tony asked. ' "The wicked are *estranged* from the womb: they go astray as **soon as they be born, speaking lies.**' I have another reference that goes with it, I'll read *it* and then get back to this one. We'll hold *this* place, and turn to Proverbs chapter 14, verse 25. It says, 'A true witness delivereth souls: but a **deceitful** *witness* speaketh *lies*.'

And remember when we looked up some of the meanings for 'lie'? 'Deceitful' was one of them. Okay, hold *that* thought. Now back to '**being born, speaking lies**.' There is no way this scripture can be taken literally. Remember where it says, you first must be **born** of water, and then, ***born again of the spirit?***

"Well, there are two kinds of water, the waters of confusion and *living* waters. First Timothy 5 and 23, says to 'Drink no longer *water,* but a little wine for thy stomach's sake and thine often infirmities.' In this context, we are told that instead of drinking water, we should drink **wine.** I believe you know what *wine* represents: *the spirit of the* **word.** When used in a negative sense, water is called the 'waters of gall.' Let's back up to verse one, and read through verse three, then we can get a better picture of who these wicked are, *teaching lies.*

'Do ye indeed speak righteousness, O congregation? Do ye judge uprightly, O ye sons of **men?**' Let's think about verse one for a second. What congregation is the scripture referring to? There is only one congregation I know of, and they are the ones that say, 'the Lord saith, the Lord saith.' Isaiah chapter 58 gives a good explanation.

"The word 'man' means one with no spiritual understanding, when it's used in the negative. Remember, the word 'understanding' and the word 'Christ' mean the same. So in verse one, the scripture is questioning the righteous teachings and judgments of those who teach.

"Verse two says; 'Yea, in heart ye work wickedness; ye weigh the violence of *your hands in the earth.*' Here, 'heart' means 'intent,' 'motive.' 'Hand' or 'hands' means 'teaching.' The 'earth' means the

THE TWO WITNESSES

Chapter 4
The Anger

letter or the law.

"Remember, 'the letter killeth' by way of 'the curse of the law.' Now, you can see what it means 'to be born,' into this way of thinking and immediately start teaching the law or the letter, which is filled with scorn and condemnation. That is not the way of Christ, or truth. The 'letter' is nothing but the *image*, ***the lie.***

"When you first get into the scriptures, you are 'born' into the emotional aspect and want to save the world. You immediately run to anyone that will listen and try to get them saved, teaching what you have heard or have *been taught*. This is part of where we've been 'born in sin and shaped [mentally] in iniquity' or the traditional way of thinking.

"Every doctrine, whether the Bible or otherwise, in many ways, teaches it differently. But all religions around the world believe their way is the way to salvation. If you were to put a spokesman for each doctrine of the world side by side in a circle, then stand in the middle and listen to them all at once, you could grasp the *real* meaning of 'the waters of confusion.' Your mind could accommodate the different voices and their views but can only assimilate that which best fits with the convictions you already have. These 'waters of confusion,' are the waters the 'whore of Babylon' sits upon in Revelation chapter 17."

"Excuse me, Tony," Bob whispered. "Man, I have got to take a breath. Am I hearing what I'm hearing? Are all religions *teaching* the letter? If they are, then no wonder the world is in the shape it's in."

"Deena, are you still with us?" Tony asked.

"I...I think I am. I don't think I've ever heard the Bible read like that before - it *is* different. I have never read it through like you and Bob have, but you have piqued my interest. I think I'll wipe the dust off *mine*. What I *really* should do is read it all the way through and let Bob share with me from his studies with you and James. Does that make sense to you? I hear what you're saying and it sounds right, but I don't quite understand it. I think if I had a little more background of the scriptures, I could follow you with no problem. But you and Bob go right ahead, I am really enjoying it. Don't worry about me, I'll

THE TWO WITNESSES

Chapter 4
The Anger

catch up later."

"I truly do understand, Deena, I've been there, and I'm sure Bob has, too!"

"Oh, no doubt about it." Bob said. "I still get there at times, and I think now is one of them. What did you mean about the 'whore in Babylon' sitting on some water?"

"It does sound weird - until you can see who she is," Tony replied. "Keep in mind now Bob, we're still expounding on the word 'lie.' It just takes several scriptures to get to the *total* picture. And to answer your question, yes they are all teaching the *letter,* that's all they know *for now.* By the way, teaching 'the lie' is *'the sin'* of the Bible. Everything negative has been begotten *from* 'the lie.' We'll get into *that* some other time. That will probably take a whole evening at James's.

"Let's see now, oh yeah, turn to Revelation chapter 17. In verse *one* it's talking about one of the *seven* angels that was to show John the judgment of the 'great whore' who sits upon *many waters*. In verse two it's referring to all religions [kings of the earth], which have made drunk those involved in *their* teachings because of fornication.

"Fornication means *intercourse* **before marriage**, and that means communicating or teaching before they are married to *Christ.* Remember? We are supposed to *be married* to Christ. And to teach *without* understanding [Christ], is to teach the *law* or letter, and to teach the law before you are married to Him is fornication. It has nothing at all to do with 'human sexuality,' that's only an *image* so you may understand what it means spiritually. All of that will be covered later."

"Beautiful, Tony, I got it!"

"Me too!" Deena boasted.

"I love it when people can see things like that. It really is simple, when you convert it," Tony said.

"Anyway, where was I? Uh...verse three - here, he's being shown *spiritually* what is taking place in the world, but our point is the *beast* and the *water,* so I'm skipping everything else for now. John

THE TWO WITNESSES

Chapter 4
The Anger

says, 'I saw a woman sit upon a *scarlet* [which also means 'guilt'] coloured *beast*, full of names of blasphemy, having seven *heads* and ten horns.' Now let's go to verse 15. Before we read this, though, did you notice that the *waters* in verse one has changed to the *beast* in verse three? Now let's read 15: 'And he saith unto me, the waters [also beast] **which thou sawest,** where **the whore sitteth, are peoples, and multitudes, and nations, and tongues.**' This means the religious *language* of this planet! Let's skip on down to verse 18 right quick. 'And the woman which thou sawest is **that great city** [all religions in one], which reigneth over the kings [doctrines] of the **earth** [the law, the letter of the earth, earthy-carnal].'

"All of chapter 18 talks about *her* fall, and the last verse, number 24, explains about the blood, [which means 'life' in this case] that was shed, or the **spiritual** lives that had been lost by all of those who were under *her* teachings. For by teaching the *lie*, and *condemning* them to believe it, she killed their minds to the truth, or the Christ, or the spiritual understanding that is hidden in the *two - edged* sword.

"Two-edged means the 'left hand' (word or teaching) and the 'right hand.' The letter, 'the *left hand*,' **killeth**, but the spirit, 'the *right hand*,' giveth life. It's a **two-**edged ***word***, 'or sword.' Like the *word* says, 'I rain on the just [righteous], and the unjust [carnal, of the law] **alike.**' There again, *He*, 'the word,' gives unto all people the intent and desires of their hearts. It all depends on the motive one goes into the scriptures with. That's another area we'll cover later, too.

"It keeps getting better and better. Boy, I'm getting as bad as James. Am I going off on tangents or what? Let's see if I can get back to the beast and the water, so we can finish up the subject of 'lie,' at least for tonight. It looks like we're about to loose Deena there."

"I'm fine. But if you don't mind, I do think I'll stretch out on your couch for a few minutes. I can still listen to you from there."

"Go right ahead, Deena - you know it's fine. We shouldn't be but just a few more minutes, then we'll wrap it up. You all right Bob?"

"Man, I'm in la la land, but don't you dare stop now! Would you like for me to get you some more soda first?"

THE TWO WITNESSES

Chapter 4
The Anger

"No thank you, Bob. I think I'm getting plenty to drink. Okay buddy, buckle up, here we go! Are you following me?"

"No problem, it'll soak in later. I just want to listen for now."

"Okay, first of all let's establish what the word 'man' represents. Turn to 1 Timothy chapter 6 verse 16, and we'll scan verse 14 and 15 first so we can understand what 16 means.

"Verse 14 is talking about the 'appearance' of Christ; 15 says; 'He is the *only* potentate King of Kings and Lord of Lords.' Now verse 16: 'Who 'only' [speaking of the King of Kings, Jesus Christ] hath immortality, dwelling in the *light* which no 'man' can approach unto; whom no 'man' hath seen, nor can see.'

"What this is implying is, no *man* can come unto or approach God, no *man* has **ever** seen God, no *man ever* will. If this were literal, then what a farce! The word 'man' does not represent the human factor. It represents a state of mind: the *carnal mind*.'

"Now turn to Ecclesiastes chapter 3, verse 18: 'I said in mine heart concerning the estate of the sons of **men**, that God might manifest **them** and that they might see that they themselves are beast.'

"I want to show you some more to go *with* that. We'll go to Psalms 9 and verse 20: 'Put them in fear, O Lord: *that* the **nations** may know ***themselves to be but men***.' And again, Psalms chapter 49, verses 12 and 20: 'Nevertheless 'man' *being* in honour *abideth not* :: he is *like the beast* that perish.... Man *that is* in honour, and **understandeth** not, is like the beast that perish.' Here, as before, the emphases are directed to 'man' and 'beast' alike. There's one more place we should go to tie all of this together - that is if you feel like it"

"You bet! I could listen all night. Deena's asleep - a few more minutes won't matter, I'm sure."

"Since you're sure," he chuckled, "we'll go to first Corinthians chapter three, verse three. This verse, even out of context, tells us what 'man' is. 'For ye are yet carnal: for whereas *there is* among you [those involved in the scripture] envying, and strife, and divisions, are ye not *carnal*, and walk as men?' Okay, now, when you put that together with what we just read in Timothy about man, and how **he**

THE TWO WITNESSES

Chapter 4
The Anger

has not and **cannot** see *or approach* God, you can understand it's talking about the 'carnal mind.' The carnal mind, cannot grasp the spiritual interpretation of the scriptures. A very good explanation of the carnal mind is in Romans chapter eight. If you want to, we can get into that tomorrow night, if we get together."

"I'm speechless, Tony. I knew there had to be more to the scriptures than what is, or rather, has been taught. I know that I've got a ton of questions, but I understand, or I think I do, what these passages mean already. This is *really* a trip - I love it! Even what little I can see, I know what you and James mean when you say you love it!

"Oh well, I guess I'd better get Deena home. I know we all have to go to work tomorrow. I'll give you a call as soon as I get home. Man, you don't know how I appreciate you studying with me, *I know* 'it's more blessed to give than to receive.' "

"I know what you mean, Bob. Remember, I was where you are, with James."

"Tell me something, Tony - why can't everybody see how this works, don't they know what they're doing? It kinda makes you a little angry at them, at least that's the way it's been making me feel lately."

"Anger is the first thing you feel when you begin to see what *sin* is," Tony said. "What you've been feeling is perfectly normal, under these circumstances. The scripture says, 'Be ye angry and sin not,' which is a sign to us, at moments like this, when we recognize sin for what it is.

"Paul writes in Romans seven about the law, and reminds us; 'For we [the brethren, those who see spiritually] know that the *law is spiritual*.' Then naturally when we hear it taught *carnally*, being 'babes in *Christ*,' we tend to get angry. We must always remember, if they could see what we see, they could not teach it otherwise. Therefore, if there is any blame to be laid, it should be laid on those that know better. 'Father forgive *them*, for *they* know *not what they do*.'

"In other words, if they could see the scriptures spiritually, it would be *impossible* for them to teach it otherwise. This really gets

THE TWO WITNESSES

Chapter 4
The Anger

into another session, you want to get into it?"

"You know I want to, day and night," Bob said, as they both laughed.

"Yeah, that's the way it energizes you, you just can't seem to get enough. But you'd better take Deena home, or I'll keep you here all night!"

Deena was a little slow getting to the car, as she quietly mumbled some scriptures and dozed off again to the sound of the car moving through the streets to her comfortable bed. By the time Bob arrived at his apartment he was wound up.

"Man!" he thought. "The more I get, the more I want. This is the same feeling I had when I first started searching and going to church. But this time it seems to promise a much deeper understanding than I could have *ever* imagined."

As he passed by the kitchen table he couldn't help but glance at his new concordance. Thumbing through the pages he happened to notice the word 'sin.' Although he knew better he found himself scooting the chair back, and it wasn't long before he was off and running. After an hour of reading references, he nodded off toward the bedroom.

One minute before the alarm sounded, Bob sat straight up, waiting a second before opening his eyes, wondering if he was awakening to reality or to another dream. Shaking his head cautiously and then opening his eyes, he sighed upon seeing that in fact it was his bedroom. Hoping he could trust his legs, he meandered toward the coffee pot for sorting out the conflicts that played havoc on his sub-conscious all night. After three cups and some serious contemplation he realized he was okay. All that had ever been put in his mind relating to the scriptures, or 'God,' was just being re-categorized. One slight unconscious gesture of the hand to pick up the concordance [just for a second], *almost* caught him off guard. "Nope!" he said. "Not this time. I'll see *you* this afternoon." And with that, made ready for work.

Today was a lot better than yesterday. He made it there and back in an alpha state, not conscious of what was going on around

THE TWO WITNESSES

Chapter 4
The Anger

him, being oblivious to anything that would have annoyed him any other time. Well aware of the trap by opening the concordance, he knew he should call Tony and Deena before even attempting it. Tony was home, and they decided to study at Bob's tonight.

"Hello, Deena, is that you?"

"Of course it is, silly."

"Just checking. After last night I want to be sure everything is real again."

"What do you mean, Bob?"

"I'm just kidding, honey. I just had a lot of weird dreams, but I figured it all out this morning. They were all relative to what I've learned about the Bible, from day one till now. Some were pretty neat, though. I really can't remember them per se but they were significant, and somehow make sense, to me."

"Really?" Deena said. "I slept like a baby. Woke up feeling great. No weird dreams that I can remember. Are you and Tony getting together tonight?"

"You bet! You *are* coming over too, aren't you?"

"I don't think I will tonight. You guys go ahead I'll catch up the next time you get together. I love you -- enjoy and call me tomorrow."

"I love you and good night."

He spent the next half hour or so shuffling around the apartment tidying up. Now, to pop a gourmet dinner in the microwave and kick back with his new toy, the concordance.

"Why didn't I ever think of buying one of these? You can find anything you want about the Bible in here. I'm sure glad someone has done all this work. I'd hate to have to try to find some of these words without a concordance -- it could take days."

Somewhere in the back of his mind, he must have heard the microwave beep, but it was the doorbell that brought him back to earth.

"Hey Tony. Come on in, I was just running some references. I really like this concordance. Maybe I don't have a choice -- it is addictive, isn't it?"

THE TWO WITNESSES

Chapter 4
The Anger

"I guess you could say that. Anything that nourishes you can be very addictive. You see, I'm in the same boat. No complaints on this end." Tony assured.

"I had a TV dinner in the microwave, but I got absorbed in you - know - what and didn't hear the bell go off. I have several if you'd like me to throw one in for you"

"Oh, I'm fine, buddy. I stopped on the way home from work and had one of those famous chili cheese burgers I like so much."

"Oooh, that sounds delicious!" Bob drooled. "Well if it won't bother you, I'll gobble this down while we talk.

"Ever since you mentioned it, I've been wondering about the book James is writing on how religion and physics, I mean theoretical physics, are saying the same thing. Does it have any relation to what we've been talking about so far?"

Tony grinned, compassionately. "First things first, Bob. I'm just getting a hint of how it fits. When we get into that arena, James will to teach you. But I do know that you have got to get the conversion keys from the Bible. Once you can see beyond 'the veil' and can see the scriptures spiritually, *then* you can comprehend the 'ghost theory' of physics.

"Like I've said, I have a lot to learn in that area, too. It won't take you long with the background knowledge you have of the scriptures. A couple more months of study and research, the way we are going now, we can start looking into and comparing some books on the subject. James will relate some of these ideas when he takes you into the section of the law and how *it* works. The principles of the law of words, and the principles of the universal law work hand in hand with the operation of energy in matter. Anyway, he'll get into that with us."

"I can't wait, Tony, I want it and I want it *right now!* I'm sure you've never felt that way, have you?"

"Right, Bob, *right*. Well, where were we?"

"I think we were going to look up in Romans the concepts of carnality, and death or that to be carnally minded *is* death."

"Oh yeah. I guess to cap it off, we can safely say the word

THE TWO WITNESSES

Chapter 4
The Anger

'man,' when used in the negative, represents ego, and *this* state of mind dwells in the *human* female *and* the *human* male. So then, **man**, is neither male nor female, it is a 'carnal' state of mind. The reason it (the carnal mind) is referred to as man instead of woman is that It stands for power and authority. In what they call the old testament no one wanted daughters, they wanted sons, because sons worked in the field. We now know that the field means, 'the mind,' The woman, is the help mate, the imagination. You can readily understand why woman [imagination] should not teach, especially the things of God, or knowledge.

There is a good man in each and every one of us, and there is an *evil* man, too. Each one having their own imagination, or wife. Until both become one flesh, that is, one *word,* one mind, one accord, there will always be male *and* female, and woman always offers what she has *imagined,* to her Adam, man. Here we go on another tangent, but you can see what it means spiritually, can't you?"

"Really!" Bob agreed. "Isn't that the same meaning of Adam and Eve and the fruit thing in Genesis?"

"Yes, exactly. It is really talking about *the church*, but let's wait until we study about the Lord's body, before we get way ahead of ourselves. Let's turn to Romans chapter eight, and get into 'carnal' and how it is used and what it represents. Everything we're talking about *now* will come up several times more before, and after we get into the physics.

"Look at verse six of chapter eight: 'For to be *carnally minded is death,* but to be *spiritually* minded is life and peace.' And seven says, 'Because the carnal mind *is* enmity [which means hatred] against God: for *it* is not subject to the law of God, *neither indeed can be.'*

You'll find, when you try to talk about the scripture *spiritually* with someone, who is not *spiritually* minded, they get angry. They won't even discuss it, they'll find every excuse in the world to get away from you. These are people who profess to love the Word of God! Put a bookmark here and turn to first Corinthians chapter two. What we're going to find *here* is how *man* cannot comprehend the *spiritual understanding* hidden in Paul's epistles.

THE TWO WITNESSES

Chapter 4
The Anger

Before we start with verse one (because it references the word *brethren*) I need to bring in what he means.

Verse one of Romans chapter 7 says, 'brethren' are those, that *know the law*, and verse 14 says, 'For *we* [the brethren] know that *the law* is spiritual.' So, when he uses the word *brethren*, he's referring to those who are *spiritual--minded*, and who interpret the law (scriptures) not *carnally* (literally), but spiritually. Any questions?"

"No, I don't think so. About the time one pops up, an understanding seems to come right behind *it* causing things to make sense. Does that make sense?"

"Does it ever," Tony laughed. "It happens to me all the time. That's what I call the interpreter. I love him. Now, verse one of chapter two: 'And **I**, *brethren*, when ***I*** [the hidden truth in the scriptures] came to you, came not with excellency of speech or of wisdom, declaring unto you the testimony of God.' The point Paul is making, because he addressed the *brethren*, is how the *hidden* message is not in the array of any egotistical speech of words, such as the letter, as we'll see in the following passages. "Verse two: 'For I determined to know *nothing* among *you*, save Jesus Christ, and *him crucified*.' He is concerned if we can read through his **lies**, (stories) and see the *truth* (Christ), hung on *this* cross, which means *contradiction*. Another way of putting it is, 'all Paul wants to know is, can you readily see the spiritual truth without it being perverted or carnal?' This will become clear as we move along.

"Verse three: 'And I was with you *in* weakness [the **flesh,** the **letter**, the **stories**], and *in* fear, and *in* much trembling.' The hidden truth is *wrapped in words* of fear, condemnation, scorn -- allegories, metaphors, parables, paradoxes, all mythological symbolization and similitudes.

"Hosea 12 and 10 tells how the prophets who wrote scripture used this type of writing to convey *many* visions or ways of looking at what they wrote. Thus *they created* confusion [which also means **sin**]. Verse four: 'And *my* speech and *my* preaching *was not* with enticing words of *man's* wisdom, but in demonstration <u>of the spirit and of power.</u>' another way of saying, 'the truth of God [from the Word] hath

Chapter 4
The Anger

THE TWO WITNESSES

more abounded through my lie.'

"Remember Bob, *all* scripture is written to the *brethren*, and if you are not spiritual -- minded, there are as many ways as the sand of the sea to interpret them. '***Broad*** is *the way* [the 'lie' or 'letter'] that leadeth to destruction.' I'm getting ahead of myself.

"Let's get on to verse five: 'That ***your*** faith should not stand in the wisdom of *men,* but in the *power* of God.' Glance to the other side of the page and read verse 24 of chapter 1. It say's; 'But unto ***them***, which *are called*, both Jews and Greeks, Christ ***the -- power of God -- and the -- wisdom of God.***'

"There it is, very clear. You *must* have *understanding* -- Christ -- in order to ***see*** the Word (God). Now, verse six reiterates what we have been talking about: 'Howbeit *we* [the apostles] speak wisdom among them that ***are perfect***: Yet not the wisdom of this [carnal] world, nor of the princes [teachers] of this world, that come to naught:'

"And verse 7; 'But we speak the ***wisdom*** of God [the Word] ***in a mystery, even the hidden wisdom***, which God ordained before ***the*** world unto ***our*** glory:' Self -- explanatory. *The truth is hidden in the word.* Verse eight; 'Which none of the princes of ***this*** [carnal] ***world*** knew: for had *they* known ***it***, they could not have crucified [afresh! Heb. 6:6] the Lord of glory [the Word of truth]:' In other words, if you know *it* spiritually [the word], it is *impossible to teach **it** otherwise.*

"The next verse is in synthesis with first Timothy, chapter 6 verse 16. This is one of the verses we read before about the word 'man.' At this point, let's bring it in again. 'Who ***only*** hath immortality, dwelling in the light which **no <u>man</u> can approach unto; whom no <u>man</u> hath seen, nor..can see:**' Okay, back to verse 9 of 1st Corinthians chapter 2; 'But ***as it*** is written [*the way scriptures are written*], Eye [carnal] hath not seen, nor ear heard, neither have entered into the heart of *man,* ***the things*** which God hath prepared [in his Word] for them [the brethren] that love him [the truth].' This is just ***more proof*** the carnal mind is 'man,' and the spiritual mind is 'brethren,' as in verse 10: 'But God hath revealed ***them*** [the *stories*]

THE TWO WITNESSES

Chapter 4
The Anger

unto *us* by his *Spirit* [Christ]: for the spirit searcheth **all things**, yea the *deep* **things** of God [the Word].'

"This next verse explains that *man* only knows the things of *each other*, ***but***, the spiritual, know the heart of *man*, the unenlightened. And verse 12 says the *brethren* have not received the understanding of the *letter*, but the understanding of *the Word,* that *we* might *know* '*the things*,' freely given to *us* from the Word. Verse 13 backs that up by saying,' 'Which **things** also *we speak* [by the Gospel], not in the words which *man's* [carnal] wisdom teacheth, but which the Holy Ghost [spirit] teacheth; <u>**comparing spiritual things with spiritual**</u>.'

" Have you grasped the idea of what it means to read the scriptures spiritually yet?"

"Not yet," Bob replied. "But like I said, I think I *hear* them spiritually. You know what I mean?"

"Good. Let me put a few simple Ideas on the table, and we'll discuss them before we continue with these last three verses, and that should tie things a little closer together for you. Okay?"

"I wouldn't have it any other way. I'm totally entranced."

Tony smiled, feeling Bob's sincere sense of awe.

"Do you remember reading, 'My people are destroyed for the lack of *knowledge*'?"

"I've read it."

"Okay! Everything is based on that premise: to *teach knowledge*. Especially *spiritual knowledge* of the scriptures. Remember, the scriptures, first show the **image**. This is done through the **stories**, or the **lie**. For example, 'Lay your **hands** on one another and pray for the sick and they shall recover.' What comes to your mind when you hear or read that statement?"

Bob sat back, rubbing his face a few seconds. "Well, I see a person walking over to someone, putting his *hand* on them, and praying for them. At least that's the way I've always seen it done."

"Very good, Bob. That's what it means by 'the **image**.' That's exactly what the words paint in the mind. You read those words and the mind sees an *image*. That **image** is *the lie*. Last night when we

Chapter 4
The Anger

THE TWO WITNESSES

were talking about Babylon, 'the whore,' and *her teachings*, I said something about it meaning 'hands.' Now you'll see what I meant. Open your concordance to the word hand.

"The Hebrew word is 'yad.' Now go to the back in the lexicon and look at all of the words it stands for, and find those that will fit *equally* throughout all scripture. There are several: "Work," "ordinance," "***power***," "order," and this one for sure -- "ministry." Add an 'A' to Yad and you have yada, which is the next Hebrew word, and out of many words that fit, we find they mean ***knowledge*** *and* ***understanding***.

"Now, when reading the Bible, if we convert the word *hand* for any one of these that infer teaching, knowledge, ministry, word, logos, or power, we'll find an entirely *different* meaning, which would only apply to your soul or spirit -- the ***inner*** and **not** the ***outer***.

One of the things James will probably say or mention when he's talking to you, so you might get a better idea of who the scriptures are written to, is for you to go in his living room, lay your body down on the couch, leave **it** there, and you as a spirit being come back to the kitchen table. *Then* when you hear the scriptures read, you'll understand them. What this implies is, the scriptures are not written to the human part of us, they are written to the inner being, the one that lives forever, the one that leaves the body when the body returns to the dust from whence it came. God is '**supposedly**' *Spirit*, and if we are made in his image, I don't believe it could be dirt. I'm not trying to be gross, but only to drive the point home. Do you understand?"

"Duh! Me stupid," Bob clowned. "I think you're saying, we're made after the pattern of the word -- I think?"

"Right! Very good! The outer is the veil; the inner, the spirit. The outer is the *flesh*, the inner is the *blood*. There *is more* to be seen here but we are not ready yet, there is much to learn *first*. We'll come back when we study about the Lord's *body*. Now let's look at that scripture again, about laying *hands* on someone.

"Say you were knowledgeable about building houses and a journeyman came to you with a question about a problem he was having doing his job. He needed *help*, he was dis-eased. He was a

Chapter 4
The Anger

THE TWO WITNESSES

good worker, he was conscientious, he tried very hard to do what was right. When you understood his problem you were more than happy to instruct him in the way he should go. You *could* say his **problem** was *healed*, you had just laid *your* **hands** on **him** (the problem). To lay *hands* on the sick is to give them Christ. Give them *understanding*, allow the Holy Spirit to do the healing of their mind -- heart. Heal the *inner*, not the outer.

"If the heart is pure, then the body *must* follow suit. Remember where it was said, 'you make clean the <u>outside</u> of the cup and of the platter, but *within* they are full of extortion and excess?' There are several more passages that imply the same message. The scriptures follow *that pattern*. The *outer layers* of the scripture is *flesh*, the *inner is the blood* or the spirit. That's why in another place it reads, 'He came *in the likeness* of **sinful flesh**.' You must have the spirit or life of *the word* (flesh) in order that the outer may be healed. Then you have the outer as the inner, the inner as the outer and have made *the two -- one,* the *Living Word*. Another place says; 'Unless you *eat my flesh -- and -- drink my blood*, you have *no life* in you.' The Bible, or any sacred scripture taught 'carnally' is called the **old** testament, because it is the *law*. The law is full of **condemnation** and *scorn*. The truth *is* Christ. It (Christ or truth) is full of hope and life. *It* is up lifting, *it* create's joy and *understanding* of God's Word, in any religion on the planet.

"The books of other cultures are written in the same manner our book is - there is no difference when they are converted spiritually. This is called *the new testament*. in His blood, in His spirit, in His truth.

"Let's go back to verse 14 of first Corinthians, chapter two: 'But the natural [carnal] man receiveth not the things of the spirit of God: for they are foolishness unto him: *neither can he know them*, *because they are spiritually discerned*.' Verse 15 and 16: 'But he that is spiritual judgeth *all things*, yet he himself is judged of *no man*. For who hath known the mind of the Lord, that he may instruct him? But *we* [the brethren] *have* the mind of Christ [understanding].' Let's keep going while we're still on the subject.

Chapter 4
The Anger

THE TWO WITNESSES

Turn back to Romans, chapter 8. We've read verses 6 and 7; now let's read 8, 9, and 10. I don't want to cover *too much* of this chapter, because James will be going over it with you again when he gets into the law. 'So then they that are *in the flesh* [outer] **cannot** please God.' That statement definitely cannot mean **human** flesh!s It means the flesh that we eat, when we eat the outer part of the Word, ***without the blood***. 9: 'But ye are ***not in the flesh***, but in the ***Spirit***, *if so be* that the Spirit of God [the Word] dwell in you. Now if any *man* have not the Spirit of Christ, he is none of his.' Verse 10: 'And if Christ be in you, the ***body*** [the *outer* understanding] *is* dead because of sin; but the Spirit is life because of righteousness.' The *body* being *dead* means when you see the scriptures *spiritually* you no longer see the *flesh*, that is, *the letter*. It is *dead*, all you *see* is the understanding. And if the two are to become *one*, they can't become *carnal* because of *the spirit*. To be carnal would mean division, not unity. I'm sorry, Bob, you look drained. Let's close shop for tonight. When I get in the scriptures and get to reading to someone I forget all about time. Were you able to follow the *overall flow* of the points I made?"

"It's coming," Bob nodded. "I am, as my friend Burt would put it, 'awesomatized.' Looking at it this way makes me think I've seen an awful lot, and then turns around and gently shows me I haven't seen *anything yet*. I feel like I'm in another dimension, but I know I have all of my faculties. I just want to sit here and meditate a few years."

Tony quietly croaked with laughter. "I know, man! Sometimes when I'm *really* in the spirit, I feel just like you do. This understanding that you are learning cleans you out thoroughly. It makes the *old* fade and the *new* shine. Sometimes *it is* a little blinding, but I will hang in there for the duration. Oh, by the way I'm calling James tomorrow and I'm pretty sure he would like for us to come out. Think you'll be ready for it?"

"You know *I'd love* to go. When do you think he'll want us to come?"

"Well, if I know him, probably this weekend sometime. After I talk with him I'll give you a call. You know, now that I think about it,

THE TWO WITNESSES

Chapter 4
The Anger

didn't we discuss the possibility of having a backyard barbecue?"

"Yep. We sure did, Tony. I forgot about it, too. Why don't you check with him and see if it would be Alright to bring the girls along."

"Good idea. I don't think it'll make any difference to him either way. You know if we go for the cookout, we're going to end up studying. So, it really doesn't matter. I feel safe in saying it's okay to invite them. I don't think Cindy can make it though, weekends are usually her best time to find clients at home. I never know though, she can always schedule some time for herself if she has enough notice. I'll ask her and see. We haven't had a day or so *together* in a few weeks. You think Deena might be able to go?"

"I feel *fairly* positive that she would, that is, for the barbecue for sure. She enjoys that kind of thing anytime. I'll get in touch with her tomorrow, and I'll know one way or another by the time you call."

"Sounds good to me, buddy, I'll call you ASAP."

"I can't emphasize enough, Tony, how much I appreciate studying with you. Right now the picture's fuzzy, but I know it's going to clear up. I feel it in my bones."

They both smiled and said goodnight. And Bob was *alone*. No one to protect him from his concordance. Still on a spiritual *high* Bob cleaned the table off, putting up the glasses and the dip, straightening up his Bible and concordance. Tempted, he *almost* opened it. I'd better get on to bed, tomorrow's another day. On the way to the bedroom the thought of sleeping brought up *last night's* dreams, and he wondered if there would be another episode.

"If there is, it's going to be a lu lu," he thought. "Oh well, off to bed." About the time he snuggled up with a pillow he remembered what it was he was going to ask Tony. 'The *flesh!*' That's what it was! I knew there was something I wanted to look up while he was here. I'll check it out tomorrow over coffee."

Wrong! "This is ridiculous, I can't go to sleep, knowing all I have to do is go look it up and get it over with." Back to the table. Mumbling to himself and turning to the F's, he located the word flesh, and beside it was the Hebrew word, 'Basar.'

"Huh, here it is," he grunted. "Whoops, there are two of them.

THE TWO WITNESSES
Chapter 4
The Anger

This one says, 'flesh,' 'kin,' 'body,' 'skin.' Look at this one! 'Bear tidings,' 'bring tidings,' 'preach,' 'preach tidings,' 'publish,' 'shew forth,' 'messenger,' 'one that bringeth *good* tidings,' 'those that *published*.'

My God! There it is! Flesh means the <u>same thing</u> as the **Word**. It all comes together now. I wish it wasn't so late -- I'd call Tony and tell him I see it! Wow, wow, this is beautiful! ***This is His body! The flesh.*** Not just the *flesh*, but, ***His flesh!*** This is what Tony was talking about all night. Jesus's body, spiritually speaking, ***is the word of God***, or scripture."

With this in mind, he looked up several scriptures that had the word 'flesh' in them and read till he couldn't hold his eyes open any longer. Bob was asleep by the time he found the bed. This time as the alarm went off, there was a difference. There was a feeling of having a good nights rest, accompanied by the feeling of wanting to stay there!

THE TWO WITNESSES

Chapter 5
THE BAPTISM

The day went fine for Bob; he seemed to be meditating constantly on the concepts of carnal and spiritual. After arriving home, he decided to go ahead and prepare to meet with Tony, assuming that was the plan. But in the shower, he kept feeling he needed another night in the Bible (by himself) with his concordance. "That's what I think I'll do -- call Tony after I eat and get his feelings about it."

Tony understood explicitly! "I expected it, Bob. That's the nature of it. I was the same way. As soon I started receiving a little understanding, I wanted to go try my wings. I figured you were *about* ready, especially after last night. By the way, how *was* your night?"

Bob endeavored to explain and by the time he finished they were both wound up. Tony had readily agreed with Bob's findings on, *the flesh*. Realizing that Bob was grasping the spiritual side of the word (on his own), he suggested that Bob run reference on the word 'baptism' and 'baptize.' Then if he wanted to, they could get together tomorrow night and talk about it.

"Oh, Bob, before I forget about it, I talked to James just before you called. He said, whatever you and I and the girls wanted to do would be just fine with him and Martie. We need to let him know by Friday, so they can pick up a few things from the store. What we usually do when we get together for a picnic or cookout is, everybody bring a dish or something to pitch in -- chips, potato salad, or just whatever you felt like fixing, or buying."

"Alright, Tony. Great! I'll tell Deena and get back to you tomorrow."

She was excited for him, and thought a cookout was a good idea. She would love to go. "And if you and Tony get together tomorrow, I think I'd like to be there, too." Deena assured him.

With all of that settled, he was free in thought, to embrace his newfound love, which was calling to him from the table. After going over a few things he saw last night, he remembered Tony's suggestion. "Baptism, wonder why he chose that specific word? Here it is." There wasn't too much to offer in the Greek lexicon. Then he remembered what Tony had said to do in such a case.

THE TWO WITNESSES

Chapter 5
THE BAPTISM

"Read how it is *used* in the references. Oh! I think I see why *now*. It means to wash **the flesh!** The 'filthy-flesh.' The *letter,* the *carnal word*. Not my *human body* but the body of my mental knowledge! The words of *misconception*. The stories and the allegories, 'the flesh.' My carnal way of thinking about the scriptures. So then, to be baptized, would be, the ability to *hear the spirit of the Word*.

"That's what it means to be baptized by the Holy Ghost! Not hearing the Word only, but the *understanding* hidden *in* the Word. This makes a whole world of difference. Why didn't I see that before?

"I need to look at some scriptures on this. Let's see, there's one that looks interesting. Acts 19 and 4: 'Then said Paul, John verily baptized with the *baptism of* **repentance**, saying unto the people, that they should believe on him which should come after him, that is, on Christ Jesus.' Baptized them with repentance? Wonder what that means? I thought *it was* water.

"Hmm, Mark one and four says, 'he **preached** the baptism.' Now that makes sense. Preaching and *publishing*, sort of means the same thing. You would be giving out the word and your *spirit w*ould be baptized. I need to look up the word 'repent.' The Hebrew word is 'Nacham.' *It* says; 'Be comforted, receive comfort, *comforter*.' Here's another one, 'Shub.' There must be a hundred interpretations! 'Be converted,' that's a good one. 'Be restored,' 'be restored **again**,' that must mean, to our original **state**. Be restored *back* to knowledge!

"Yep! Here's more. 'Go **home**,' [back to God?] 'call to mind,' 'restore **again**.' I see, if we have fallen **away** from God, then we need to **return**. Like Tony said, 'my people are destroyed for the lack of *knowledge*.' That's the same thing as **words**, and **The Word**, is what John is talking about in chapter one, verse one. 'In the beginning was *The Word*, and The Word **was with** God, and The Word **was** God.' The kingdom of God, or words, is *within you*, it says.

"This is awesome, this is totally *backwards* from what I thought. Wonder why it says he baptized with '*water*'? That *has to be* symbolic. A spirit or mind, can't feel physical water. It has to mean the waters of *life*. What good would washing my human body do? It is of

THE TWO WITNESSES

Chapter 5
THE BAPTISM

the earth, and it says somewhere here, that it is of the dust, and to dust it **must** return.

"This is getting very complex, I think I'd better make some notes and see if Tony can straighten it out tomorrow. Maybe *this is the water* we're supposed to walk on? Maybe this is the *living waters* it talks about? If all scriptures are written for the edification of *the spirit*, and God or The Word is spirit, *and* the spirit is *the one* that leaves the human body; then that would mean what we've been doing, has been **backwards**. I gotta get off this subject, I'm trying to push it too hard. Besides, it said John baptized **in the wilderness**, and if that is also true, how could the *river* of Jordan be ***in a wilderness?*** That means Jordan, has got to be *symbolic* too. Good God! This could go on and on.

"But in order to fit *spiritually*, it has to be looked at in *this manner*. It just doesn't fit any other way -- too many contradictions. This is one subject we definitely have to get into." Bob spent the rest of the evening looking into different subjects and pondering the spiritual aspects of their interpretation. Still, the thoughts of 'baptism' kept arising in every area of thought or subject.

Another night with no dreams. A wonderful day at work. Some of his work buddies were beginning to notice a difference in him. After arriving home he decided to call Tony. Again, Tony was excited for Bob and was looking forward to getting into the baptism story with him.

"The baptism story really helped *me* a lot," Tony said.

After Bob explained to Deena his experience last night with his studies, she decided she should wait until he understood it enough to explain it to her.

"There is no need for me to come in with you two, right in the middle of it. That's more or less what happened last time. You know what I mean don't you? While you and Tony are doing that tonight, I think I'll do some reading of my own. I've had a desire to do that anyway. Maybe I'll find some scriptures on baptism and familiarize myself a little with that too, so when we do talk about it I'll at least have a better idea of what we're discussing."

THE TWO WITNESSES

Chapter 5
THE BAPTISM

"Heck of an idea. You're so smart, Deena."

"I love you too, Bob."

"Well, call me tomorrow, or I'll call you - whichever - and I guess we'll go from there. Tony'll be coming over in about an hour, I'm going to do a little reading before he gets here."

Steering clear of 'baptism.' he scanned a few scriptures and noticed chapter 14, verse one of Job: 'Man *that* is born *of woman* is of few days, and full of trouble.' What!? How *else* could you be *born*? That doesn't make any sense *at all*. 'Man that is born of a woman.' '**Man** that is **born of a woman**.' There's no other way to look at it. Here's another one - in chapter 15 verse 14: 'What *is man*, that he should be clean? <u>and</u> he **which is born of a woman**, that **he** should be righteous?' Something's wrong here! This is trying to tell me *something*, I can't wait till Ton -, I guess I can, there's the doorbell. Buddy have I found something! Man, I just ran into one heck of a contradiction!"

"Slow down, Bob, we'll figure it out." Tony couldn't keep from laughing, as he patted him on the shoulder. "What have you found, my friend, that's got you so bouncy?"

"Well, remember yesterday when you suggested I run reference on 'baptism'? I did. And by the time I went to bed I was so confused, I was going to wait for you before I went any further. Today, waiting for you to get here, I thought I'd get into some other area and stay away from anything to do with 'baptism'. But I ran across something just as mind blowing as that. I'm sorry Tony, I'm so wound up I forgot to offer you anything to drink. What will it be? Coffee, water, or soda?"

"A cold glass of ice water sounds delicious."

"Water? Don't you know the Bible said not to drink water anymore, but a little wine for the stomach's sake?"

"Never mind Bob, the water will do just fine."

They both chuckled.

"Anyway, it was in Job. Listen to this."

As Bob was explaining his feelings about being '*born of a woman*,' Tony was laughing. When Bob finished, he asked Tony what

THE TWO WITNESSES

Chapter 5
THE BAPTISM

was so funny:

"Don't tell me -- I know. You've been there too. Well, is that one of those contradictions you were talking about?"

"You bet! And a beautiful one it is."

"Is this anything to do with *man*, I mean the one we studied?"

"You got it! This subject is another one - or two - nighter, so I'll just bring in a couple of scriptures so you can get the gist of what its talking about, then we'll get back to 'baptism.' Unless you want to go ahead with this one."

"No, you're right. I don't want to get too scattered, but darn it, I want to know it all...now! You know, Tony, I can see where you really need patience when you get into these contradictions. I guess everybody's that way though."

"I'm sure they would be. I haven't run into anyone that could follow it long enough, outside of James of course, to catch those little crosses. I enjoy it very much when *you* find them."

"Why did you call them crosses? "Bob perked."

"I thought we got into that the other night, Bob. Maybe we didn't. 'Cross' means 'contradiction.' "

"Well, I'll be. I can see how that might fit. I've heard the expression, 'crossing someone.' It does mean *to contradict* when used like that, doesn't it?"

"That's *one way* of putting it. It is a joy for the *Christ mind* (in us) to *find* the contradiction and overcome *it*. That's in Hebrew's chapter 12, verses 2 and 3. Here we go on another tangent. But don't worry Bob, there are enough little nuggets, to keep us busy for a long time.

"Okay, turn to Matthew, chapter 11 and verse 11 and you read it aloud so I can hear you."

Excitedly, Bob began to read.

"Verily I say unto you, Among them that are **born of women** there hath not risen *a greater* than John the Baptist: [wow!] notwithstanding **he that is least** in the kingdom of heaven *is greater than he.*' John the Baptist? I thought *'to be born of a woman'* was not a *good* thing, according to what I read in Job. And *right here* it says *John* didn't even make it to heaven. Everyone knows he went to

51

THE TWO WITNESSES

Chapter 5
THE BAPTISM

heaven, or so *I thought*. What's going on, Tony?"

"I thought you'd *never* ask."

"Ha! You couldn't shut me up for a million dollars right now!"

"Well, you think about *Matthew*, and read one more verse: Job 25 and verse 4."

Bob thumbed through the pages and found it, and began to read: "How then can man be justified with God? ***Or how can he be clean that is born of a woman?*'** I can see now, Tony, this is going to be absolutely beautiful once I get it."

"Okay, I'll really show you a contradiction. But hold on to your chair, it's a winner! Turn to Galatians 4, verses 4 and 5 and read them"

Bob found it and began: "But when the fullness of *the time* was come, God sent forth his Son, [***made***] *of a woman*, **made** *under the law*....To redeem them that were *under the law*, that we might receive the adoption of sons.'"

Bob almost looked pale and was quiet for a moment, and then said, "Jesus was not **born** of a woman? He was **made** of a woman? The Jesus of the Bible? Tony what does all this mean? Something is very, very strange here. I *really* feel weird."

"Look at Romans one and three, Bob."

"I don't know if I can, man."

"Don't worry, your mind is just having to readjust. These are things that the intellectual mind skips, because right there, it would be assumed, '*born*,' instead of '*made*.' "

"I can't even find Romans, Oh, Okay - one and three; 'Concerning his Son Jesus Christ our Lord, which ***was made*** of the seed of David ***according to the flesh***.' My God, Tony, this is awesome. What's it trying to say?"

"Well, this is an area that James will have to explain to you. Which I know he will, in due course. He has a certain method of tying it in with other things so you can comprehend the whole picture. I just wanted to show you a few that were *obvious* since you asked me about being 'born of a woman.' I know James will take you through

THE TWO WITNESSES

Chapter 5
THE BAPTISM

this part also, because you have to understand what the *difference* is before you can see what it means.

"But, I really need to finish what I started with the scriptures I was showing you so I won't leave you hanging and befuddled. I'll read from here, so I can emphasize certain areas for you and make it quicker. Look at Psalm 139 and verse 16: 'My substance was not hid from thee, **when I was made** in secret, *and* curiously wrought in the *lowest* parts of the *earth*.' This is the Son speaking from *out of* the Word *in* which *He* is wrapped.' And the *wrappings* are referred to as '*earth*,' or 'knowledge.'

"Hold your thoughts. *One more*, to verify *that one*. Turn to Hebrews two and seven: 'Thou **madest him** a little *lower* than the angels....' Did you notice He was *made lower* than 'the angels' this time? Last time it was the 'earth.' The reason being, *earth* and *angels* are in a way synonymous, 'Earth' means the *law* or *knowledge*, and 'angels' means the messengers in **the Word**.

"Now verse 17: 'Wherefore in all things it behoved him to **be made** like unto *his* brethren..,' Look at 6 and 20: '...*even Jesus*, **made** an high priest....' And 7 and 16: 'Who **is made**, not after the *law of a carnal commandment*...' And verse 22: 'By so much was *Jesus* **made** a surety of a better testament.'

"Every one of these scriptures, and there are more, say Jesus was '**made**.' **This** Jesus they are talking about *was not* 'born' of a woman,' as are **men**. This Jesus is the one **made according to the flesh**, or scripture, as it said in Romans one and three. Now, on the other hand, going to Matthew chapter one and verse one, we read, 'The book of the generation of Jesus Christ, **the son of David**, the son of Abraham.' So, *here*, we have Abraham, and *then* David, and so on down the line to Joseph in verse 16. Read 16 with me and pay close attention to how it turns around and takes Jesus out of the lineage of *flesh* and says He's **born of a woman**.

"And **Jacob** begat Joseph **the husband of Mary,** of *whom* was <u>born</u> **Jesus**, who is <u>called</u> Christ.' Remember that Mary was a 'virgin,' she was found with child before she and Joseph 'came together.' Consequently, Joseph was not Christ's father, only his

THE TWO WITNESSES

Chapter 5

THE BAPTISM

stepfather. I know it sounds confusing, but hang on a few more minutes and go back to Hebrews seven and let's read verse 28.

"For **the law <u>maketh men</u>** high priest which have infirmity, but the **word of the oath** which was *since the law*, **maketh the Son**, who is consecrated for ever more. This Jesus, that was **made** under the **law**, meaning **words, earth** or **letter**, is the one 'of the **flesh.**' The one of Abraham, the one of Joseph, the one of David. Then, the one of the **oath,** or by promise, is the Holy Ghost or *the Spirit*.

"When the law is read, or the scriptures taken **carnally**, it portrays an **image or fleshly picture**, the one we worshiped when we hereunder **the law** taking the scriptures literally or rather, carnally. But **since the law**, we worship Him in Spirit, as it says in second Corinthians chapter 5, verse 16: 'Wherefore henceforth know **we no man** [carnal stories] after the **flesh:** yea, **though we have <u>known</u> [Christ]** *after the flesh, yet [now]* henceforth **<u>know we Him no more.</u>'**

"What all *this means* is, there are **two ways** of looking at the scriptures. They have to be *divided,* **they** are a **two-edged** [s]**<u>word.</u>** One, is called 'the Son of **man**,' the other is called '**the Son of God.**' *One* is of the **flesh** and *one* is of the **Spirit**. This is what Paul was referring to in second Corinthians chapter 11, verse 4: 'For if *he* **that cometh** [and **he will**] preacheth <u>**ANOTHER JESUS**</u>, whom we have not preached [not openly], or *if* ye have received *another* spirit [understanding], which ye have not received, or another gospel, which ye have not accepted, **ye might well <u>bear with him.</u>**'

"Here, he's *inferring* someone *is coming* 'preaching **another** Jesus,' and **for us** to **bear with <u>him.</u>** One word for 'bear,' in the Greek is 'Bastazo,' and it means to '**take up,**' or' <u>might well</u>, **take up with <u>him</u>.**' 'Him,' in this case, means the *message* of the '*other Jesus.*' The *first one* we see when we read the scripture is the 'Son of man,' the one we knew 'in the flesh.' Now, 'know we **Him**' no more.

"Another clue to this verse is in Luke 9, 49 and verse 50: 'And John answered and said, Master, we saw **one** casting *out devils* **in** *thy name*; and we forbad him, **because he followeth not with us**.' Another Jesus? If <u>his</u> ministry is 'truth,' well, Jesus said, 'I Am the

THE TWO WITNESSES

Chapter 5
THE BAPTISM

truth.' Anyway, verse 50: 'And Jesus said unto him, forbid *him* not: for *he* that is not *against* us--*is for us*.' Or you could say, 'Satan does not cast out Satan.'

"Remember, the word has *two* sides to it, that's why it has to be 'rightly divided'. The *'left hand of God,'* (or the carnal, the word of *men*,) and the *'right hand of God'* (or the spiritual, the word of the brethren). Remember, He came in the *likeness* of sinful *flesh*, or words of confusion - the stories.

"One more verse then we'll get off this subject for now. Second Corinthians 5 and 21: 'For he hath *made* him *to be sin* for *us*, who knew no sin; that we [the spiritual] might be *made* the righteousness of God [the Word] *in* him.' There is one side of the scripture which the *carnal mind* sees, and the other side sees them *both*. Making the twain *one*. How'd, you get me started on this. It's *hard to stop* right in the middle of it. There *is more* we should get into to make it more understandable, but it looks like you've had enough for now. Did I lose you too badly?"

"Oh, not too bad. Just about a thousand light years back. You know, Tony, I really can't assimilate it all *right now*, but by the time James goes over it, I bet I'll have read all of these scriptures *again*, over and over, and run my own references to the point where at least I'll be familiar with the terminology. I know there is something here, *there is a double message!* I can feel it."

"You're right, and I can't wait until you see it. Well, are you ready to get back to 'baptism' yet?"

"I don't think I could hear another word. Tomorrow, for that one; I'm numb, I don't think I can make it to the bedroom. Did it make *you* this weak?"

"Oh yes, and sometimes it still does. Especially when I receive revelations like you've been getting, or you could say, *baptism of the spiritual understanding*."

"Oh! I *see that!* That's what that means. Being baptized by the Holy Spirit, 'seeing the *spiritual* understanding of the Word.' Whew! It's all going to make sense, I just know it. How many times have I said that now? How long did it take you to remember all of these

THE TWO WITNESSES
Chapter 5
THE BAPTISM

scriptures, Tony?"

"There is a *pattern*, Bob, that flows with 'key words' in the text. Suppose you read something about the resurrection? If you have studied the Bible much, the word 'resurrection,' would immediately, like DNA, seek it's own. So, *any scripture* that was significant with what you were reading would *call itself* to your remembrance and relate immediately.

"Remember where it was said, 'think not what *you* will say,' well, that's what it means. He, the Holy Spirit, brings them to *your remembrance* as you need them. Don't worry about remembering. *Find understanding*, know what ***He's*** talking about. Look for the *hidden spiritual meaning*. That universal knowledge: 'seek ye *first* the kingdom of God and all of *its* righteousness,' these other *things* will be added unto you.

"And remember where it says, 'the kingdom of God is ***within you?*** Since God represents ***words*** then where do ***words*** dwell? Here *again*, ***within you!*** Think about it, Bob - with whom else do you have to deal with, but ***your mind?*** "

"Wow Tony! I gotcha. That's so true, how *simple*, the only enemy *you can* have *is yourself*. Or should I say, what's *in* you. That's what this book is all about isn't it?"

"*You* think about it, buddy, I'm outta here. Don't forget tomorrow we need to finish up on baptism, Okay?"

"Oh don't worry! *I definitely* have to know the rest of the story."

"You will." Said Tony. "You will."

With all said and done Bob was off to dream land. Pleasantly *surprised* the morning brought no remembrance of any dreams, at least none that he could recall. One thing did dance in his head: "*This is Friday!* One more day! Then a long weekend of study and research." Bob's office would be closed for inventory on Monday - he wouldn't have to work but he'd get paid for it. Today on the way home from work, he stopped to get a notebook so he wouldn't be caught without a place to write his references, knowing there were going to be many.

THE TWO WITNESSES

Chapter 5
THE BAPTISM

After leaving the office supply place he remembered that famous hamburger spot Tony mentioned, and he couldn't pass it up. Headed toward his apartment from the parking lot he noticed Cindy getting out of her car.

"Hello! Haven't seen *you* in a few days. Keeping you pretty busy, huh?"

"Oh, somewhat. How are you, Bob? Getting ready for the barbecue tomorrow?"

"You bet! But I think I'm really looking forward to talking to James more than the barbecue."

"You sound like Tony now. When he and James first met, that's all he did was go to James's. I guess it was close to a year before he finally mellowed out and now he spends all his spare time trying to show others what he's seen.

"Don't get me wrong, it doesn't bother me, I'm glad for him; he really loves it and it keeps him out of trouble. Besides I have been busy these past few months, trying to establish some new accounts for the company I work for. He tries to keep me updated in the mean time. Is your girlfriend - Deena isn't it? - going with us to James's house?"

"Oh yeah! I couldn't keep her away with wild dogs. She really enjoys outings."

"Are you and Tony planning on getting together tonight to study?"

"Well, we thought we might. I'm supposed to call him when I get in, then we'll decide. Are you working tonight, Cindy?"

"Not actually. I was considering going out to eat with Tony, if you guys weren't going to study. Ask him to call me before you hang up would you?"

"I'll do you one better than that, I've got some research I can do on my own, so why don't you and Tony go ahead and have a night for yourselves, I would like that better. Settled?"

"Thank you, Bob, that's very noble of you. I know what these study sessions mean to you guys. I really appreciate your attitude. I made arrangements for my appointments to be cleared tonight and

THE TWO WITNESSES

Chapter 5
THE BAPTISM

tomorrow and to be rescheduled for Sunday. This will work out great."

"Well, that makes me happy too, Cindy. I'll go and call him and give him the good news. No! I'll leave that for you, I'll just tell him I'm going to do some research on my own tonight, which is the truth, and you call him. Give me about fifteen minutes."

Bob had just finished talking to Tony, and thought tonight would also be a good time to be with Deena. Maybe go to the show, and later fill her in on some of the things he'd been into by himself and with Tony. It was a nice break, physically, to get away from the books and to be with Deena, but his heart still yearned for more understanding.

Pushing that aside, knowing he had all weekend to satisfy that desire, he now needed to share some of himself with someone who cared for him. After all, he could sense that marriage was not far in the future. It was a nice evening, Deena grasped most of what Bob was trying to relate and was quite intrigued with what she did understand.

Explaining to her though, brought up a lot questions for himself. After capping things off with the late news and weather, they called it a day and fought the sandman all the way to the slumber chamber. Then closing his eyes, he imagined tomorrow, as he slipped out of today, into the future. It was a real treat waking up to the smell of coffee and having someone you love moving around in the kitchen. The sound of bacon and eggs frying blended in with the humming of a song.

"What a morning to be alive!" he thought. Hopping out of bed and trotting to the commotion he joined in singing. She laughed, they hugged and skipped around the table like two kids playing in a meadow.

While eating breakfast Deena asked, "How are we going to James's? Are we riding with Cindy and Tony?"

"When I talked to him yesterday he suggested we take both cars. Because when Martie and Cindy get together, there's no telling when they'll stop yakking. No feminine slight intended, sugar. He

THE TWO WITNESSES

Chapter 5
THE BAPTISM

thought in case that did happen and we were ready to leave, we would have our own transportation.

"I remember how to get there. We just need to stop by the store and get some soft drinks and maybe some chips. James bought the meat. Tony and I are chipping in six bucks apiece for our part. Cindy is bringing some beans and some buns for Martie and me. She likes hot dogs and cheeseburgers better than brisket, too. We're supposed to meet there around 10 or so. That should give us enough time to get the little stuff ready. James has been cooking the brisket since 7 this morning. They're good people, you'll like them. I say 'them,' But I haven't actually met Martie. She was over at her sister's. Well, I guess we can tidy up and head on out of here. I'm getting more excited by the minute."

"You're getting me that way too, silly. Come on, let's get on our way."

Holding hands and skipping, they headed for the car.

THE TWO WITNESSES

Chapter 6
The Barbecue

It was a nice drive to James's house Bob and Deena highlighted a few things and talked about their future somewhat. They felt good with each other, but Deena still had some reservations about James.

"Oh, good!" Bob said. "Tony and Cindy are here. I was hoping they would get here first. No big deal, I just thought we'd feel a little more comfortable. When I know him better it won't matter."

As Bob was getting his Bible and concordance out of the back seat, Tony came out to see if they needed any help bringing things in. As they went into the house, Cindy and Martie were standing by the sink talking. After excusing himself, Tony made the introductions and Deena fit in almost perfectly. It wasn't long until it seemed like they had all known each other before and were talking over old times. Tony and Bob meandered out to the backyard to see if they could give James a hand with the meat.

"Smells good!" Bob complimented.

"Hello Bob! I thought I heard someone pull up. Did Tony get your girlfriend squared away with Martie and Cindy?"

"Sure did. They hit it right off. Tony and I slipped out here and left it to them. They're three peas in a pod right now. I'll bring her out to meet you in few minutes."

"Sure! No hurry. How you doing with your studies, Bob?" James asked.

"I'm like a jack rabbit. it's hard to slow down. Tony has shown me some wonderful and beautiful things. I wouldn't know where to begin telling you the things that I've seen since last Saturday. I do know it begins to dominate all your waking moments, and some of your sleeping ones too!"

James and Tony couldn't help it, they laughed loud enough for the girls to come out to see what was so funny. Having explained it to them, Bob introduced Deena to James. Everyone visited for about thirty minutes and got to know each other a little better as they talked about different things including science and religion, and just everyday life.

When Bob asked Deena how she was doing, she said she felt

Chapter 6
The Barbecue

THE TWO WITNESSES

right at home and that she really liked Martie and, of course, Cindy. The girls drifted back off toward the kitchen and the guys were discussing their jobs and what kind of work they did there.

They barely touched on the scriptures, knowing once they did they would be in the kitchen studying. Finally the meat was done and they went inside. It was around two o'clock by the time they finished and cleared the table. As they were talking, James asked Tony and Bob how far they had gotten on the subject of baptism.

"Well, like I said earlier, Tony had come by to go over it with me but I had run into the part about being 'born of a woman,' and when he got there, we started on *that* and never got back into baptism. The night before and a little the next evening I had run some references and looked up some scriptures on it. Once we got started on the two Jesus's we didn't have time for baptism; I was getting a spiritual one, I think."

"Yeah, Tony had mentioned that you'd been getting some pretty good understanding, and if that is the case then you *have been*, baptized by that understanding. The key that set me off on baptism, was in first Corinthians chapter one. Did you happen to read that one yet?" James asked.

"No, I don't think so, it doesn't ring a bell. What does it say?" Bob replied.

"Get your Bible and we'll read it," said James. "We'll start at verse 10 and read down through verse 16. Paul is trying to show there are *divisions among them* (the new believers) and *questions* if they were baptized by anyone other than Christ. Anyway, I'll try to explain it as we go. Okay, verse ten; 'Now I beseech you brethren, by the name of *our* Lord Jesus Christ, that ye **all speak the same thing, and that there be no divisions among you**; but that ye be **perfectly joined together in the *same mind* and in the *same judgment*.'**

"The reason he said this is that they each had a different way of interpreting the scriptures. As he says in verse 11, 'For it hath been declared unto me of you, my brethren, by them *which are of the house* of Chloe, that there be contentions **among you**.' The word Chloe means, 'those *who can discern* **spiritual truth.**' To be in this state of

THE TWO WITNESSES

Chapter 6
The Barbecue

mind (house), is *without* contention or division. Verse 12: 'Now this I say, that *everyone of you* saith, I am of Paul; and I of Apollos; and I of Cephas; and I of Christ.' The implication here is that each is of a different doctrine - definitely implying *division*, and we know a divided house, or mind if you will, can't stand.

This would be the same thing as casting lots for his garment, or His flesh, which is His Word, for which many have cast lots or carved out an *image* (doctrine). There are many references. One good one is Isaiah chapter four and verse one. Turn to it and we'll read it.

"'And in *that day* [speaking of the *third day*] seven women [meaning *the seven churches*] shall take hold of *one man*, [in this case, the carnal doctrine or dogma] saying, we will eat *our own bread,* [again, doctrine] and wear *our own* apparel [bear rule by their means]: only let us be called by thy name, to take away our reproach.' And that, brings us back to verses 12 and 13 where one is of this faith and another of that, and so forth. I could go on and on with this subject, but we're getting away from baptism. Do you have any questions, Bob?"

"No, I'm fine for now. Go right ahead!"

"Okay, verse 13: 'Is Christ [truth] divided? was Paul crucified for you? or were you baptized in the name of Paul?' And verse 14: 'I thank God that I baptized none of you, but Crispus and Gaius;' 15: 'Lest any should say that I had baptized in mine own name.'

"The baptism he's referring to here is in Acts chapter 18, verse 8; let's look at that one along with this one. 'And Crispus, the chief ruler of the synagogue, believed on the Lord with all his house [mind]; *and* many of the Corinthians *hearing* believed, and were *baptized*.' As you will see in the next verse of Corinthians, *this* baptism is by *hearing*.' Verse 16: 'And I baptized also the household of Stephanas: besides, *I know not* whether I baptized *any other*.' Now here is the part that *really* showed me *what* baptism Paul was talking about.

"Paul is an 'apostle,' which means that he is an ambassador for Christ, and of Christ, which means, 'one like unto.' In other words, an apostle would be *the same* as *who* he represents. In this case it

THE TWO WITNESSES

Chapter 6
The Barbecue

wouldn't make *any difference* if it was Christ *or* Paul. Anyway what I'm trying to say is, Paul said he baptized Crispus and Gaius; and *also* the household of Stephanas. Let's assume (literally) the household of Stephanas is, Stephanas himself, a wife and some children. Hypothetically, let's give him three, maybe four children. So what we would have is, Crispus and Gaius, that's *two*, and the household of Stephanas, that's *six*. Six and two is eight; here we have eight people, and one *like unto* the Son of God--Paul. Now, Paul knows he baptized *eight* people; outside of these *eight*, **he doesn't know** if he baptized *anyone else* **or not!**

"Hold *that thought* and let's take a scenario with a modern-day preacher, and a modern-day baptism. Assuming this preacher *does not* have the mind of God or Christ, *as Paul did*, do you think they could tell you who they baptized? And if they could, do you think they would or would not know if they baptized *more than eight people* **or not**, even if they couldn't remember their names? Common sense would tell you, with just *eight people*, you would know the difference. Although, according to the story Paul evidently knew these folks quite well. But somehow-he doesn't *know* if he baptized anyone else or not. And *this apostle* is supposed to have *the mind* of Christ.

"Well, to make a long story short, those are some of the scriptures which helped *me* understand that baptism was for our souls -- the way we **think**, not our **human** flesh. *Flesh* and blood cannot enter the kingdom of heaven. Why even wash it symbolically? What Paul meant was, he was *preaching*, and he knew *some* **heard** (or were baptized) but he **knew not** if anyone else had *heard*. I have found myself in the same situation. Sometimes people understand what I'm saying and others don't, some are baptized and some may not be."

"You know, James," Bob interjected. "I just knew it was going to turn out like that. It's the same way I've felt all along about baptism but somehow couldn't quite put it all together. Too much tradition, I guess. But it is so beautiful to see it all come together without any doubt.

THE TWO WITNESSES

Chapter 6
The Barbecue

"Being baptized by water is *hearing the stories*; being spiritually baptized is *hearing* the spiritual interpretation, which is the same thing as being baptized by *fire*.

"Exactly," James replied. "You're coming along pretty fast, Bob. If you want, we can get into the *circumcision* now. That always brings up a lot of questions. You're pretty quiet, Tony. Did you want to add anything?"

"No, everything you said will do just fine."

"Ha, I knew Tony would say something like that," James grinned.

"What did you mean, James" Bob asked. "About getting into the circumcision?" "Well, the circumcision is the cutting away of the *flesh*. It's sort of like the baptism story we just went through. You take a *carnal story* and convert it into a *spiritual* one. Let's take the tower of Babel story in Genesis, for example. Remember that one"

"Sure, let's do it." Bob urged.

"Okay, turn to Genesis 11 and 1: 'Now the whole *earth* was of one language [everyone interpreted scriptures the same -- carnally, earthy], and of **one speech** [or they all sound alike].' Remember the seven churches or women taking hold of **one** man or doctrine? It's the same as *one speech*.

"Verse two: 'And it came to pass, as they journeyed *from* the *east* [rising of the *light*], that they found a plain in the land of Shinar [Babylon; confusion at it's *fullest* extent], and they dwelt there.' Verse three: 'And they said one to another, go to, let us make brick, and burn them throughly. And they had brick for stone, and slime had they for mortar.' These are the teaching materials **men** use for building the temple of God, or the *word,* which is in our minds.

"Verse four: 'And **they** said, go to, **let us build us** a city and a tower, whose top may reach unto heaven; and let **us** make **us** a name [in the minds of men], lest **we** be scattered abroad upon the **face** of the whole **earth**.' Now so far, *men*, meaning those who are carnally minded, are telling everyone how to live for God, or they are trying to build a tower to heaven. Same difference, but they are using slime for mortar -- this slime will not hold up in the storms of life or

THE TWO WITNESSES

Chapter 6
The Barbecue

when truth appears, and the house or tower they're building for God will fall when the scriptures are understood spiritually. This tower of Babel, is the *same Babylon* in the book of Revelation. That's another story.

"Pay close attention to what happens next in verse five through nine: 'And the Lord *came down* to see the city and the tower, which *the children of men* builded... And the Lord said, behold, the people *is one*, and they have *all one language* [one motive, one intent, or *ecumenism*]; and **this they** begin to do: And *nothing* will be restrained from them, which they have **imagined to do**.' Here again, '*imagined*' refers to the *woman*.

"Verse seven: 'Go to, **let us** go *down*, and **there** confound their language, that they may not understand one another's speech.' Did you notice, more than *one* is coming down?

'So the Lord **scattered** them abroad from thence upon the **face** of the whole *earth*: And they left off to build the city [tower].' A reference you may not understand just yet, but you will later, is Luke 1 and 51. Let's look at it quickly and we'll get back to verse nine: 'He hath shewed strength with his **arm** [the *power* of *his word* which is Christ, the *power* of God, and the wisdom of God]; he hath **scattered** the proud [*men*] in the **imagination of their** hearts.' Now verse nine: 'Therefore is the name of it Babel; because the Lord did **there** *confound* the language of **all the earth:** and from thence did the Lord **scatter** them abroad upon the face of **all the earth**.' Have you noticed anything *strange* about this story, how it would be *impossible* to take literally? It is a beautiful example of how the carnal mind has been trained by *the letter*, to overlook the spiritual meaning behind these *stories*."

"Wow, James!" Bob interrupted. "By the way you were emphasizing, none of it makes sense the way it used to. I know it has to be spiritual, and it's talking about the one world religion that he had to **scatter** because of their power over others. What am I missing?"

"You're going to love it, Bob." Tony interjected. "I couldn't keep from falling out of my chair when James showed me *this one*. I'm sorry James, I just couldn't help it, you know this is one of the ones

THE TWO WITNESSES

Chapter 6
The Barbecue

that really got me."

"Yeah it was Tony. He really 'got off' on that one Bob. It *was funny* though."

"What? What? What *am I missing?* Bob said, almost begging."

"Okay," James continued. "Remember when I read the part where God had to come down and *'here'* confound their language? If it were a literal situation, don't you think God had enough knowledge to know that building a tower to heaven would have required *oxygen...* in such an undertaking and there was really *nothing* to worry about? We couldn't have gotten far enough for him to even think about coming down, let alone to bring a whole cast of angels *to scatter us*. But, there again, this is *just a story*. This is *not* a physical tower. This 'tower that **men** build' is a religious *empire,* delegating **their will**, dogma, condemnation, and scorn on us to serve *their interpretation* of God in the way their leaders **have *imagined*** for us to worship him."

"Oh my God! You're right! I would never have noticed that in a million years! I can't believe how simple that was. How could they have carried oxygen with them? That's simply beautiful! Just awesome!

James and Tony both laughed as Bob ranted and raved.

"I'm not throwing stones at them," James said. "Because they don't know what they do. As a matter of fact, there was a time when I taught scriptures carnally myself-- all have sinned. But I kept running into these little contradictions, and I couldn't let well enough alone until I *could understand* why anyone would want to write the scriptures *that* way.

"Now, I understand this is *truly* the inspired word of those who understood the *spirit of creation*. The scriptures *were written* by **holy men** (spiritual minds) of old, as the **spirit of God** *or* knowledge moved upon *them*. Or as they *understood* the operation of creation. Or you could say the operation of energy in matter. That's saying the same thing as *truth* (spirit - energy) hidden in the Word. 'Word' also represents 'earth,' 'matter,' 'flesh,' *or* 'image,' a **thing made**. Lets read

THE TWO WITNESSES

Chapter 6
The Barbecue

Romans 1 and 20 where it says, 'For the invisible [or spiritual] **things** of Him [the Word] from the creation of the world **are clearly seen, being understood by the <u>things</u> that are made, even his eternal power and godhead; so that they <u>are without</u> excuse**:' Well, that's how scriptures were written, by observing the *things* that are *made*. When these *stories* are read they **make** a *mental picture* in the mind. This mental picture is called an *image*, this image is made **by the Word**, or if you will, God.

"This *thing* that is made, is called the ***left hand*** of God, and is referred to as the 'letter.' This *letter* is the one that is referred to when it says, 'the **letter** killeth, but the *spirit* giveth *life*.' The spirit that 'giveth life' is referred to as, the **right hand** of God, or the '*Living Word*.'

"The 'left hand' is ***the curse***, and the 'right hand' is the savior, or Jesus, the 'good Word' of God - Life, not the 'image Word' or the *liar*. Now don't think all of this is wrong, or that God doesn't know what's happening. This is the beautiful part of the paradox. For without this '**war of words**,' or **controversy**, there could be no 'life' *or* understanding. Why don't we follow this ***hand*** theme for a little while? It will help with all of your studies into the mysteries of *all* scripture and also physics, for they (physicists) have also encountered the same dilemma.

"I'll throw out a few scriptures for reflection. In his hour of darkness, Job knew where he was, but he couldn't see clearly. Turn to Job, 23, verses 8 and 9 'Behold, I go forward, but he is not there; and backward, but I cannot perceive him: On the left hand, where he doth work, but I cannot behold him: he hideth himself on the right hand, that I cannot see him:' Look at Job 40, and verse 14: 'Then will I also confess unto thee that *thine own right hand* can save thee.' More proof!

Isaiah 29, and verse 18 'And in that day shall the deaf *hear* the words of the book, and the eyes [understanding] of the blind see out of obscurity, and out of darkness [the letter].' Isaiah 30 and 21: 'And thine ears [spiritual] shall hear a word behind thee, saying, This is the way [Christ, the truth the life and the way], walk ye in it, when

THE TWO WITNESSES
Chapter 6
The Barbecue

ye turn to the right hand and when ye turn to the left.'

Here's a good one about making the two hands one. Turn to Isaiah 48, verses 12 and 13: ' Hearken unto me, O Jacob and Israel [the Son of Man], my called; I am he; I am the first, I am also the last [the first, is the law, the last is the Spirit]. Mine hand hath also laid the foundation of the earth, and my right hand hath spanned the heavens [the law]: when I call unto them, they stand up *together*.' Is that plain or what? It takes friction to create energy. This is what the writers of Genesis are telling us, but they are saying it in such a way to *include* the creation of *all things*, with the creation and operation of the mind at the *same time*, with the *same words*. Not only is this a Trinity, it is also a trilogy. Three stories in one. We'll cover that later.

"Turn to 1st Timothy chapter 3 verse 16, and let's follow how this controversy plays a part in creation. 'And **without** controversy great is the *mystery* of **God**liness [there is the clue, you must have **controversy**]: **God** was manifest in the *flesh* [**word**], justified in the Spirit [understanding], seen of angels [messengers], *preached* unto the Gentiles, believed on in the world, received up into glory.'

"Remember now, 'the flesh' is 'the story,' and the story *wars against* the spiritual interpretation. Look at Galatians 5 and verse 17: 'For the *flesh* [the letter] lusteth against the Spirit [understanding], and the Spirit *against* the flesh: and these are **contrary** [or the controversy] the one to the other: *so that ye cannot do the things ye would* [understand it spiritually].' This is an area of Romans and Galatians we'll get into when we get into the law. Now, there are a few verses I want to read through in different books that will help paint the picture on controversy. In Isaiah chapter 34 it refers to how God is going to destroy *His* enemy, and verse eight implies the end era: 'For *it is* the day of the Lord's *vengeance* [the revelation of the truth], *and* the year of recompences for the **controversy** of Zion [the spiritual church].' Another thing we will see later: *God's vengeance* is always the truth.

"Next is Jeremiah, 25 and 31: 'A noise shall come *even* to the ends of the **earth** [the letter, the lie]; for the Lord hath a **controversy** with the nations [religions], he will plead with **all flesh** [doctrines]; he

THE TWO WITNESSES

Chapter 6
The Barbecue

will give them that are wicked [carnal] to the sword [the sword of truth will destroy their way of thinking], saith the Lord.'

"Okay, Hosea four and one: 'Hear the word of the Lord, ye children of Israel [the church**es**]: for the Lord hath a **controversy** with the inhabitants of the land [religious land], because *there is no truth*, nor mercy, nor **knowledge** *of* God [the Word] in the land [or in their teachings].' And Micah, six and verse two: 'Hear ye, O mountains [teachers of the letter, or lie], *the Lord's controversy*, and ye strong foundations of the **earth:** for the Lord hath a controversy with his people, and he will plead with Israel [the Son of man, the church].'

Here's what the Jews were saying against Paul in Acts 18 and 13. Remember 'Jews' teach the 'law' or letter, saying; 'This *fellow* persuadeth **men** to worship God **contrary** to the law [of men].' Paul was converting the law from carnal to *spiritual*, which is **contrary** to the law or letter. Colossians 2 and 14: 'Blotting out the **handwriting** of ordinances that was *against* us, **which was contrary to us**, and took *it* out of the way, nailing **it** to **his cross**...' What he's saying is the truth *took away* the image so we could see the **left hand** writing spiritually. When you are seeing or teaching the scriptures spiritually, they cannot be contradicted or argued with, and this is what Paul is saying in Titus two, verses seven and eight. 'In all things shewing thyself a **pattern** of *good* works: in **doctrine** *shewing* **uncorruptness**, gravity, sincerity,...sound speech, that *cannot be* condemned; that he that is of the **contrary** [carnal] part may be ashamed [confounded], having no evil thing to say of you.'

"This is true; when you are in the *spirit* of the Word, no one can say anything against what you are saying, and that's the beautiful thing about the truth - the negative *cannot* come *against it*. Like the Bible says, truth is the Lord's vengeance. Oh yeah, that's another scripture I was going to show you. Turn to Romans 12 verses 19 and 20. Here Paul is talking to the brethren - or the spiritual minded: 'Dearly beloved, avenge not *yourselves*, but *rather* give place unto wrath: for it is *written*, Vengeance *is* mine; I will repay, saith the Lord.' And 20: '***Therefore*** if thine enemy [the carnal - minded] hunger, ***feed***

THE TWO WITNESSES

Chapter 6
The Barbecue

him; if he thirst, give him drink: [now listen to this] for in so doing thou shall heap coals of fire on his head.' His head meaning his *source* of knowledge.

"Did you grasp what's going on here? Before you answer that, let's understand the *enemy* situation. We'll cover some of this again later, when we get into the *body* of Christ. But for now we'll stick to the part about *the enemies*. We're still in Romans, on the next page there, chapter 11 verse twenty 8: 'As *concerning the gospel, they* [Israel, the varied doctrines] *are enemies* for *your* sakes: *but* as touching the election, *they are* beloved for the father's sake.'"

"Excuse me, James. Wasn't he referring to the Jews there?"

"Well, in a way, Bob. In this case he is referring to Israel, 'his Son.' I guess I should set the stage before we go any further. As you know, people go to church for many different reasons, and at this day and time, approximately one - third of the people on the planet that go to their respective churches, whatever religion that might be, for no other reason than to find the truth. I'll explain why I said about a third when we get into how everything falls into a pattern of one - and two - thirds, like space and matter. But, for now, this third represents those that 'walk with God.' These are the true Jews, these represent 'Israel, many members in particular, making up *one* body,' His **first** born. Now there are those who *say they are Jews* and are not. We'll get right back to the 'enemies,' but first let's look at Revelation two and verse nine: 'I know thy works and tribulation, and poverty, [but thou art rich in carnal knowledge] and *I know* the blasphemy of them **which say they are Jews, and are not**, **but are of the synagogue of Satan**.'

"Now put this with chapter three and verse nine: 'Behold, I will make *them* of the synagogue of Satan, **which say they are Jews, and are not, but do lie**; behold, I will make them come and worship before thy feet, and to know that I have loved thee.' So here we have some calling *themselves* Jews that are not actually *Jews*. Just because someone is Hebrew does not always mean they are **a Jew**. Look at Esther chapter 8 and verses 16 and 17: 'The *Jews* had **light**, and gladness, and *joy*, and *honour*.... And in every province, and

THE TWO WITNESSES

Chapter 6
The Barbecue

in every city, [this is all spiritual, but read it literally for now] whithersoever the king's commandment and his decree came, the Jews had joy and gladness, a *feast* and a good *day*. And many of the people of 'the land' *became Jews*; for the fear of the Jews fell upon them.'

"If being a 'Jew' means a race of humans, then this wouldn't make any sense *at all*. How could a white person go around calling himself a black person and get away with it? Or anyone else of a *distinguishable* race for that matter. Romans chapter 2 and verses 28 and 29 will clear it up beautifully: 'For *he is not a Jew*, **which is one outwardly**; neither *is that* circumcision, which is *outward* in the flesh: But he is a Jew, **which is one inwardly**; and circumcision *is that* of the heart, in *the spirit and* not in *the letter*; whose praise *is* not of *men*, but of God.'"

"My, my. Man! All these years, all this time, I thought the Hebrew people were the Jews of the Bible, but after what you just read, it's *impossible!* Being a Jew is a state of spiritual mind. Anybody can be a Jew if they set their *heart* to it. If everybody knew this, maybe the poor Hebrew people wouldn't have been persecuted all these years. How in the world are you going to let everybody know this, or how can you tell them?"

"Well, that's what I'm trying to do now, Bob," said James. "In this new book I'm working on in my spare time. Sessions like this help, though, believe me. Anyway there are, as the *two* Adams, the *two* Jews, those *that say* they are, and those *that are*. One set of Jews takes the scriptures carnally, and one set takes them spiritually.

"The ones that teach them carnally are referred to as 'men.' The others are referred to as 'brethren.' This brings us back to Romans 11. This time look at verse 25: 'For I would not, *brethren* [the spiritual - minded], that ye should be ignorant of this **mystery**, lest ye should be wise in *your own* conceits; that blindness in part has happened to Israel, until the fullness of the Gentiles be come in.' In verses 26 and 27 he says they are going to be saved when *their* sins (which means the teaching of the letter), are taken away, which will be done by *the brethren*.

THE TWO WITNESSES

Chapter 6
The Barbecue

"This is a beautiful mystery and paradox. Remember there has to be a falling away first, that's what's meant by the 'blindness in part.'

"Now, we got off on a tangent at verse 28, Romans 11; see if you can understand it better. 'As concerning the gospel, **they** are enemies for your sakes: but as touching the election, *they are* beloved for the fathers' sakes:' 29: 'For the gifts and calling of God are without repentance.' Verse 30: 'For as ye in times past have not believed God [the spiritual word], yet now have obtained mercy **through their unbelief**: 31: 'Even so have these *also now* not believed [spiritually], that through *your* mercy they *also* may obtain mercy.' 32: 'For God [the scripture] hath concluded them *all* in unbelief [or sin], that he might have mercy upon all.'

"Turn to Galatians 3 and verse 22; 'But the **scripture** [God] hath concluded *all* under sin [the *image*]. That the promise by faith *of* Jesus Christ might be given to them that believe.' Now, Jesus Christ means the **living Word.** You have the '*dead* letter' and you have the '*living* word.' If you have the spirit of **understanding**, then you have Jesus Christ, **the living Word**; His body is the **Word**, and his blood is His **Spirit.**

"Remember where it says, 'Unless you eat *my flesh* [Word] **and** drink *my blood* [Spirit] you have no life [understanding] in you'? **Men** eat only the flesh, the letter. **Brethren**, eat the flesh **and drink** the blood. So now back to what brought all this on: vengeance. Can you now understand what he meant by feeding your enemy, **and** giving him **drink?** Food **and** drink, flesh **and** blood. Simply tell them, the truth, *that is* the 'Lord's vengeance.'

"There are no words, James," said Bob. "There are *none* that I can see that can be said *against* what I've just witnessed in my mind. I've got chills all over me. I want to run and tell everybody, I mean everybody!"

"We know Bob. Tony and I both have that desire, and it will *never* leave you. It just keeps getting better and better. You can probably understand a little more by now, why I have to go off on several tangents at a time to get back around to the point."

72

THE TWO WITNESSES

Chapter 6
The Barbecue

"Oh yeah, definitely, but you've really got to know your scriptures."

"True, Bob, but even the *enemy*, knows the scripture. It's the intent and desire *behind* your search that makes the *difference*. For as with the 'sands of the sea,' there could be an interpretation for *each* grain. *Broad* is the way that leadeth to *death* and destruction (the letter), and there are many that go therein. They are trapped in the bondage of the lie.

"What that implies is, without a pure intent and desire, you will never *find* the truth. That's how well it's protected. If someone told it to you, and your heart was impure, you wouldn't understand. They have 'ears to hear and eyes to see' but *don't understand*, as *one* scripture puts it.

"The scriptures had to be written the way they were because they follow the laws of the universe: they follow *that* which came first, **the Arc**, which parallels what scientists call the big bang, which out of chaos brought about creation and its laws. You remember the arc of God, the arc of the covenant, don't you?"

Bob nodded.

"Well, in the beginning absolute positive and negative energy arcked. We'll get into how all of that came about when we get into creation in Genesis. Anyway, the Bible, through breaking down some words, says, out of necessity, *and* by occasion, there was a *heaviness* in this infinity of **nothing**, yes 'nothing' (you'll understand later), and it refers to *this* **heaviness** as a 'tiny chamber.' Over the course of eons this 'tiny chamber,' *because* of the 'heaviness,' began to sag and then move. And *time* 'rolled' on, and on, and on. And roll it did. As a sphere as tiny as or smaller than an atom. As this happened, it began to heat around the perimeter of the sphere and formed a 'disk' in the midst of the sphere. The faster it traveled the faster it heated, the faster it heated, the more it accumulated positive and negative charges, until the negative charges outweighed the positive.

"At this point, the Bible says it starts to fold in on itself, or compress. One word is called 'Galgal' in Hebrew, and 'heaven' *in* English. It's very, very interesting when you run reference on this

THE TWO WITNESSES

Chapter 6
The Barbecue

word. I ran it in the dictionary and in Hebrew. In the dictionary, 'heaven' is defined as 'The space surrounding or over arching the earth, in which the sun, moon, and stars appear. Visible sky; Firmament; **God**; Providence.' That was the dictionary, but wait until you put it *and* the Hebrew together. 'Heaven,' [in Hebrew means Galgal] '**Rolling** cloud [sphere], **Rolling thing**, Wheel [the disc]. Another Hebrew word for heaven is Galil, and its definition is; **Folding ring**. Remember *that one*, it is the key to the arc. Here's some more on heaven: 'Shamayim; Material; Sky; Lofty; **Heaved up things**.' Another is 'Raqia,' and it means 'firmament; **Celestial expanse**.' This fits the *'expanding* universe theory.' The arc *heaved up - things*: matter, the law all in chaos at *this stage*.

"Okay, let's see if we can put this all together. We have a tiny *round* chamber, the sphere, the 'rolling cloud,' the *'folding ring.'* And celestial *'expanse.'* To get a better mind's-eye view of this, look at a drawing of the yin and yang. We'll assume that black is the negative and white is the positive. These are two powers in a *womb*. As time has it, this charged disc, because of the imbalance, folded in on itself and arced. I guess a good way to conceptualize it is to take this rubber band, and as I twist it, you can see where the two sides slowly come together. Just at the point of *touching*, this 'absolute' energy is embedding that image into *all things*.

"But if you notice, this image is in the shape or configuration of the numeral, *eight*. Through the ages, people used pictures or symbols as signs to those who understood the mysteries. The first one is the circle with the disc (some used just a dot), representing 'the **one** in *the midst*.' God refers to *himself* as 'dwelling in the midst.'

"The 'yin and yang,' represents several things: the positive and the negative, good and evil, male and female, the Father-Mother principle, Esau and Jacob, light and darkness, the letter and the spirit, energy and matter, and so on.

"Can we take a break for just a minute?" Bob meekly asked. This has got my head spinning, I feel like *I* just came out of the big bang."

James and Tony both smiled and chuckled as they looked at

THE TWO WITNESSES

Chapter 6
The Barbecue

him, and James said, "Sure, Bob, I forget that you're relatively new to this way of thinking. We can break as long as you want. You know how I am - stop me *anytime* you need to. Did you have a question, or do you just need a little time for it to soak in?"

He shook his head, took a deep breath and said, "Both. You know James, *if this is true*, and I can't see any way that it isn't, where or how does the creation theory fit in? What about God, the one we've all been taught created everything ?"

James grinned and said, "Somehow I knew you were going to ask that."

Tony laughed and shook his head. Then all three started laughing with an inner joy. The girls came and looked in and they started gigging. James briefly told them what was going on and that it felt good to see someone like Bob walking in their footsteps, having the same questions as they had.

"Whatever." James said. "We just felt like laughing."

Deena said she couldn't help but overhear some of the conversation. She said it sounded very interesting, and wondered if she could sit in for a while.

"Of course" James said. "Please do. We were talking about the big bang and how the scriptures explained it by calling it the *arc*."

"I'm somewhat familiar with the theory and tend to agree with it. I would like to hear what *you've* found." Deena replied.

After moving a chair over next to Bob, James asked if she would like to borrow a Bible so she could follow along with them.

"Sure, I'd love to. Thank you, James."

"Happy to, Deena. Well, let's see, I guess the first place to start would be more or less where we left off because that's where everything was leading. I recapped a little of it for you awhile ago, Deena. Did you follow what I meant by the 'heaved up things'"?

"Yes, the things that came from the bang, right?"

"You got it. The *bang* or the *arc* they're the same. What happened *then* was total chaos. Everything was banging into everything else. Collisions, explosions - there was *no order*. Here in the dictionary under 'chaos,' it says, 'Utter disorder and confusion.' And,

THE TWO WITNESSES
Chapter 6
The Barbecue

'The supposed *unformed* original state of the universe.' And when we look at Habakkuk chapter three verse three, it reads, 'God *came from* Teman.' Running reference on *Teman* back through Esau, we find 'God came from chaos.' So out of chaos comes order. Out of order comes law. Remember in chapter one and verse one of John, it says, *'In the beginning* was **the Word**, and **the Word** was *with* God, and **the Word was God**'? In the beginning were heaved up *things*. In order to get a full picture of this, we need to see just what the *word* 'God' means. I've already run reference on it.

"Tony, if you'll hand me that folder there on the shelf, I'll read it for you. While we're at it, I think I should go ahead and read what the word 'beginning' means so you'll have a better overview. Bear with me on this, there are a lot of words, but when it all comes together, you'll understand how necessary it is to have them as a foundation.

In the dictionary under **'beginning**:' 'Starting or commencing; The time or place of starting; Birth; Origin; Source; The *first* part; Begin; To come into being; Originate; Setting into motion some action: Process of course; Leaving a point of departure; A beginner; A person or thing just beginning to do something. Hence, inexperienced; Unskilled.' Or, no order.

In Hebrew, the word **'beginning**' means (**A z**) 'Fierce; Mighty; Strong; Power; Heat; Be heated; Hot.' Another Hebrew synonym, **Rosh**: 'Head; Captain; Chapiter; Chief; Chiefest place; Chief man; Chief *things*; Company; Highest parts; Ruler; Sum; Top; Excellent; First; Principle; On high; To lead; *Gall*; Hemlock; *Poison*; Venom.' **Rasha:** 'Fault; *Wickedness*; Wickedly.' **Rishon**: 'Afore time; Ancestor; Before; Before time [matter]; Eldest; Foremost; Former; First; First estate; Principality; Power; Magistrate; Rule; *Logos*; *The Word*; Prince; Author; Chief; Sheppard; High priest.'

Now the word, 'God.' Dictionary: 'An *image* that is worshiped; *Idol*; A person or thing deified.' Now the **Hebrew** - God *as number* **six**; (**El**): 'Mighty one; These; Those; Power; Elm, oak, teal tree; *An object* of worship.' (**Elohim**): 'Angels; Mighty; Great; Judges.' [**Tsur** means]: 'Assault; Beset; Besiege; Lay siege; *Adversary*; Cast;

THE TWO WITNESSES

Chapter 6
The Barbecue

Fashion; Bind; Bind up; Distress; Fortify; Enclose; Put up in bags; *Edge*; *Mouth*; *Sword*; Mighty one; Rock; Stone; Strength; God; Mighty God; *Sharp*; Strong.'

What all of this is saying is, there is *nothing* that is not God. You could say, the *creator* and the *created* are one. But to make a person or an entity out of what I have just read doesn't make sense. Where all of this leads now is into the area of biology and the origin of species. That's another story, and it is important to the *overall* understanding. It will be covered later on. Anyway, we now have the arc, and the 'heaved up *things*,' which we understand to be the universe or the heavens.

"Let's move on to the time the cavemen came on the scene, before there was language. Can you imagine the difficulty of trying to communicate without words? I use *cavemen* for this generation. There have been many civilizations before *them*. It took many, many years of learning and experience for us to become communicative. Do any of you, besides Tony, know what a waka-paka looks like? Of course you don't, I made up the word for this example.

"Now watch my fist as I open and close it. Okay, now I'm going to put my hand down, and watch in your mind as I say the word again. Waka-paka. Did you notice, you *now* have an **image?** I can now say the *word*, and you don't have to try to *imagine* what I'm talking about. This also works in reverse. I can show you an **image** with *no word*, and you will have the same problem.

The mind *cannot* assimilate without having one *and* the other. It must have an *image* to reflect off of. You can't *name it* if you haven't *seen it*. So, I can imagine that the beginning of communication was making the right grunt for the right *image*. These are laws of the mind. When there is **no-thing** or *image*, how can there be an observer? With no-thing made, how could there have been a **mind?** For that fact, how could there have been a **thinking** creator?

"Don't get me wrong, I see your faces. Believe me, *there is* a God, and *there is* a Jesus, and *there is* a Christ, and *there is* the Father-Mother. How to comprehend how all of this works is what we're after. It has been long and arduous, but after you see and

THE TWO WITNESSES

Chapter 6
The Barbecue

understand it, you will see the *simplicity* of the whole puzzle, the *mystery*.

"Remember where it says to 'let this *mind* be in *you* which is **also in** Christ Jesus?' And Romans 1 and 20; 'we're *without excuse* for **not having** the **mind of God**'.... 'Let *us* go on unto **perfection**'....'Be ye therefore *perfect even* as your father which is in heaven [universe, heaved up things] is *perfect*.' It is our God-given **birthright** for our understanding to be *like* His. We must deliver *ourselves* from hell, which means confusion or chaos. All of this will make much more sense to you after we get into the two Adams, and what the word '*man* ' means throughout the scriptures.

"This Bible could not have been written any other way to get the message across, and fit hand-in-glove with the operation of energy and matter and energy *in* matter of the universal laws. I realize I may have gotten a little ahead of myself by saying some of the things I did. But if you're really serious about understanding the universe and how all things came into being, I hope I have stirred up your pure conscience enough to give you the mental stamina to make it your life's quest. I cannot see any other reason for living, except to know and understand why, **and to know it** in its totality.

"There are many different scriptures that *must* be brought in to make a simple point. It's like a painting, it takes many *brush strokes* to make the picture, *but* you have to perform each one before you can see the completed picture. You really have to want to see it and have patience for the finished product. Similarly breaking down these words to find their spiritual significance is an absolute *must*, and the scriptures cannot be understood without doing this. I want you to understand *this* because of the 'brush strokes' I will have to use before you can get the 'picture.' If there is another way of explaining what I see, I haven't found it yet. This is the only way, at this point, that I can relate what I've found to anyone.

"Hopefully by the time I finish this book, I'll have found a more simple way of presenting it. One thing that does help though, is when the people I talk to have pretty good knowledge of the scriptures, or as the Bible would say, 'the *good earth*.' It *really* helps if

THE TWO WITNESSES

Chapter 6
The Barbecue

they have read or studied it at least once.

"I know you have a lot of questions at this stage, but like I said, when we get through, the majority of them should be answered."

"I can see how that works," said Bob. "During my discussions with Tony several times I started to ask him something and a few minutes later it answered itself. For now, the only thing I'm curious about, of course, is how God fits in. But I know it will makes sense later as you explain a little more, so I'm content to just listen and wait."

"There you go, Bob. It'll all come together, but it takes study and research. But what I have already done will save you a lot of time in your personal studies. After we have finished with what I *can show* you, then we can discuss anything that comes to mind. Then if there is an unanswered question we'll know how to run research until we find the answer. If you want to take a break or get something to drink or munch on, feel free to make yourself at home. Like I told Bob when he first came over: first time, you're a guest; second time, make yourself at home."

"Thanks, James. I do think I'll get some more potato salad," said Deena. "It's delicious."

"While Deena's getting her plate, I'll give you a run down of where we're going next. What I would like to do is get into the area of the word 'man' and how it is used, and then into the 'law.' We've brushed on it some, but a more comprehensive study is in order for what comes after.

"You don't have to try to remember anything, just weigh what it's talking about and see how *it's used*. I'll be taking some excerpts out of what I've already written, and will read *them* to you, it'll save time rather than having to look the verses up. The places where I'll be reading scripture, you can follow along in *your* Bibles, if you like.

This will probably take a couple of hours, so anytime you do want to ask anything or break, please go ahead. I'm sure I'll be covering some of the ground that you and Tony have already covered, Bob, but it'll be necessary for a more complete picture."

"Don't worry about me, James," Bob was happy to reply. "I

THE TWO WITNESSES

Chapter 6
The Barbecue

could listen to it over and over again. It helps to embed it in my mind. I'm getting like you and Tony, I could do this day and night and I don't think I'd ever get tired of it."

"Okay then, looks like Deena's ready. We'll get started. What we're going to see is what God thinks about *man*, and how the word 'man' is used, so we can grasp the terminology and understand why it is used the way it is. I know you've already read this verse, but I want to start off with it because it **assures** us that 'man' can **never** be saved, and to me, that is some kind of statement, taken literally.

"It's in first Timothy, chapter 6, verse 16 if you want to read along. 'Who only hath immortality [Jesus], dwelling *in the light* which *no man* can approach unto; whom *no man hath seen*, *nor can see*.' By listening to *that*, we don't have a prayer. But let's go on. Ecclesiastes 3, verses 18 through 20: 'I said in mine heart concerning the estate of *men*, that God might *manifest them* and that *they* might see that **they themselves are beast**. For that which befalleth the sons of *men befalleth beast*; even one thing befalleth *them*: as the one dieth, so dieth the other; yea, they have all *one breath*; so that a *man* hath *no preeminence above a beast*: for all *is* vanity. All go unto *one place*; all are of the dust, **and all turn to dust again.**'

"Matthew 22 and 16; 'Master, we know that thou art true, and teachest the way of God in truth, neither carest thou for **any man**, for thou **regardest not the person of** *men*.' Psalms eight and four: 'What is *man*, that thou art mindful of him? and the son of *man*, that thou should visitest him?' Psalms 9 and 20: 'Put them in fear O Lord that **the** __nations__ [carnal minds] may know **themselves to be but *men*** .' Galatians one and ten; 'For do I now persuade *men*, or God? Or do I seek to please *men?* For if I yet pleased *men*, **I should not be the servant of Christ.**' These are some heavy statements, and if this were the case, why should **we as men** even try to serve God? "First Corinthians chapter three, verses one through three will help clear up the discrepancy: 'And I, *brethren*, could not speak unto *you* as unto *spiritual*, but as unto *carnal*, *even* as unto babes in Christ. I have fed you with milk, and not with meat [through his writings, or epistles]: for hitherto ye were unable to *bear it*, neither yet now are ye able. For

THE TWO WITNESSES

Chapter 6
The Barbecue

ye are yet **carnal**: for whereas there is among you *envying*, and *strife*, and *divisions*, are **ye not yet carnal, and walk as** *men?*'

Remember what we read earlier in Romans about one being of *this religion* or faith, and one of *another?* Let's go ahead and read verse four: 'For while one saith, I am of Paul; and another, I *am* of Apol'-los; *are ye not carnal?*' So, what we are getting out of this is, when you are *divided* in your *opinions* of the scripture, there is going to be *strife, envying, arguments*, and the fostering of **many negative attitudes and actions**. Again, the multitude of doctrines on the planet. You'll find throughout your studies in the Bible that the only enemy it speaks of, **are men**. Those who take or teach the scriptures literally, or carnally.

"Your *so-called* sinners, do not even read *or* teach the Bible. When they do take occasion, they read it with the interpretation handed down for thousands of years and have no choice but to interpret them carnally, because all they *can see* is **the image**, the story. And believe me, I throw no stones, this has been handed down by our forefathers, and *we're all innocent* until we know the truth.

"As we go along through our studies, keep in mind when you read the words, 'men,' 'man,' or 'carnal,' it's referring to the image-makers, or if you will, the story tellers. The word 'man,' simply refers to a *state of mind,* not a human being of either gender. Remember all scripture is *two* handed, the *left* hand, and the *right*. The left is carnal, the right is spiritual. The left is 'men,' the right is 'brethren.' There is only one place in the Bible where I found *the clue* to what the word 'brethren' means- well, two actually. Let me show you right quick and we'll come back to where we left off.

"Turn to Romans chapter seven and verse one; '**KNOW** ye not, *brethren, (**for I speak to them that know the law**),* how that the *law* hath dominion over a *man* [carnal] as long as *he* liveth [or as long as he is *carnal*-minded].' Okay, turn the page and look at verse 14 [same chapter]: 'For *we* [brethren] **know** that the *law is* spiritual: but I am carnal [outer message], sold under sin [the stories].'

"As long as we are carnal, the law or letter has dominion over us, but when we are spiritual, we are free from that law of sin and

THE TWO WITNESSES
Chapter 6
The Barbecue

death and are alive with Christ or the spiritual understanding of the Word. I'll be covering some of this again later on, but you need this as background for now. Well, I'd better add *one more* before we go back. See what I mean about these tangents? It's in first Corinthians, chapter 15 and verse 56; 'The sting of death [the letter] is sin, and the strength of sin *is* the ***law***.' The *law* is not what you've been led to believe, it is not what *they* call, the *old* testament.

The law the Bible speaks of is ***all scripture***, *from* Genesis *through* Revelation, taken or taught literally, which is carnally. The new testament, is ***all*** scripture, taken or taught spiritually, which is in Christ, that is, understanding-another reason for 'rightly dividing the Word.' The new testament is in his *blood*, which is the *life* of His Word, or His Flesh, which is written in this case in this book. There are many other books that have the truth written in them also.

"We will cover some of *this* shortly, but listen to the point that can be made by putting these verses together. There are *two* kingdoms: the kingdom of God and the kingdom of Satan. Satan said he was going to set *himself* up *as* God, showing that *he is* God, and if it were possible, he would deceive the very elect. And to read the scriptures carnally, they do look like they will save you, which Paul expounds on later.

"Where does this opposing spirit dwell? Remember the *controversy*, the war of words? You guessed it **in the same Word**. This leads us back to where we left off. What I'll do now is read from what I already have typed, the first part will touch on what we just talked about, but we'll wade on through that to get back into the word, 'man.'

"Galatians 3, verses 21 and 22: 'Is the law then against the promises of God? God forbid: for if there had been a law given which *could have* given *life* [understanding], verily righteousness should have been by *the law* [the golden rule]. But the scripture [Genesis through Revelation] hath concluded *all* under sin, that the promise by faith of Jesus Christ [the Living Word] might be given to them that believe.'

"So, the ***scriptures*** have concluded *all* under sin. All this

THE TWO WITNESSES

Chapter 6
The Barbecue

should shed a little light on the location of the deceiver. *He is intertwined in the scriptures*, showing the carnal intellect that *he is* God or the truth, and this gives him power *in men* to become the priest. 'Or the *law* maketh *men* high priest.'

"If Satan's kingdom is close enough to God's that it's **almost impossible** *even* for the *very* elect to tell the *difference*, then it's obvious he's not talking about what we have been taught sin is. Drinking, adultery, murders, and so on are all just the *effect of sin*. It is **not the cause**.

"What *has been sought* in the scriptures feeds the 'man,' the ego, pride. It seeks for things like a new car, public recognition as one 'like unto God,' a *new* doctrine, fortune, all the things of the human world. The word does not lie when it says it feeds 'every intent,' as numerous as the sands of the sea. There is nothing wrong, from what I can see, with having these things, but we have had it backwards. We're to seek the kingdom of God (knowledge) *first*, then all *these things* will be added unto us. I know it sounds like I'm picking, but how can I explain where *we* went astray unless I show the other side?

"I cannot point out any negative thing about anyone that I haven't thought or done. Like we just read, 'the **scriptures** hath concluded *all* under sin.' That also means *me*. I cannot emphasize enough, I **cannot** condemn or scorn anyone, or anything for I feel I can understand why and what brought it about, no matter what anyone has done. *Enough* boasting.

Okay, back to 'men.' James three, verses 14 through 16; 'But if ye have bitter **envying** and **strife** in your hearts, glory not, and lie not *against the truth*. **This wisdom** descendeth *not* from above, but is *earthly* [carnal], sensual, devilish. For where **envying** and **strife** is, there is **confusion** and *every* evil work.' As in first Corinthians 3:3, 'Are ye not carnal? And walk as **men**?"

Now verse nine: 'Therewith bless we God, *even* the Father; and therewith curse we *men*, which are made after the **similitude** of God.' First Corinthians 16 and 13 says 'Watch ye, stand fast in the faith, quit you **like men**.' As you can see, he doesn't *want us to be like men*. God is spirit, men are carnally minded and **cannot** see spiritual

THE TWO WITNESSES
Chapter 6
The Barbecue

things, especially in The Word. *Men can only see the flesh*, 'the outer,' not the 'inner.' They see the letter, the stories, the image.

What's the matter, Deena? Did I loose you somewhere? You had a puzzled look on your face a moment ago. It's Okay to stop me when you have a question. I want you to - I won't bite you."

"Oh I know, James," she smiled. "It was something you said a few minutes ago that really hit home. Something about Satan's kingdom **so close** to God's. I had never even come close to looking at it like that, even though I remember hearing it before in church and I've read it."

"Yeah, me too, Deena," said Bob. "That *was* good. It helps make more sense of what sin is. I'm sorry, I didn't mean to cut you off, but this stuff really excites me and I find myself getting carried away."

"That's okay, honey, I understand. I can see why now. All of what I've heard from you and Tony, and what James has been saying makes a world of difference, compared to what I've heard all of my life. It's much more simple understanding it *this way*. Go ahead, James. I just wanted to think a little longer on that."

"Anytime, Deena. Am I going too fast for anybody? Okay. As you know, sometimes I too get carried away, and if you need to slow down at any time, just let me know. Let's see... where was I? Oh here we go, '...the stories the image.' The flesh is the letter, the story, the image that is painted in the mind when the *words* are read.

The *story* of Ishmael and Isaac, the *story* of Lucifer and Jesus, the *story* of Esau and Jacob, the *story* of Cain and Abel, the *story* of Saul and Paul, the *story* of the *two* Adams, and so forth. As you've probably noticed in these sets of *two*, the *first* one is always the *bad guy*, the *second* is always the *good guy*. The *first* Adam: 'of the earth, earthy.' Cain: *slew* his brother Abel. Esau: whom 'God hates,' Ishmael: 'son of the bondwoman.' Lucifer: who set himself up as God or *as* good. Saul: who destroyed the church. The *flesh* and then the spirit; the *lie* and then the truth; darkness and then the light. All of these and many many more are stories, and the first impression that comes to mind when these stories are read is 'the image,' the *lie*.

THE TWO WITNESSES

Chapter 6
The Barbecue

"The deceiver is the bad guy, and he tries to convince the Eve within us, to partake of the forbidden fruit, which is the flesh, *the image*. And looking at it *his way* convinces everyone to believe the lie, and be damned to hell or confusion. And after two thousand years of looking at it *this way*, there has been such fear instilled in us, that we tremble to think there could be any other way of looking at the scriptures at all.

"Understanding or Christ sets us free from this fear, so that we may see the Word spiritually, or see Him as He is. If you have read the *story* of Cain and Abel, you might remember when Eve 'bore' Cain, she said, 'I have gotten a **man child** from the Lord.' The scriptures we're written this way intentionally, they are like *fish hooks* (**man child**), they are supposed to *catch* your attention. Taking it as a story Eve could have said, 'I've just given birth to our son' or, 'the Lord has blessed us with a son.' But noooo, it has to be a '**man** child.' I don't mean to be silly, but it is joyful to consider *the way* the scriptures were written, but never understood until now.

"Anyway, that was in Genesis four and one. Then she 'bore' his brother Abel. Abel was a keeper of the *sheep*, a shepherd. Cain was a 'tiller of the **ground**,' of the earth, earthy, a farmer. Verse 3: 'And in process of *time* it came to pass, that Cain brought of the ***fruit of the ground*** an offering unto the Lord. And Abel, he also brought of the firstlings of *his* flock and of the fat [anoint or precious] thereof. 'And the Lord had respect unto Abel and *his* offering. But unto Cain and *his* offering he had not respect. And Cain was very wroth, and his countenance fell.' What this *story* is telling us here about Cain is that he is a *farmer* and has tilled the **ground** and planted it, watered it, and grew all the necessities of life that his farm could yield, then in the heat of the day, picked and gathered it. Worn out and tired after all this toil, he brought the best he had to offer to God. But God didn't think too much of *that*, and had no respect *for him*. Abel, on the *other hand*, really didn't do too much labor at all, he just lay around under the shade trees or went fishing, or did anything he wanted to do as long as he made sure the sheep had a pasture to graze in and no animals attacked them. He took one of *his sheep* to God and **killed it**,

THE TWO WITNESSES

Chapter 6
The Barbecue

and God had respect *unto him*. Now something has got be wrong here somewhere! Why does God prefer shepherds over farmers? It does seem pretty silly if you look at it like that. So, the point here is, Cain's offering is *from the ground*, 'the earth.' Abel's was '**living** sheep.'

Remember Romans 1 and 20, where it' says, 'the invisible or spiritual things of God from the creation of the world are *clearly seen*, being **understood** by the things that are **made**?' Well, these stories **make** an **image** in our minds of a literal translation which is the *first* impression, which is the bad guy. Let me bring in another analogy.

"Back in the cowboy days, the cattlemen and the shepherds had had a problem with feeding cattle and sheep in the same pasture. The problem was, when the sheep went to graze first, there wasn't any grass left for the cattle. They found if you let the cattle graze first, then there would be plenty left for the sheep. The moral of this story is, the sheep go to the root. That is why those that follow Christ are called sheep, they go to the *root*.

"This is what *we're* supposed to do in our studies. Don't be content with the top of the grass, as cattle are -- that's the letter. If something seems contradictory, don't pass it up and forget about it. We are told to break it in pieces, grind it to powder, get to the root, find out what *it means*. Get to the bottom of it, so to speak. Cain's fruit was of the ground, and a clue to what kind of fruit Cain tilled is in one John chapter three, verses eleven and twelve. It says, 'For this is the message that ye heard from the beginning, that we should love one another. **Not as Cain,** who was of that *wicked one,* and slew his brother. And wherefore slew he him? Because his *own works* [farming?] *were evil* and his brother's righteous.' Well, here we go again.

"What kind of deal is this? God prefers shepherds over farmers? I wouldn't think so in the human sense, but this is *only a story*. Let's read a couple more verses, then break the word 'Cain' down to the root meaning. Then we can understand better what this allegory is trying to tell us.

"Hebrews 11 and verse 4: 'By *faith* Abel offered unto God a

THE TWO WITNESSES

**Chapter 6
The Barbecue**

more excellent sacrifice [**sheep**] than **Cain** [vegetables], by which he obtained witness that he was righteous, God testifying of his gifts: and by it he being dead *yet speaketh*.' Now Jude, verse 11, where he's talking about those who corrupt themselves with **strange flesh** (teachings): 'Woe unto them! for they have gone in **the way of Cain**, and ran greedily after the error of Balaam [Lord or Word of *the people*. Or the letter] for reward [ego, pride], and perished in the gainsaying of Cor'-e [false teachers].' One of the Hebrew root words for Cain is Hephek, and it means, 'contrary, opposite, reversed ['my people, have gone away backwards'], and perversity.' So, what all of this is telling us is that the nature of the *spirit* of Cain, is to teach the carnal interpretation of the scriptures, because it is of the earth, 'earthy,' of the ground. The spirit of Abel teaches the spiritual side.

"I guess it would be like me, as in the past, trying to save someone and get them to go to church, and worship **in the letter**, or the graven image. On the other hand, if I taught someone how to break down the words to the root meaning so they could gain spiritual understanding and not interpret them carnally, then I would be offering unto God a spirit minded-person, to where the *Christ within them* could teach them the Living Word. And if I guided them in their studies, then I would be classified as a shepherd, and they would be like sheep, eating to the root.

"The same works in the mind. If your intent and desire is pure and spiritual, then the understanding *within* you becomes your shepherd. This would be an offering unto God that He could respect. The kingdom of God is within us. Do you see what I'm saying?"

"I think I do," Bob said. "What you're saying is, to teach the scriptures the way all religions teach them is the way of Cain, and to teach them spiritually, is the way of Abel -- or something like that."

"That's the idea, Bob. The part of scripture which is strong in illusion compels you to believe the letter; this is the part that *looks like* it is directed to the human factor rather than the eternal living spirit, the one that leaves the body at *its* death. The spirit is who the scriptures are written to. Ideally, you could go in my living room, 'and if you could,' leave your body *there*, and you, as a spirit, come back in

THE TWO WITNESSES

Chapter 6
The Barbecue

here, *then* read the Bible. You could understand it with no problem because you would be applying the scriptures to your spirit not your physical being. Like Cain and Able, the spirit and body are *two* brothers, one of the earth (carnal) and one of the spirit These *two*, must become *one*. There is a human nature and there is a spiritual nature. The *first*, has been deceived: 'the son of the bondwoman.' The *second*, is the Lord or *spirit of life*, the all knowing one: 'Christ in you, the hope of glory.'

"Oh well, that's another tangent. Anyway, we're going to cover it shortly as we get into the *two covenants*. But before we do, it's going to be necessary to take a *detour* into the **law** and how *it* works. For these two covenants are Ishmael and Isaac, the two brothers. Some of this you might have already heard -- I was talking about it earlier when I was trying to explain something else.

"Okay, the two covenants, carnal and spiritual. First and foremost, *know the law*; that you may be free, from the law of sin and death and *its* curse.' The curse of the law compels the mind to believe the stories and *their* images. Let's look at the Hebrew words for *law*, some of them are rather interesting. One of them is **Dath**, and it means, 'commandment or decree.' Another is **Choq**, and this one says' '*necessary food*, *ordinary food*, statue. **Mishpat**: 'judgment, *custom*, crime, sentence, *sin*.' Another, **Asham**: 'trespass, be found faulty, be found guilty, destroy.' And **Chata**: 'to err, to miss the mark.'

The law, is *ordinary food*, but as it says, *necessary* food. You're found faulty or guilty under the law, and you will err and miss the mark, its sentence *is* confusion, sin, and spiritual death. Second Timothy, chapter two and verse five reads, 'And if *a man* also strive for masteries, yet is he not crowned, except he strive lawfully.' Put that with Hebrews chapter 7, verse 28, then verse 16: 'For the *law* maketh **men** high priests [did you catch that?] which have infirmity [here it's telling us the law feeds the intellect and gives *men*, a *false* sense of divinity]; but the word of the oath, **which was since the law**, *maketh the Son*, who is consecrated for ever more. Who [the Son] is **made**, not after the law of a **carnal commandment** [literal interpretation], but after the power of an endless life.'

THE TWO WITNESSES

Chapter 6
The Barbecue

"As you know, the law is the veil, a wrapper, the flesh, the outer, a protector of the truth, and '*it* seemeth right unto *a man*, but the ends thereof are *death*,' and could be debated forever, and 'never come to the knowledge of the truth.' And 'they that are unlearned, and unstable, wrest, as they do also the *other* scriptures, **unto their own destruction**.' To live of the *flesh*, is to live of the law. 'The *flesh* profiteth nothing, it is the spirit [understanding] that giveth life.'

"To live of the flesh is to live of the human intellect, ego, pride and arrogance, which begets manifold offspring. Again, first Corinthians, chapter 15 and verse 56: 'The sting of death *is sin*, and the strength of sin *is* **the law**.' The 'law' is the entire Bible taken literally. The spirit or the blood, is the entire Bible taken spiritually. For **we** know, that the law **is** spiritual. The Old Testament is the law. The New Testament is the Life or the *blood* of The Word, His flesh. Let's look at second Corinthians, chapter 5 and verse 15 again in light of what we just talked about.

THE TWO WITNESSES
Chapter 7
BARBECUE PART TWO

'Wherefore henceforth, know we *no man* [carnal teachings or 'the law'] after the **flesh**: Yea, though we have known Christ [the story] after the flesh, yet **now** henceforth know we **him** *no more.*' What this is saying is, we once looked at the scriptures carnally, but **now** -- spiritually.

Remember, *brethren* are those that *know the law, and* know **it** spiritually. **Men**, know **it** carnally, and this situation is what the **controversy** is all about. Turn to Romans seven and verse four where Paul's starting to talk about the law and how it held **us** (*the brethren*) in bondage when we read it with the carnal mind. 'Wherefore, my *brethren*, ye also are become *dead* to the *law* by the body [Word] of Christ [truth]; that ye should be married to another, *even* to him who is raised from **the dead**, that we should bring forth fruit [offering] unto God' [as Abel].

Verse five reads, 'For when we **were in the flesh**, the motions of sins, which were **by the law**, did work in our members [thinking body] to bring forth fruit [offering] unto death [**as Cain**].' Let's go on to verse six: 'But now *we* are delivered from *the law*, that being dead **wherein we were held**; that we should serve **in newness of spirit**, and not *in* the **oldness of the letter**.' Are you following this so far?"

Bob and Deena looked up at him like two kids caught with their hands in a cookie jar, and Bob said, "I think what I'm getting out of this is, none of the scriptures taught literally is the true way of looking at them, and if that is the case, *the whole religious community is teaching a lie.* And another thing, James, I don't know how to ask this, but, it has been on my mind for a while now. In reality, did any of this ever happen, physically that is?"

"I'll tell you what, Bob, wait until we finish studying in Romans about the law, then ask me *that* question again. Okay?"

"Sure. I see what you're saying. I think I know the answer, I just can't believe it."

"What you're after, Bob, *must* come by revelation of the *Living* Word. That's why I suggested waiting just a little longer, and I think you'll see it. You know what I'm saying?"

THE TWO WITNESSES
Chapter 7
BARBECUE PART TWO

With that, Bob smiled and nodded his head, and James continued.

"Now, Romans, seven and seven. 'What shall I say then? Is the law [or Bible] sin? God forbid. Nay, I had not known lust [ego, pride], except *the law* had said, thou shalt not covet.' And eight; '**But** sin, taking occasion *by* the commandment wrought in me all manner of concupiscence [over desire, lust]. for *without* the law, sin was dead.' What Paul is saying here is, since sin is *in* the law; where there's *no* law, there's no sin.

Verse nine: 'For I was alive *without* the law *once*: But when the *commandment came* [the hearing of the stories], sin revived and I died.' Remember where it says, 'The **scripture** hath concluded *all* under sin?' Okay, verse ten: 'And the commandment which was ordained to life, *I found to be unto death*.' Verse eleven. 'For sin, taking occasion **by the commandment** [scriptures], *deceived* me, and *by it slew me*.' Did you get what he was saying there? Paul said; the *very thing* (which was the scripture) I thought would save me -- deceived me. He's talking about the letter or the law. How plain can you be? What this infers is, you just have to be aware of 'Satan' when you read the scriptures. Because he, 'as he said,' is walking up and down, to and fro, *in* the earth; 'which is the scripture, or the earth or the letter or the Word of knowledge,' seeking whom he may devour; **those who read or hear him.**

"Since I'm going to be using *these* metaphors about **earth** and **ground** and *the word*, I guess I need to put in the scriptures that explain what I'm talking about. Do you remember the story about *the seed* and the *sower* of the seed? Never mind, let's read them then we'll come right back where we left off. It won't throw us off, but will help clarify what we're about to see.

Turn to Mark four, verses eleven through twenty: 'And he said unto them [the disciples], unto you it is given to know **the mystery** of the kingdom of God: but unto them that are without [those who are carnal], *all these things are done in parables*:.... That seeing they may see, and not perceive; and hearing they may hear, and not understand; lest at any time they should be **converted** [and

THE TWO WITNESSES
Chapter 7
BARBECUE PART TWO

see spiritually], and *their sins* should be forgiven them. And he said unto them, Know ye not this parable? and how then will ye know all parable's?....**The sower soweth the word**. And these are they by the way side, where the **word is sown**; but when they have heard, Satan [the image, the liar] cometh immediately, and taketh away the word that **was sown in their hearts**. And these are they likewise which are sown on stony ground [not much earth -- knowledge]; who, when they have heard the word, immediately receive it with gladness;.... And have no *root* [of **the** tree] in themselves, and so endure but for a time: afterward, when affliction or persecution ariseth for the word's sake [**controversy**], immediately they are offended. And these are they which are sown among thorns; such as hear the word, and the cares of this world, and the deceitfulness of riches [ego,pride], and the lusts of other things entering in, choke the word, and it becometh unfruitful [or non-spiritual].... And these are they which are sown on good ground; such as hear the word, and receive *it*, and bring forth fruit, some thirtyfold, some sixty, and some an hundred.'

"Now we can see that earth, ground, knowledge and the Word mean the same thing, in the spiritual understanding. Okay, back to where we left off.

"His ministering angels or *messengers*, are presenting themselves ***also***, right along ***with*** the rest of the scriptures, showing that ***he*** (Satan) is God, or the ***true*** Word, sitting in the temple of God, which is our mind where the *words* dwell. Another reason for the scriptures saying that is, the Word has to be *rightly* divided. It also explains the next verse, verse twelve: 'Wherefore the law **is** Holy [spiritual], and just, and good.'

"The reason that the law is good, is because it is our *necessary* food. You *have to have the controversy* -- controversy **is the friction which gives it energy** or life. The controversy within the law *is the schoolmaster* that leads us to understanding, or Christ. The *image* is for reflection *only*, not for worship. Paul endeavors to explain in the following verses -- I think thirteen was next.

"Was then that which was good [the law] made death unto me? God forbid. But sin, that it *might appear* sin, *working* death *in* me

THE TWO WITNESSES

Chapter 7
BARBECUE PART TWO

by that which is good; that sin *by the commandment* might become exceeding sinful.' Now, here it is *again*, verse fourteen: 'For we [brethren] know that the *law is spiritual* [making *it* good]: but I am carnal, sold *under* sin.'

"Remember where he said, 'for if the truth of God hath *more abounded* **through my lie** [his epistles] unto Gods glory; why yet am I also judged as a sinner?' In other words, if it takes this kind of writing to *hide the truth* and *still get the point across*, why look at me as one that would pervert the word of God? Paul agrees he *hates the lie*, and says I'm doing the very thing I hate.

Let's go on. Verse fifteen: 'For that which I do I allow not: for what *I would*, that do I not [**plainly** tell the truth]; but what I hate [the lie], *that* do I.' Verse sixteen: 'If then I do *that* which I would not, I consent unto *the law* that *it* is good [because of the controversy].' Verse seventeen: 'Now then, it is no more *I* that do it, but sin that dwelleth in me [his epistles].' 'in him' means **in** *his words*, because in Pauls words are also **hidden** the lie. At the reading of the Bible for the first time, one would not think there is a lie interwoven in it. Like it says in second Thessalonians chapter two verse eleven: 'And for this cause God shall send them [the carnal-minded] *strong* delusion [he sent his Word], **that they should believe a lie**.'

"We'll be covering that part later. Okay, back to Romans seven and eighteen: 'For I know that **in** me (that is, my *flesh*) dwelleth no good thing: for to will is present with me; but how to perform that which is good I find not.' The law cannot perform that which is good. But I don't think the scriptures could have been written any other way and say what they have to say in order to cover everything about creation and that within it. Anyway, verse nineteen: 'For the good that I would I do not: but the evil which I would not, that I do.' Verse twenty: 'Now if I do that I would not, **it is no more [I] that do it**, but sin that dwelleth **in** me [his epistles].' Verse twenty-one: 'I find then a law, that when I do good, *evil is present with me*.' That's a little paradox, did you catch it?"

"Which one?" Bob asked. "I think I saw a hundred or more. No, I'm kidding, James. Did you mean the part where he said, 'when I

THE TWO WITNESSES

Chapter 7
BARBECUE PART TWO

do good, evil is present with me?"

"Right! It really is a very bold statement when you understand he's talking about what *he writes*. It reminds me of second Corinthians chapter two, verse fifteen and sixteen where he says; 'For we [those who know, *and those* who write] are unto God a sweet savour of Christ, in them that are saved, **and** in them that perish: to the one *we are* the savour **of death** unto death; and to the other the savour **of life** unto life. And who is sufficient for *these things?*' That's sort of like, '*I rain on the just and the unjust alike.*' One word, *two* sides -- or two stories in one.

"Death unto death' means, when you read the scriptures and and you are carnally-minded, you will receive the things *that are* carnal. If you are spiritual-minded, you will receive the things of eternal life. It is a *two edged* sword. One Hebrew word for *edge* is '**peyah**.' And it means 'mouth.' Have you heard the saying, 'he speaks out of both sides of his mouth'? Here we go on another tangent. Okay, back to Romans 7 and verse 22: 'For I delight in the law of God after the *inner man*' [of the Word, and of self]. A clear distinction between the **outer** and the **inner**. He's talking about the *inner* law, not the *outer*, that he delights in. Verse 23: 'But I see another law in my members, warring against the law of my mind, and bringing me into captivity to the law of sin which is **in my members**.' "

"Excuse me, James, he can't be talking about his human body when he uses the word *members*, can he?"

"Good question, Bob. Turn to the word *members* in your concordance and get the Hebrew word for it."

"Okay, here it is: **yetsurim.** Here's the meaning, beside it, '**things formed.**" Okay, now to the lexicon to check it out. It only says, '*members.*'"

"Back up to the singular word *yetser*, Bob, and see if it doesn't have a few more," James guided.

"Oh yeah, it has *five*. '*Frame, imagination, mind, thing framed, and work.*' I see! I see! it's talking about the **image**, the story, **his work**. So his **members** would be the writing or **the flesh**, sort of like a **word body**. That *is* the outer man, and the **understanding** is

THE TWO WITNESSES

Chapter 7
BARBECUE PART TWO

the inner or hidden man. That is absolutely beautiful!"

"Understanding that," James said, "will help interpret the next two verses, 24 and 25: 'O wretched *man* that I am! Who shall deliver me from the **body of this death?** [Only the spiritual minded can *deliver him* from the *pages* of the Bible].... 'I thank God through Jesus Christ *our* Lord. So then with the mind *I myself* serve the law of God; but with the **flesh** the law of sin.' What he's telling us, is *how the scriptures are written*. The **outer** or the **flesh** serves the **law**, the **hidden** understanding serves the **spirit**. You can see now what is meant by, 'He came in the **likeness** of sinful flesh,' and, 'The **scripture hath** concluded **all** under sin.'

"I'll throw in a few more scriptures to help paint the picture, then we'll get into chapter eight of Romans where it's still talking *about the law*. Turn to second Corinthians chapter 4 verse 18: 'While **we** look not at the **things** which are seen [the stories -- image], but at the things which are **not seen**.' Let's put that with Romans 1 and 20: 'For the invisible [or spiritual] things of him from the creation of the world are **clearly seen**, being understood by **the things** that are **made**, *even* His eternal power and Godhead; so that they are **without excuse**.'

"Did we discuss the example of seeing '**the things** that are made' by using the **word** *hand?* I think we did, but look at it again. 'Lay your *hand* on some one and pray for them.' What comes to mind when those words are read is an image of someone physically putting *their hand* on another person, and speaking into the air for God or Jesus to *physically* heal them? The image of the story creates the **first** impression. And if one believes that (the image) with all their heart, *it will* happen: *'thy faith* has made thee whole.' It gives the one who laid their hand on another the sense of power that God did it *because* of *them*. There again, giving them a false sense of divinity. The point *in* this is, if you believed with the same intensity that a certain piece of cloth had that kind of power, then the cloth *would heal* you, or anything you give *that kind of power to*. But -- even still -- it was *'thy* faith that made the whole,' not the one who laid their hands. If you're eighty years old and were healed of cancer you would still have to die

THE TWO WITNESSES
Chapter 7
BARBECUE PART TWO

of old age, sooner or later, never having the mind healed. Heal the mind and the body will be healed also.

"What good is it to have a healthy body and a carnal mind? The word *hand* spiritually means 'to minister' or teach the *spiritual* understanding of the word; *that* heals the spirit mind *and* body. To lay your **hands** on someone, would be to minister the understanding needed to correct the misunderstanding that made them sick in the first place. In other words, a pure mind then a pure body. 'Seek ye first the kingdom of God, which is *within you*, and all other things will be added unto you.

Remember where it was talking about where the kingdom of God is and that we could do *everything* in our mind without having to move our body anywhere? Let's read it right quick. Turn over to chapter ten of Romans where he's talking about those who have a zeal of God and we'll read verses four through eight: 'For Christ *is* **the end of the law** for righteousness to **every one that believeth**.... For Moses describeth the righteousness which **is of the law**, That the **man** which doeth those things shall live **by them**.... But the righteousness **which is of faith** speaketh on this wise, Say not in thine heart, Who shall ascend into heaven? (that is, to bring Christ down *from above*:) Or, Who shall descend into the deep? (that is, to bring up Christ **again** from the dead)....But what saith it? The word **is nigh thee**, *even* **in thy mouth, and in thy heart**: that is, the word of faith, which **we** preach;' And which **we** are reading at this very moment. What this scripture is talking about was written in Deuteronomy chapter 30, verses 10 through 20. Be sure and read them later.

"Let's go back to Romans chapter eight, and we'll start at verse one and go through verse ten. '**THERE** is therefore *now* no condemnation to them which are *in* Christ Jesus who walk not after the *flesh* but after the *spirit* [in other words, the Living Word *has no* condemnation, its *the letter* that condemns and scorns].' 'For the law of the spirit of life *in* Christ Jesus hath made me free from the law of sin and death [condemnation].'

As you've probably noticed the 'law of sin and death' is not

THE TWO WITNESSES

Chapter 7
BARBECUE PART TWO

drinking, smoking, drugs or sex. However, these things can kill you physically. This is where you need common sense. You have to obey the laws of the land, which also means the 'outer,' or physical - the law. You are at liberty to do *anything* you wish in Christ, but you also have to obey the laws of the physical body. Like it says, 'Happy *is* he that **condemneth not** himself in *that thing* which he alloweth.'

Anyway, back to verse three: 'For what the law could not do, in that it was weak **through the flesh**, God sending his own Son [His Word] in the **likeness** of sinful *flesh*, and for sin, condemned sin in the flesh.' Okay.., in order to grasp the spiritual entirety of that verse, do we need to bring in anymore scriptures to help explain at this point? We are going to get into more detail with it a little later."

"Fine for me," Bob replied. "I'm following it so far."

"Don't worry about me, James," Deena said. "I'm going to have to sort it all out later anyway. I enjoy this very much. Just the way you've been going is great."

"Yeah, don't worry about me either," Tony chuckled.

"I never worry about you anymore Tony. I gave that up quite a while back. Usually I can't go fast enough for you. Well, does anyone need to take a break for anything?"

"I think I'll get a glass of tea. Do you guys need anything while I'm up?" Deena asked.

"That sounds good, Deena." Tony said.

Bob and James declined. While Deena made the drinks, the guys chatted about what they had just read. After coming back to the table with the tea, Deena asked James if they were going to have a discussion after the studies.

"Oh, no problem there, Deena, that is a difficult thing to get around, especially with Tony here. Don't take me seriously -- Tony loves it."

"You bet," Tony agreed. "Just try and leave without one. After all we've been looking at, it always helps to hash it out later. That's the fun part."

"Good." Deena said.

"Okay then," James said. "We were talking about God

THE TWO WITNESSES

Chapter 7
BARBECUE PART TWO

sending his *own Son* in the *likeness* of *sinful flesh*. I think we have determined what *sinful* flesh is. We left off at verse four of Romans eight. I'll read verse three again so we won't lose our train of thought. 'For what *the law could not do* in that *it was weak through the flesh*, God sending his own Son in the *likeness* of sinful flesh and for sin, condemned sin *in the flesh*.' Now verse four: 'That the righteousness *of the law* might be fulfilled in *us*, *who* walk not after the flesh [or the letter], but after the spirit.'

"Verse five: 'For they that are after the flesh [or you could say religion] do mind the things of *the flesh*; but they that are after the spirit the things of the spirit.' Verse six: '**For to be carnally minded is death** [remember, *sin* brings death, and the strength of sin is *the law*]; but to be spiritually minded is life and peace.' Seven: 'Because the carnal mind is enmity [warring - the controversy] against God: for it is not subject to the law of God, **neither indeed can be**.' Eight: 'So then **they that are in the flesh cannot please God.**' It's quite obvious *he's not talking about humans* here.

Verse nine: 'But *ye* [the brethren] *are not in* the flesh, but *in* the spirit, if so be that the spirit [spiritual understanding] of God dwell in you. Now if any *man* have not the spirit of Christ, *he is none of his*.' Verse ten: 'And if Christ be *in* you, the body [flesh] is dead because of sin; but the spirit is life because of righteousness.' Here it doesn't mean your physical body being dead, it means your mortal, or carnal mental word - body, the body of flesh. To have spiritual understanding is to have Christ, and in order to have Christ, *you*, the carnal must die. As Paul writes, 'I *die* daily.' In other words, our carnal outlook toward the scriptures no longer holds a *physical impression* when we read or think about the Word. You can finish this chapter later in your personal studies at home. I don't think you'll have any trouble interpreting it now.

"Let's go to Galatians chapter one and verse one. Through several chapters Paul shows the story of Ishmael and Isaac to be nothing but an **allegory**. Anyway, verse one: 'Paul, an apostle, (not of **men**, neither by **man**, but by Jesus Christ, and *God* the *Father*, who raised him from the dead);' He was raised from the dead, **according**

THE TWO WITNESSES
Chapter 7
BARBECUE PART TWO

to *Paul's gospel*. The Father, in this case, means 'the Word.' Write these scriptures down, so you can look them up at home: 'Romans 2, and verse 16, also chapter 16, verse 25. Ephesians chapter 6, and verse 19. Colossians chapter 1, verse 23. Second Thessalonians chapter 2, verse 14. Second Timothy chapter one, verse 8, and 10. And first Peter 1, and verse 25.'

Now, Galatians one, and verse two: 'And all the *brethren* which are with me, unto the church[es] of Galatia:'... Galatia represents those, who at the first, had some insight into the spiritual interpretation of the law, but kept mixing it up. Not quite ready to be diligent in their search, they were hanging on to *their* religious fathers' teachings or orthodoxy.

Let's go on to verse six: 'I marvel that ye are soon removed from him that called you into the grace of Christ unto **another gospel**.' As you now know, there are *two* ways of looking at the scriptures. Here he wants to know why they went back to the law, or letter side of them.

Verse seven: 'Which *is not another* [gospel -- implying it's the same *one*]; but there be some [men] that trouble you, and would pervert the [spiritual] gospel of Christ.' Did you get the point there? He's asking them why they are listening to the carnal interpretation after having begun in the spiritual. When he referred to the **two gospels,** he was talking about the two edged sword, which is really not *another gospel*, it's **two in one**. Let's look at it again.

"Second Corinthians chapter 5 and verse 16: 'Wherefore henceforth [since we know it is *spiritual*] know we no *man* after the *flesh:* yea, though we have known Christ **after the flesh**, yet henceforth know we *him* **no more**.' One Word, **two gospels**. The first gospel is when we first believed -- when we were *born of water*. The second gospel is when we gain understanding into the *invisible things* that aren't **made**. Or you could say, that aren't reflected as an *image*. When the spiritual mind reads the gospel, *it* no longer sees the man, or the letter, the flesh, or the image. We see it in a universal way that fits and explains *all* things, witnessing the scripture that refers to God as, 'in all things, is *all* things.' There is nothing that *is* **not** God.

THE TWO WITNESSES

Chapter 7
BARBECUE PART TWO

God dwells in **all** things. Understanding this is more than the most beautiful thing you can imagine. That will come in time. You must endure these scriptures until you can find *and* see how that works.

"Okay, Galatians one and eight; 'But though we, or an angel *from heaven*, preach any *other gospel* unto you than that which *we* have preached unto you, let him be accursed.' He's going to say this again in verse nine. But look at the *difference*. Verse nine 'As we said before, so say I now *again*, If any *man* preach **any other** gospel unto you than that you have received, let him be accursed.' Did you notice in verse eight he said, 'though we or an [now get this] **angel from heaven** preach **any other gospel** than that which Paul has preached, which was spiritual, let him be accursed.' First of all if it were literally an angel *from heaven*, that angel *could not*, in no way, teach the gospel other than spiritually. This is a great clue. The word 'angel' means messenger. There are messengers of the law and messengers of the truth. They **both exist in the Word**. Remember, it is a two-edged sword or word.

"In other words, an angel from heaven could not come down to this planet and teach the carnal interpretation of the scriptures. Then why did it say that? Because he's emphasizing the *two sides*, and in verse nine he reiterates by using the word **man** instead of **angel**. **Anyone** teaching the *letter* is accursed because he is under the law. No matter how Paul has to write his epistles, he does it so that the truth will abound through the lie. It's like this saying I use sometimes, 'he always tells the truth, even though he has to lie about it.' Do you follow me?

"I think so," Bob replied. "Why would he say, 'if an angel from heaven preached another gospel,' if an angel from heaven has to tell the truth?"

"Good question," James answered. "Remember the paradoxes we talked about? This is part of it. And remember when we looked up the word heaven? One of those words was 'Shamayim,' and its meaning is, '**heaved up things**.' When the big bang took place, it heaved up the universe, which is energy and matter. This **matter** is symbolized as 'the things that are made.' It is also referred to as earth,

THE TWO WITNESSES

Chapter 7
BARBECUE PART TWO

which is also referred to as the 'law,' as we saw earlier. By the way, have you noticed *the word* 'universe'? It actually stands for 'one word.' Uni equals one, and verse equals word. One Word. The Lord *our* God is *one*. Anyway, 'an angel from heaven' simply means a carnal interpretation from the *law*, not the spiritual law. Nevertheless, all of this will become very clear as we go on with our studies.

"We left off at verse ten: 'For do I now persuade *men*, or God? or do I seek to please *men?* for if I yet pleased *men*, I should **not be** the servant of Christ.' That pretty well answered some of what I was saying a moment ago. Pauls purpose in writing is to feed the spiritual *not the carnal*.

"Verse eleven: 'But I certify *you*, **brethren**, that the gospel which was preached of me is not after *man* [though it should appear so, outwardly or literally].' Verse twelve: 'For I neither received it of *man*, neither was I taught it, **BUT** by *revelation* of Jesus Christ.' Let's look at this scripture right quick, it helps to tie this together. One John, chapter 2, and verse 27: 'But the *anointing* which ye have received of *him* abideth in you, and ye need not that any [carnal-minded] *man* teach you: but as the **same** *anointing* teaches you *all* things, and *is* truth, and is **no lie**, and even as *it* hath taught you, ye shall abide *in him*.' Notice here it calls **the anointing Him.**

"Let's move on to Galatians chapter three and we'll start at verse one: '**O FOOLISH** Galatians, who hath bewitched you, that you should not obey the truth, before whose eyes Jesus Christ [the Living Word] hath evidently been set forth *among* you?' Verse two: 'This only would I learn of you, received ye the *spirit* by the works of *the law* [**image**], or by the *hearing* of faith?' Verse three: 'Are ye so foolish? *having begun* in the Spirit, are ye now *made perfect* by **the flesh?'**
This is what I was saying earlier. How the Galatians had heard the gospel spiritually, and had gone back to the carnal. Also, the word 'bewitched' has a bearing on what witchcraft and magic mean in the scriptures. We'll cover that later.

"Now, we're going to skip on to Galatians chapter four. Remember, they have heard the gospel spiritually before, and here

THE TWO WITNESSES

Chapter 7
BARBECUE PART TWO

Paul is going to try and tell them again.

Chapter 4, verses 19 and 20: 'My little children of whom I travail **in birth again** until Christ be **formed** in you,... I desire to be present with you now, and to *change my voic*e [speak plainly]; for I stand in doubt of you.' Verse 21: 'Tell me, ye that desire to be **under** the law, **do ye not hear the law?'**

"Verse 22: 'For *it is written*, Abraham had *two* sons, the one by a **bondmaid**, and the other by a **freewoman**.' Now verses 23 and 24: 'But he who was of the *bondwoman* was born after the **flesh** ; but he of the free woman was by *promise.* **Which things are an allegory: for these are the two covenants**; [Isn't that beautiful?] the one from mount Sinai [the intellect], which gendereth to bondage [under the law, wherein we were held], which is Agar [or Hagar, which means wandering, flight, *fugitive*].' As you've probably guessed by *now* there are also *two* Abrahams. We'll also cover that in the course of our studies. The Galatians [as the story goes] were under this scenario. They started out right, spiritually, but were bewitched by the letter or *curse* of the law, and it caused them to wander or flee back toward bondage. Did you notice Agar is a '**hand** 'maid?

"Okay, Galatians 4 and verse 25: 'For this Agar **is mount Sinai** in Arabia [dark swarthy *waters* and confusion], and answereth to Jerusalem [*mans* religion] which **now is**, *and is* in bondage [to the law] with her children.' All religious scripture in all cultures are written the same way -- In allegory, parables, metaphors, and paradoxes. Jerusalem is supposed to represent the *city of peace*. But *this one* is *man's* Jerusalem, and it is under the law; under bondage. It is not the spiritual Jerusalem, it is **the image**, made in the **image of God** by **men**.

Verse 26: 'But Jerusalem which is *above* [or spiritual] is free, *which is the mother of us all.'* This scripture relates to Revelation chapter 21, especially verses one and two: 'And I John saw the holy [or spiritual] city, new Jerusalem, coming down from God out of heaven, prepared *as a bride* adorned for her husband.' As you can see, *two* Jerusalem's.

Now, verse 27: 'For it is written, Rejoice, thou barren that

THE TWO WITNESSES

Chapter 7
BARBECUE PART TWO

bearest not; break forth and cry, thou that travaileth not: for the *desolate* [non-spiritual] hath many more children [followers or members] than she which hath an husband.' That's referring to where it says; 'we're *espoused* unto one, even Jesus Christ.' Remember, the spiritual- minded are the bride. We are to be married unto *Him*. Verse 28: 'Now we, **brethren**, as Isaac was, are the children of promise.'

Verse 29: 'But as then, he that was born after the *flesh* persecuted him *that was born* after the spirit, even so ***it is now***.' It's the same as when we read the scriptures, and the intellect tries to put us in bondage to *the story*. The controversy is woven *in* the scriptures. *It* is also referred to as, '*the sin* that doth so *easily beset **us***.'

And verse 30: 'Nevertheless what saith the scripture? *Cast out* the bondwoman and *her* son: for the son of the bondwoman shall not be heir with the son of the *freewoman*.'

Verse 31: 'So then, *brethren*, we are not children of the **bond***woman*, but of the free.' As it says, 'And if Christ sets you *free*, you're free indeed.' And the way that happens is, *when you receive* the **hidden** revelations from beneath the words *written*. One of the joys of finding the hidden message of the Bible *is to look* for the controversy, or the contradiction. The contradiction is referred to as the *cross* in Hebrews chapter 12. Have you gotten into that yet, Bob?"

"I think Tony and I touched on it some. Then what you've read about the controversy. That's about all. Wasn't it, Tony?"

"Seems like it. We've gone over so much. I think you're right though, Bob. I don't believe we *really* got into it *that* heavy."

"Well let's touch on it some," James said. "What reminded me of it was a second ago when I mentioned '*the sin* that doth so easily beset us.' To see how that relates to the cross, let's go to Hebrews chapter 12 and we'll start at verse 1 and read through verse 3: '**WHEREFORE** seeing we also are compassed about with so great a cloud of witnesses [meaning the *repetition* **in all** of the stories], let us lay aside every weight, and **the sin** that doth so easily beset *us*, and let us run with patience the race that is set before us.... Looking unto Jesus **the author** and finisher of *our* faith; who for the *joy* that was set before him *endured* the **cross**, *despising* the shame [confusion],

THE TWO WITNESSES

Chapter 7
BARBECUE PART TWO

and is set down at the **right hand** of the throne of God. For consider him that *endured* such *contradiction* of sinners against himself, unless ye be wearied and faint in your minds.'

"Oh, oh wow!" Deena blurted. "I just got it! It just hit me! That *is* neat. That's *beautiful*. I see how it comes together now."

"What's that, honey?" Bob asked.

"The part about the controversy being the same as the contradiction. What *I* got out of it was, the contradiction, or the story, is against the truth, or Jesus, *which means* the truth. And the sinners are the ones that teach the controversy. Which means the sinners are against him, like it just said. So to me, that also means, when we search the scriptures for the truth, the contradiction of the scriptures will be against us, too. "Because James read earlier that **the scriptures** has caused *all* to be under sin. And that also shows me what the *joy* part means. If you know what you're looking for, you will find it hidden in the contradiction. I have just never considered anything like this before in my life. It's beautiful.

"And the part of him sitting at the *right* hand of the throne of God -- That means the truth is sanctified or set apart from the *left* hand. And the part about enduring -- Well, that means you have to keep digging until you overcome the contradiction."

"Well, Deena," James smiled. "I think I'll just let you stand in for me. I don't think I could have said it much better. Isn't that wonderful though. That's what this is all about. When the spirit reveals something to you, there is no doubt, *or* contradiction."

"Oh, another thing," she gleamed. "I see the part about the cross. It shows it plainly, now that I understand what it's saying. In verse two it said, '*He* **endured** the cross,' and in verse three it said '*He* **endured** the contradiction.' Meaning the cross, the contradiction, and the controversy *are* the *same thing*."

"Right again, Deena," James assured. "And the death of *this cross*, means the death of the contradiction. If there's no more contradiction, then there is no more cross. The blood, or the life of *it* is no longer there. And it means his **hands** are no longer fastened to *the tree*. One of the meanings for *tree*, is knowledge. The controversies

THE TWO WITNESSES

Chapter 7
BARBECUE PART TWO

over the cross and the tree no longer exist when you understand *that*.

"Do you remember *in Acts* where Paul said they hung him on a tree? Well there have been a lot of arguments over that. Some say he was hung on a tree, and some say he was hung on a cross. When we understand *the tree* is *the Word*, and the Word has *two* sides, and the word *hand* means *teaching or ministry*, then it doesn't make any difference which one you use. That's a beautiful example, of how you can say it *more ways* than one. Which makes up a *part* of the controversy.

"Let's get into first Corinthians chapter two. It'll wrap up a lot of what we've seen about the spirit and the controversy. We'll read all of the chapter it's only sixteen verses."

"Alright!" Bob said. "I've been *wanting* to get into this one. As a matter of fact, it's the one I was going to read the other night but I got off into something else. You know how that goes, I'm sure."

They all chuckled and agreed.

"Good!" James said. "We'll just start at verse one until we're through. Notice in this chapter he's referring to the *brethren*. Any questions before we start?.... Okay then, verse one: 'And I, *brethren*, when I came to you, came not with excellency of speech or of wisdom, declaring unto you the testimony of God.... For I determined **not to know anything** among you, save Jesus Christ, and him *crucified*.... And I was with you in weakness, and in fear, and in much trembling.... And my speech and my preaching *was* not with enticing words of **man's** wisdom, but in demonstration of the Spirit and power:... That your faith should not stand in the wisdom of *men*, but in the power of God. [Or you could say, in the power of the *Word*. Remember, Christ **is the power** of God, and the **wisdom of God**. Or, the **life** of the Word, the blood or the spirit, and so forth].... Howbeit we speak wisdom among **them that are perfect**: yet not the wisdom of this world, nor of the princes of this world that come to nought: [He's referring to the *world* of *men's* teachings. These next few verses will explain what I mean].... But we speak the wisdom of God in a *mystery*, *even* the **hidden wisdom**, [it's hidden in the scriptures] which God ordained before the world unto **our** [brethren] glory:... Which none of

THE TWO WITNESSES

Chapter 7
BARBECUE PART TWO

the princes of *this world* knew: for had **they** known *it*, **they would not have crucified** the Lord of glory [or taught it carnally].... But as it is written, Eye hath not seen, nor ear heard, neither have entered into the heart of **man**, the *things* which God hath prepared for **them that love him**.' Did you notice how it separated man and brethren? One clue for this is in Hebrews chapter six. I know we're going off on a tangent, but again, it's necessary to get an overall view. Bear with me a few minutes and we'll come right back to our text. Flip to chapter six, verse six of Hebrews: 'If they [*men*] shall fall away, to renew them again unto repentance; seeing **they crucify** to *themselves* the Son of God **afresh**, and put **him** to an open *shame*.' The word **afresh**, means in the same manner as before, or *again, once more, over again*. **The exact same way He was crucified before**. By teaching the scriptures *carnally* we crucify to ourselves the *spiritual* understanding and put the truth to open confusion, and nail fast the spiritual **hand**, or truth of the message. Now, the part where he said that it hasn't entered the *heart of man*, the things which God [the Word you read] hath prepared for them *that love him*.

"Okay, that takes us to Proverbs chapter 8 and verse 17: '*I love them that love me*; and those that *seek* me early shall **find** me.' Proverbs 8 verse 14: 'Counsel is mine, and sound wisdom: *I am* understanding; *I* have strength.' Proverbs 8:8 and 9 '*All* the words of *my* mouth *are* in righteousness; *there* is nothing froward [troublesome] or perverse in them....**They are all plain to him that understandeth, and right to them that find knowledge**.' This goes with verse seven of first Corinthians, chapter two: 'But we speak the *wisdom* of God [Christ] in a *mystery* [puzzle], even the **hidden** wisdom, which God ordained before the world unto *our* glory.' Back to Proverbs eight verses 20 through 23: '*I* lead in the way of righteousness, in the **midst** of the paths of judgment [scriptures].... That *I* may cause those **that love** me [Christ or truth] to inherit substance [faith]; and I will fill their treasures.... The Lord possessed me in the *beginning* of his way, before his *works* of old.... I was set up from everlasting, *from* the beginning, or ever the **earth** was.' Verse 30 and 31: 'Then I was *by* him, *as* one brought up *with him*: and I was

THE TWO WITNESSES
Chapter 7
BARBECUE PART TWO

daily *his* delight, rejoicing always before him:...For whoso **findeth** me **findeth life**, and shall obtain favour of the Lord.'

Some of the things we are to *find* is *wisdom* and *understanding*. It is **hidden**. It *has been* **hidden** from the beginning and was not to be **found** until the end of this age, *now*, when the **mystery** of God should be finished. At this point, let's bring in *that* which was from the beginning. Turn to John chapter one and verses one and two: '**In the beginning** was the **WORD**, and the **WORD** was **with** God, and the **WORD** was God.' 'The **same** was *in* the beginning **with** God.... In Him was life; and the life was the light of *men*.' Remember, 'Whoso *findeth* **ME**, *findeth* life,' I am hidden *in* the word or scripture. 'And the light [truth] shineth in darkness; and the darkness comprehended it not.' In other words, the truth is hidden in the word but unless you love the truth with all of your heart soul and mind, you will not comprehend it. *I love them that love me.*

The **light** is in the **letter**, and it shines out of this *dead letter* or darkness to those who can *see it*. Look at first John chapter one verses one and two: '**THAT** which was *from the beginning*, which we have *heard*, which we have *seen* with **our** [spiritual] eyes, which we have looked upon, and our hands [thoughts] have handled, of the **WORD OF LIFE**.... (For *the life* was manifested, and we have seen *it*, and bear witness, and shew unto you *that eternal life*, which was **with** the Father, and was manifested unto us;)'

When you can read scripture and not see an *image*, you are seeing the *spirit of the word*, or the **spirit** of God is shining through. This **spirit** is called *understanding* or **Christ**. Another reason for saying if you have **Christ** you have no **sin**. Sin is the worship of the **image** [or Devil] that words first present to the *carnal* or unenlightened mind.

And that brings us back to where we left off In first Corinthians two, verse ten: 'But God [the Word] hath revealed them unto *us* [spiritual-minded] by his Spirit: for the Spirit searcheth all *things*, yea the **deep things of God**.' Verse eleven: 'For what *man* knoweth the things of a man, save the spirit *of man* which is in him? even so the things of God knoweth *no man*, but the Spirit of God.'

THE TWO WITNESSES
Chapter 7
BARBECUE PART TWO

Verse twelve: 'Now *we* have received, not the spirit of the world [carnal-mind], but the spirit which is of **God**; That we ***MIGHT KNOW THE THINGS*** that *are freely given to us of God.'* Verse thirteen: 'Which *things* we also speak, not in the words which *man's* wisdom [religion] teacheth, *but which the* Holy Ghost teacheth; ***comparing spiritual things with spiritual***.'"

"Beautiful! Beautiful!" Bob exclaimed with joy. "I just love it when it comes together like that. It seems to come right out and show plainly you can't see the inner by looking at the outer. Or you can't see it *spiritually* if you're worshiping the *image*. And you know? The *image* is what has been taught for the last six thousand years. Right, James?"

"That's true, Bob. For the last six thousand years. And this is the dawning of the seven thousandth year.

"What do you mean by that, James? Or should I say what does that imply? The *dawning* of the *seven thousandth year*," Deena asked.

"Well, do you recall having heard or read the scripture somewhere in Peter where he mentions, 'One day with the Lord is as a thousand years, and a thousand years is one day'?

Bob and Deena nodded, James continued.

"Looking at that statement Spiritually this would be the seventh day, the day on which God rested from all his works. If you look at Genesis literally or, carnally, from *that* point on, throughout what is considered the Old Testament, you'll find God had *quite a lot* of work to do with Israel *after* the seven days of creating everything. It was nothing but wars and wars, until the *story of Christ* comes on the scene - as the story goes.

There were four thousand years of the *Old Testament* teaching before Christ. It has been two thousand years since. Four thousand and two thousand are six. So counting time from the story of Christ until now, it has been two thousand years, and this is the dawning of the *third* thousandth year. You can look at it this way: it was *four* days until Christ, and it has been *two* days since, and this is the dawning of the *third day*, the **day** of the *first* resurrection.

THE TWO WITNESSES
Chapter 7
BARBECUE PART TWO

　　Do you recall over in Hebrews 11 and verse 35 where it was speaking of those that suffered certain ways so they might receive a ***better resurrection?*** And in the book of Revelation chapter 20 and verse 5 it's talking about the end of the *third* day, or the *third* thousandth year or the end of the thousand year reign, or the millennia that the *elect* should rule and reign with Christ until the thousand years were finished. Like it says, '*this* is the ***first resurrection.***' And the beginning of *it is the* morning of the ***third*** day it speaks of throughout scripture. This is the beginning of the *first* resurrection; and the following thousand years is the millennium of ruling and reigning with Spiritual understanding, or Christ. *Jesus* arose on the morning of the *third* day, this is in process ***spiritually right*** now. But like it says in Hebrews 9 and verse 28: He will appear the second time ***only to those that look for Him***. It is a ***spiritual awakening***, not a physical one otherwise everyone would see Him.

　　"Anyway ***now*** is the morning of the *seventh* day in which God is to rest from *all* His works. It has taken six thousand years for the spiritual mind to develop and for the information age of the natural laws such as theoretical physics, the *DNA, in **all*** things to reach their evolutionary fruition. We'll cover all that later, but let's get..., are you lost Deena? You look a little puzzled."

　　"I was for a minute, but I think it's sorting its self out. There are so many ways of looking at it. That really is most beautiful. You know, it sort of reminds me of those poster *magical eye* things."

　　"Exactly!" Bob exclaimed. "That's a good example, Deena. When you look at the poster everything is jumbled up, then from out of the blue it grabs you, and you can see the many different levels that make the picture."

　　"It really is a good example, Deena," James replied. "That tells me a lot about what you see and how you weigh the scriptures. That brings us to the brush strokes we talked about earlier."

　　"Oh my goodness!" Deena exclaimed. "I hate to interrupt, but I just noticed the time. It's nearly eleven o'clock. I hate to leave now, I was just getting into it, but I've got a lot to do tomorrow and I guess I really should go. I was so engrossed I even forgot about the discussion

THE TWO WITNESSES
Chapter 7
BARBECUE PART TWO

we were going to have. Oh well, next time I guess. By the way, Tony, I haven't forgot about the *ox* yet."

"I apologize, Deena," Tony said. "I think you understand by now. We'll get into that soon."

"No problem, Tony. I truly do understand. It just happened to me. And anytime is fine. Bob, you don't mind leaving now do you?"

"Not at all. I didn't realize it was that late either. James, I can't tell you the pleasure I've had listening to your interpretation of the scriptures. It makes more sense than anything I've *ever* come across. Would you like to get together tomorrow for a little while? I think Deena's going to be tied up most of the day."

"Of course, Bob, if you would like to, I'm always ready. We'll just pick up where we left off at verse 14."

"Great!" Bob replied. "Tony, are you coming tomorrow?"

"You bet, buddy. We can ride together if you want to, Cindy has to work tomorrow also."

"Alright then, I'll give you a buzz when I get up moving around," said Bob.

After saying goodnight to everyone, Bob and Deena drove off into the night. It was mostly quiet on the way back, both of them reflecting on what James had shared with them.

THE TWO WITNESSES
Chapter 8
The weekend

The birds chirping outside the window, gently woke Bob. 'What a beautiful day" he thought. 'What a *beautiful* day to study. I can't believe it's only seven o'clock. Good! I'll have time to do a little reading before we leave. No need to call Tony just yet -- maybe around nine would be more like it."

With that, Bob showered, dressed, and sat down for coffee. It didn't seem like ten minutes had gone by before it was time to call Tony.

"Good morning, Tony," Bob said with anxiety in his voice. "Are you on your way yet? I'm kidding! I'll be *more* than happy to come by and get *you* whenever you are, though."

"No problem," Tony replied. "I'm ready whenever you are. James has already called to see when we were heading out. I'll call him and tell him you're on your way to pick me up and we'll be coming that way."

"I'm walking out now Tony, see you in a minute."

Tony had just walked out toward the parking lot when Bob pulled up and they were on their way to James's.'

"You know," said Bob. "I go to sleep with what we've talked about and I wake up with it. Seems like basically that's all I want to think about. I'm not complaining, by no means -- it's beautiful. It really changes you."

"Isn't that a beautiful witness to the scripture, Bob?"

"What's that?" he asked.

"You know, Bob, 'pray without ceasing.' "

"I knew that!" Bob chuckled. "That's exactly what it is. You can't help but pray without ceasing once you've seen the *spirit*. Can you?"

"It's impossible, Bob. 'Lo I'm with you always,' *He* says. Once you've been born of the Spirit, you have it with you constantly. *He* also said, 'I will *never* leave you.' To pray without ceasing in the traditional sense is *also* impossible. You can also add to *that*, once saved, always saved."

"That's what it is, Tony! That's exactly what it is. That's also part of the grace thing we talked about. You know, 'saved by grace.'

THE TWO WITNESSES

Chapter 8
The weekend

Grace is sort of like a cattle prod. It keeps after you until you *find* the truth."

"It's the most beautiful thing I've ever seen," Tony remarked. "Here *we* are. There's James carrying out the trash."

Without much adieu, the three headed toward the kitchen to rehash what was discussed the night before.

"Bob, I was quite impressed with your girlfriend," James said. "She really catches on quick. I feel she'll be right up there with us very soon. Looks like you and Tony have been keeping her up to date. Tony, did you or Bob have anything in particular you wanted to get into, or do you want to take up where we left off last night?"

Bob and Tony both agreed they would like to go ahead with last night's discussion.

"There was something I wanted to add to Deena's statement about the poster," James continued. "When it does come into focus, it also appears *three* dimensional. That's a little play on the trinity. I sort of thought that was apropos.

"It really *is* the same thing. It follows the pattern pretty closely," Tony said.

Bob just nodded and grinned.

"Okay, we left off talking about comparing spiritual things with spiritual things," James continued. "And that was in first Corinthians chapter 2 and verse 13 and in 14 it reads, 'But the carnal mind receiveth not the things of the *spirit* of God: for they are foolishness unto him: *neither can he know them*, **because they are spiritually discerned**.' Now again, if you compare that with first Timothy chapter 6, verses 15 and 16 where it's referring to Christ as the spiritual light, you can see the relevance, especially where it says, 'which **no man** can approach unto; whom **no man** hath seen nor can see.' Why? Because the scriptures *are spiritually* discerned.

"Now, verse 15, 'But he that *is* spiritual ***judgeth all things***, yet he himself is judged of **no man**.' And the last verse, 16, 'For ***who*** hath known the mind of the Lord, that he may instruct him? ***But we have the mind*** of Christ.' Looking at chapter two, we can understand the scriptures *must be* spiritually discerned if we are to

Chapter 8
The weekend

THE TWO WITNESSES

find the **hidden wisdom** that has been **sealed** from the beginning, but now *in* the end, is revealed. This relates to the scripture in Daniel 12 and 4 where the book was to be sealed *until knowledge increased.* And *this is* the age of information.

"As for instructing Christ, as in verse 16, *those who converse spiritually* are instructing the Christ within each of them. And in turn when the scriptures are read with a spiritual mind, the hidden spiritual understanding is revealed to the inquirer. As for *judging **all things***, the spirit of Christ *cannot* condemn. Therefore, to judge spiritually, means to *weigh*. Like it says, 'weigh **all things** and hold fast to that which is good.' Any questions?"

"What wonderful understanding!" Bob smiled. "That brings to mind where the scriptures said, 'you shall know them by the fruit they bear.' In answer to your question, 'are there any questions,' the questions that do cross my mind seem to fall away soon after. It seems like the answer is right around the corner. It's all hidden but then it's not. What a beautiful contradiction."

"Speaking of contradiction, that's where we are headed. Let's get into some more of them," said James. "Off and on I will add the conversion word or words in place of the written text. It saves time explaining what it means. Look back at chapter one in first Corinthians and we'll go through verses 18 to 26. Verse 18: 'For the preaching of the cross [contradiction] is to them that perish foolishness; but unto us which are saved it is the power of God [the Word].' In the next few verses he explains it was done this way so he could hide the truth from *men* **by** the way it is *written*. Verse 19: 'For it is ***written***, I [truth] will destroy the wisdom of the wise, and will bring to nothing the understanding of the prudent.' Verse 20: 'Where is the wise? Where is the scribe? where is the *disputer* of **this** world? hath not God [the Word] made foolish the wisdom of **this** world?' Verse 21: 'For after that in the wisdom of [knowledge] the world by wisdom knew not *God*, it pleased God by the *foolishness* of *preaching* [the letter] to save them that believe.'

"Let's throw in Titus chapter one and verse three right quick. 'But hath in due times manifested *his* [Son] **through** *preaching*,

THE TWO WITNESSES

Chapter 8
The weekend

which is committed unto me *according to the commandment* of [truth] our savior.' And two more in Romans chapter 16, verses 25 and 26: 'Now to him that is of power to stablish you according to *my* gospel, and the preaching of [the *Living* Word], according to the revelation of *the mystery*, which was kept *secret* since the world began.' Verse 26: 'But now is made manifest, and *by* the *scriptures of the prophets*, according to the commandment of the everlasting [Word], made known to all [religions] for the obedience of faith:'

"Turn to Hosea chapter 12 and verse 10: '[The Word] has also spoken *by the prophets*, and the [Word has] multiplied *visions*, and *used similitudes*, **by the ministry** of the prophets.' There it is in a nut shell! The mystery! It is *all* in parables, allegory, visions, similitudes, paradoxes, metaphors, et cetera. This is how the prophets wrote. This is how *it is written.*

"And for good reason. There are *seven* levels, as is there are seven levels of flesh on his *word body*. Some words that are despised by many scribes, are most necessary for *each level* of interpretation. Words like 'durst,' 'thou' 'ye,' and *many* more. It is for *this* reason they have written 'the living Bible,' 'good news Bible,' and this Bible and that Bible. Trying to make it fit the *human experience* instead of the *spiritual* one. Trying to make it fit the *outer* and not the *inner*. Seeing it only on the first level, **the outer** of the **word body**. The outer level of the skin on our human body is *dead flesh*, and *that* is what the carnal mind eats when *it* eats *His flesh*. The Bible, or any ancient writ, was written to the inner mind and not to the carnal intellect.

There I go again. Okay, back to first Corinthians 1 and 22: 'For the [carnal] require a sign, and the Greeks seek after wisdom:' Verse 23: 'But *we* preach [the truth] crucified [or contradiction], unto the [carnal] a stumbling block, and to the Greeks *foolishness*.' See, Romans 11 and verse 19, Isaiah 57 and 14, Ezekiel 3 and 20, Revelation 2 and 14. Also run references on the phrase stumbling block; it means the 'image.'

"Verse 24: 'But unto them which are called, both Jews and Greeks, *Christ* the *power* of [the Word], *and* the *wisdom* of [the Word].' Verse 25: 'Because the **foolishness** [preaching] of the [Word]

THE TWO WITNESSES

Chapter 8
The weekend

is wiser than **men**; and the weakness of [the Word] is stronger than **men**.' And 26: 'For ye see your calling **brethren**, how that not many wise **men after the flesh**, not many mighty, not many noble, *are called*.' John 6 and 63: 'It is the spirit that quickeneth; **the <u>letter</u> profiteth nothing: the words** that **I** speak unto you, **they** are spirit and **they** are life.' That should be very clear. The letter or the stories cannot save you from *themselves*, it must be the spirit or the life of the Word. The **Son** of what we are destroyed for the lack of -- Knowledge -- the Word."

"Whew, what a message! I like the way you changed those words out, it does seem easier to grasp, and *quicker*. What a most beautiful understanding," Bob said excitedly. "That's what it means when he said '*my* people are destroyed for the *lack of knowledge!* And God *is* knowledge.' If He is the Word, then we are destroyed for the lack of God, and 'the god of many shall wax cold.' It all means the same doesn't it?"

"True Bob," James said. "But don't forget you have to have the Son also. The father *and* the Son; the flesh *and* the blood."

"That's right." Bob said. "Well, I knew that. And in my mind I *meant* that. You know what I mean don't you?"

"Yes I do, Bob. I was fluffing your spiritual feathers," James chuckled. "A good scripture to tie that in is where we left off in John six. Look at verse 44: 'No **man** [what about women and children?] can come unto me except the Father which hath sent me draw him: and I will raise him up *at* the **last day** [or third day].' And verse 65: 'Therefore said I unto you, that **no man** can come unto **me**, except it were given unto him of my Father [in this case, the Word, because *that's where He is*]. Looking at *His* Father as the Word, and the Son as the *life* of the Word, and then comparing it with, 'In the beginning *was* the *Word*, and the *Word* was **with** God, and the *Word* **was** God. **The same** *was in the beginning with* God.' Here it's talking about **two** things. Now turn to first John chapter 2 and verse 23: 'Whosoever denieth the Son, the same hath not the Father: **but he that acknowledgeth the Son hath the Father <u>also</u>**.' You can't help it. As He said, 'my Father **and** I are **One**. If you have seen truth, you

115

THE TWO WITNESSES

Chapter 8
The weekend

have seen the Word *also*. In other words if you have seen the Son, you *must have* seen the Father, or you could not have seen the Son. The truth or the Son is *wrapped* in the Father Word, swaddling clothes.

"Flip back to chapter one and we'll start with verse one, and what we've already covered should become clear to what has been said. '**THAT** which was from the beginning, which [we the brethren] have heard, which [the spiritual] have seen with our [understanding], which *we* have looked upon, and our [***thoughts***] have handled, of the **Word** of life.' Verse two: 'For the [truth] was manifested, and *we* have seen *it*, and bear witness, and shew unto you *that* eternal [Christ], which was *with* the [Word], and was ***manifested*** unto [those that are spiritual].' Verse three: 'That which *we* have seen and heard declare we unto you, that *ye also* may have fellowship with us: and truly our fellowship *is* with the Father, and with his Son [the ***living*** Word],' 'And he that ***seeth me seeth him*** that sent me.' That was John 12 and 45.

Turn to Phillipians two, verses five and six: 'Let this mind be in you, which was also in Christ Jesus: who being in the form of [the Word], thought it not robbery to be ***equal with*** [the Word].' Again; 'I and my Father *are* one.' The *Word is the veil* that protects the *inner* message. The *swaddling clothes* that are wrapped around Him, the 'Flaming Sword.' Remember in Romans where it says, 'And the commandment *which was ordained to life*, **I found to be unto death**. For sin, taking occasion by the commandment, deceived me, and by it slew me'? By looking at the scriptures *carnally*, or *literally*, the stories do the teaching. These stories ***appear*** to be the truth, it's in 'the likeness' of truth, but as he says, ***it is sin***. It is only the letter, and the ***letter killeth***. Let's listen where the letter tells us this.
"Turn to Deuteronomy 32 and verse 39: '[Understand] now that *I*, even *I*, *am* he, and *there is* no god with me: *I* kill, and *I* make alive; *I* wound and *I* heal: neither *is there* any [man] that can deliver out of my ***hand*** [Word].' Another scripture for that is Galatians 3 and 22: 'But the [Word] hath ***concluded all*** under sin.' And the ***law*** is the ***strength*** of this sin, which also brings spiritual death.

THE TWO WITNESSES

Chapter 8
The weekend

"Speaking of, 'the letter killeth,' maybe you and Tony have been here before in your studies, but I'd like to bring it in again. Turn to second Corinthians chapter three and we'll start at verse six: 'Who **also** hath made us **able** ministers of the **new** testament [truth]; ***not of the letter***, but of the spirit: for the letter killeth, but the spirit giveth life.' Or, 'the *flesh* profiteth nothing.' Verse seven: 'But if the ministration of [the letter], written *and* engraven in stones [or the law], was glorious, so that the children of Israel could not steadfastly behold the face of Moses [deliverer from water, or bondage] for the glory of his countenance; which glory was to be done away:' Eight; 'How shall not the ministration of [understanding] be rather glorious? Nine: 'For if the [teaching] of [the stories] be glory, much more the ministration of [understanding] ***exceed*** in glory.' This is what it meant in Romans when he said, 'For if the truth [understanding] ***hath more abounded*** through my [gospel lie] unto his glory,' et cetera. Verse ten: 'For even that which was made glorious [the stories, the veil] had no glory in this respect, *by reason of the glory that excelleth.*' Which is the spiritual understanding. Before we go further, Tony, have you and Bob discussed what Moses represents?"

"I don't think so, have we, Bob?"

"It doesn't ring a bell. At least not that I can remember."

"Okay then," James said. "Moses represents 'the drawer out of ***water***,' a deliverer like unto Jesus. Moses *is the message in scripture* that leads you out of 'the story bondage.' It is that spiritual attitude within us that sets us free from being bound by the letter. He helps free your mind to where you can search in different areas, or the wilderness, for freedom from the condemnation and scorn. Or, you could say, from the lashes of the whip by the Egyptians. 'Egypt bondage' means, bound under ***the law***. When you are bound by traditional ways of reading scripture you are most always beaten by the task masters. Moses brings you out of *that* through the 'red sea' or guilty waters, into the wilderness. As a matter of fact, Bob, that's where you were when we met you. The *stage* for scripture is in our minds.

"Remember you said you had gotten into some self-help

THE TWO WITNESSES
Chapter 8
The weekend

books and other things looking for answers anywhere you could? Well, in your heart you were **wandering** and searching, but it was not in the Bible. The veil had been removed from Moses' *face*, and you read into the scriptures something different than they were teaching, and it made you want to look elsewhere. If you are bound by the law and are afraid to question the contradictions, you cannot pass through the sea of guilt. The word 'blood,' has *two* meanings, one is life, and the other is guilt.

Let's get back to the text. We left off at verse 11: 'For if *that* which is done away *was* glorious, much more *that* which remaineth [your *new* understanding].' Verse twelve: 'Seeing then we have such hope, we use **great plainness** of speech:' Now 13: 'And not as Moses, which put a veil over his *face*, that the children of Israel [those who read the Bible literally] could not steadfastly look to the end of *that* [the law, the stories] which is abolished [in Christ].' And 14: 'But their **minds** were blinded: for until **this day** [yes, *even* now] remaineth the **same veil** untaken away in the **reading of the old testament** [the letter], which veil **is** done away in [understanding].' Verse 15: '**But even unto this day**, when *Moses is read*, the veil is upon *their* heart.' Or, 'Wherefore **henceforth** know we **no** [scripture] after the [veil], yea, though we have known [understanding *by* the letter], yet now henceforth know we *him* [the veil] **no more**.'

"Let's turn to Romans chapter eight and verse four: 'That **the righteousness of the law** might be fulfilled in *us*, who walk not after the flesh, but after the Spirit.' Five: 'For they that are after the *flesh* do mind the things of *the flesh* [strife, wars, et cetera]; but they that are after *the Spirit* the things of the *Spirit*.' Six: 'For to be carnally minded *is* death: but to be Spiritually minded *is* life and peace.' *No* strife, *no* wars. Look around you! Evidently life and peace hasn't come yet. And so it is true, 'All that came before *ME*, are thieves and robbers;'

Seven: 'Because the carnal mind *is* enmity against God: **for it is not subject to the law of God, <u>neither indeed can be</u>**.' Eight; '**So then they that are i<u>n the flesh</u> cannot please God.**' That should be *proof positive*. To read or teach the scriptures literally, is

THE TWO WITNESSES

Chapter 8
The weekend

SIN. *The* Father of SIN. Everything else is the *offspring* of *it*. There again clarifying *where* Satan's kingdom *is*. Sitting in the temple of God in the Word *and* mind, *showing* that *he* is *the Word*. Walking up and down and to and fro *in* the **earth**. The *earth* represents the carnal *knowledge*, or the *letter*, of the scriptures. It represents the *lie*. And the carnal intellect is the Father of it.

Let's elaborate a little more on the earth and earthen vessels, and then we'll get into the contradiction of *woman* and what she represents. Turn to second Corinthians chapter four and verses three through seven. 'But if our [*spiritual*] *gospel* be hid, it is hid to them that are lost [carnal]: In whom **the God of this world** [the deceiver, the letter] hath blinded the *minds* of them which *believe not* [spiritually], lest the *light* of **the glorious gospel** of [understanding], *who* is the truth of [the Word] should shine unto them.' Five: 'For we preach not our selves, but [the *Living* Word] the Lord; and ourselves your servants for [truth's] sake.' Verse six: 'For God, who commanded the [understanding] to *shine* out of [the law], hath shined in our hearts, **to give t*he light* of t*he* knowledge** of the glory of [The Word] in the [personality] of Jesus Christ.' Verse seven: 'But *we have this Light* in **earthen vessels**, that the excellency of the power may be of God, [spiritual understanding] and not of us.'

"This *earthen* vessel is the same thing as the *flesh*, or the *veil*, it is the *outer* garment, it is the *outward appearance*. It is the **thing made**. It is the flaming sword in Genesis 3 and 24 which turns *every which way*, to keep **the *way*** of the tree of life. And the tree of life, as *we* know, *is* Christ. '*I am* the truth, **the life**, and ***The Way***.' The truth is hidden in this veil. This outer image. The flaming sword. 'Is not our God a consuming fire?'

"Remember in Romans 1 and 20, where Paul said, 'For the invisible things of [the Word] *from* the creation of the world are **clearly** seen, being understood by the **things that are made** [the image], **even** his eternal *power* and Godhead; **so that they are without excuse**'? The *power* of the *Word* of knowledge, *is spiritual* understanding. This message is to those who study the Word. You, they, we, me, anyone who sets their *hand* to the plow is *without*

THE TWO WITNESSES

Chapter 8
The weekend

excuse for not having the mind of God. He said the truth is **clearly seen**, being *understood* by the **things that are made** -- the image.

"Look at second Corinthians chapter 4 and verse 18: 'While *we look not* at **the things** which *are seen* [the image], but at the things which **are not seen**: [understanding] for the things which *are seen* [image] are temporal; but the things which are not seen are eternal.' This goes along with, 'Let *this mind be in you* which was *also in* Christ Jesus.' And '*Be ye therefore* **perfect**, even as your Father which is in heaven.' 'Let *us* go on unto perfection.' Some of this will come up later as we go through different areas of scripture. It's not that I *want* to be repetitious, but the *scriptures* are that way, and it takes the repetition to build the allegorical levels."

"That makes *sense now* about Jesus's body," Bob said. "The church, or churches I should say, are the ones teaching the letter. And the letter is the same as Jesus's flesh, which is His body. That's also the *outer*. And if *this* is the *third day*, then His body is about to be resurrected. Wow! That's beautiful. That means this is the *first resurrection*. God, or the Word, is about to go into the body and raise *it* from the dead."

"That's right on the mark, Bob. That's exactly what's going to happen as soon as the 'son of perdition,' which is Satan, who has them bound to the law is *revealed* to them," James added. "We'll be covering the resurrection and how that fits, pretty soon. For now, we'll go ahead with the contradiction of women and see how that works in the spiritual understanding. Any questions before we start?"

"None from me," Bob said. "Unless Tony has any, I'm ready."

"Shucks, James knows I'd interrupt if I had anything to say," Tony chuckled.

"Well, again, some of this might have been mentioned before, but here we go. Turn to Job 14 and we'll read verses one through 4. '*Man* **that is born of a woman** is of few *days*, and full of trouble. He cometh forth like a flower, and is *cut down*: He fleeth also as a shadow, and *continueth not*.... And dost thou open thine *eyes* on such a one, and bringest me into judgment with thee?... Who can bring a

THE TWO WITNESSES

Chapter 8
The weekend

clean thing out of an *unclean?*' Now, Job 15 and verse 14: 'What is *man*, that *he* should be *clean?* And he which is **born of a woman**, that *he* should be *righteous?* ' And Job 25, verse 4: **'How then can MAN be justified with God? or how can he be clean that is born of a woman?'** Put *this* with Matthew chapter 11 and verse 11: 'Verily I say unto you, **among them that are born of women** there hath not risen a greater than John the Baptist: notwithstanding **he that is least in the kingdom of heaven is greater than he** [John].' After we get through with the subject of women, we'll see why he said *that* about John.

"Turn to first Timothy chapter 2, verses 11 through 14: 'Let the *woman* learn in silence with all subjection. But I suffer not a *woman* to teach, nor to usurp the authority over the *man*, but to be in silence. For Adam was first formed then Eve. And Adam was not deceived, but the *woman* being deceived was in the transgression.' Genesis 3 and verse 16: Unto the *woman* He said, I will greatly multiply *thy* sorrow and thy conception; in sorrow thou shalt bring forth children; and *thy* desire shall be unto *thy* husband, and he shall rule over *thee*.' First Corinthians 11 and verse 3: 'But I would have you know that the head of every *man* is Christ; **and the head of the woman is the man**: and the head of Christ is God.'

Let's skip on to verses eight and nine: 'For the *man* is not of the *woman*; **but the woman of the man** [but in the human situation, it has been quite the *contrary* ever since, taking it literally that is].' Okay, first Corinthians 14 verses 33 and 35: 'For God **is not the author of confusion**, but of peace, as in all churches of the saints.... Let your women [this means the woman within all humans] keep silence in the churches: for it is not permitted for **them** to speak; **but they are commanded** to be under obedience, as also saith the law.... And if *they* will learn anything, let *them* ask their husbands at home: for it is a *shame* [confusing] for *women* to speak **in the** church.' Romans 2 and 11: '**FOR THERE IS NO RESPECT OF PERSONS WITH GOD.**'

"Well, how do you think this makes the ladies feel? What kind of design could this possibly be? What kind of God could command

THE TWO WITNESSES

Chapter 8
The weekend

such a thing, and then turn around and give the following scriptures, after what he just said about *women?* James chapter two, verses one and nine: '**MY** brethren, have not the faith of our Lord Jesus Christ, the Lord of glory, with *respect of persons*.' 'But if ye have **respect to persons** *ye commit sin*, and are convinced of *the law* as transgressors.' Proverbs, chapter 28 and verse 21: '*To have respect of persons is not good*: for for a piece of *bread that man* will transgress.' Ephesians six and nine; 'And, ye masters, do the same things unto them forbearing threatening: knowing that *your* Master is *also* in heaven; *neither is there respect of persons with him*.' First Peter chapter 1, verse 17: 'And if ye call on the Father, **who without respect of persons** judgeth according to every *man's* work, pass the time of your sojourning *here* in fear:' Colossians 3 and 25: 'But he that doeth wrong shall receive for the wrong which he hath done [karma]: and *there is no respect of persons*.' Acts 10 and verse 34: 'Then Peter opened his mouth, and said, **Of a truth I perceive that God is no respecter of persons**:' And the list goes on. If God is **no respecter of persons**, then why did he give all those *negative* commandments **concerning women**? Taking all this *literally* would definitely be hypocrisy on God's part.

According to this, *women* don't quite stack up to *men* in the eyes of God. And as it's written in first Timothy chapter 6 and verse 16, speaking of *men* approaching unto God, men *never* have and they *never* will stack up either. And if *men* are no good because they were **born of women**, where does that leave anyone if we are to believe these stories?

The scriptures have been taught by *carnal - minds*, or the first man Adam, *of the earth*, earthy, the scriptures are *first* given to the woman, the imagination, or the *wife* of 'the man,' in this case the carnal imagination in all humans. *She* (the carnal imagination) saw that they (the stories) were good for food. So she gave *them* to her husband to eat, or believe in. The serpent being *the lie*, interwoven in *with* the truth *in* the scriptures, deceived the woman and she gave to her husband to eat. This *first man* Adam was the *corporate mind* of the human race in its intellectual infancy, along with the *imaginative*

Chapter 8
The weekend

THE TWO WITNESSES

factor that was borne of **man's** experiential knowledge, that lead him to the place where his imagination was born *of him* or *from him.* Thus we have the story of the woman taken from the man. The *rib* represents what is referred to as the 'substance of the Word' and also represents faith.

The *story* goes on. But let's get back to John the Baptist and why it looks like he never went to heaven because he was *born* of a woman. Remember, it said that **the least** in the kingdom of heaven is *greater* than John. And then compare that with the question he asked in Matthew 21, verse 25: 'The *baptism of John*, whence was it? from heaven, or of *men?'*

"First of all, let's look at where the *least* in the kingdom of heaven are, so we can appreciate John's position. To find that, turn to Matthew 5 and verse 19 where the Word is talking about fulfilling the law. 'Whosoever therefore shall *break* one of these **least** *commandments*, and shall teach **men** to do so, he shall be called the **least in the kingdom of heaven**: but whosoever shall *do and teach them*, the same shall be called great in the kingdom of heaven.' Now look at Matthew 11, verses 12 and 13: 'And *from* the days of John the Baptist until *now* **the kingdom of heaven suffereth violence**, and **the violent** take *it* by force.' 'For all the prophets **and the law** *prophesied until* John.' And compare this with John ten and verse eight: 'All that ever came **before me** are thieves and robbers: but the sheep did not hear **them**.' John came *before* Him.

"And there's Paul's account of what John the Baptist said in Acts 13 and verse 25: 'And as John *fulfilled* **his** course, he said, whom think ye that I am? I am not *he*. But, behold, there cometh one **after** me, whose **shoes** of *his* feet I am not worthy to loose.' And there's several more that are relative to that verse. Continuing what *they* said in the rest of Matthew 21, verse twenty-five: 'And they reasoned with themselves, saying, If we shall say, From heaven; he will say unto us, Why did ye not believe him?' Verse 26: 'But if we shall say, Of men; we fear the people; for all hold John as a prophet.' John's message was *against* established religion -- Israel -- saying there was a better way *coming.*

THE TWO WITNESSES

Chapter 8
The weekend

Right now let's go to verse 14 of Matthew 11 and it will tell us *who* John represents: 'And if you will receive *it*, this is Elias, which was for to come.' Now, in the same chapter look at verse ten: 'For this is *he*, of whom it is written, Behold, I send **my** *messenger* before *thy* face, which shall prepare ***thy way before thee***.' At this point I want to remind you of where he said, 'The sting of death is sin, and the *strength of sin* is **the law**.... And all the prophets *and the **law*** prophesied ***until*** John.'"

"Excuse me, James." Bob said. "That's what you were talking about a few minutes ago. It was when you were showing how all the prophets wrote the scripture by *allegory*, or *similitudes*, which is the same as the *image*. And now I can see how *that* represents **the law**, and how also *it*, the *story*, can include anyone under sin who reads it *that* way.

"So then, if the law, which is the *strength* of sin, and **all the prophets prophesied until** John, that tells me that John showed them they were in error and *under the law*, and by doing so, those *that* **heard** him were baptized with water. Now the only kind of *water* that I know of, which is in a desolate, dry and barren wilderness, is *spiritual water*. I'd wondered how that worked *before* when I ran across it while checking out my concordance."

"Excellent.," James replied. "John is sort of like Moses in a way. Moses brings us out of condemnation and mental bondage of the law, into the wilderness where we wander around trying to get to the promise land, which is the mind of Christ. John *is* that part of scripture which reassures us, 'after all the *men of war* have died,' we can cross over Jordan into *that* 'promised land.'

"These '*men of war*' represent the scorn and condemnation that we had for those who abused us while we were in bondage under the law. Or you could say when *we* condemned the religious system. You've heard it said in scripture, 'we're all born in sin and shaped in iniquity.' What this indicates is that part of scripture which includes us all under sin that study, or understood them carnally. John's the part of scripture that finds us *already* out of the heavy bondage of Egypt, wandering in *the wilderness*, where he is *a voice* crying. And

THE TWO WITNESSES
Chapter 8
The weekend

his crying or heralding is for **us to prepare** for the next step in our quest for righteousness and truth, or the Christ.

"Well, I'll save the best for last. I think we'll go on a little more in our studies and let you find out how John fares *today* as he does his wonderful thing in the scripture and in the minds of all disciples of truth. Remember, John had a little condemnation against the *system*, or you could say, the woman *he* was born of. If he [literally speaking] had the mind of Christ, it would be impossible for him to condemn anyone.

Okay, before we went off on the subject of John, we were talking about God not being a respecter of persons. And this *woman* that is being referred to was the imaginative part of the mind and not a *physical* human female. This *woman* also represents Babylon and *her* harlots. Which is a representation of global church*es* plural, and not *the* church singular, those that are called out.

There again, when traditional *male* ministers or preachers say that a human female cannot teach in their churches, they are saying females do not or cannot have Christ. Thus, these ministers are **respecters of persons**, which we have seen, **is sin**. It simply shows who is taking the scriptures carnally. Why should the female even attend *their* ceremonies in the first place, if they can't receive the Christ of their teachings that is, the Christ as they perceive him in the religious community?

"Let's look at Colossians chapter three, verses nine through eleven 'Lie not one to another, seeing that ye have put off the *old* **man** with his deeds; and have put on the *new mind* which is renewed **in knowledge** after the image of him that created him: Where there is neither Greek nor Jew, circumcision nor uncircumcision, Barbarian, Scythian, bond *nor* free: But Christ *is* all in all [even *human* women].' Okay, let's turn back to Galatians chapter three, and couple *that* with what we've just read; then we'll comment on it. Galatians 3, verses 26 through 28: '**For *ye are all* the children of God by faith in** [the *Living* Word]. For as many of you as have been baptized *into* [not by] Christ have put on [understanding].... There is neither Jew nor Greek, there is neither bond nor free, **there is neither male nor female**: **for**

THE TWO WITNESSES

Chapter 8
The weekend

*ye are **all one** in* [the Living Word].'

"What more can be said? The essence here is, if you have Christ, you have Christ! No matter what gender you are. Looking at these scriptures, *we just finished,* literally or carnally the way the system does, they stand without excuse for not letting the human female teach scriptures with the same theological connotations that they all use. Bless their hearts, *they'll soon* understand and rejoice.

Whether taught or read by male or female, **these scriptures** must be taken spiritually to understand the true significance of their meaning. *This woman* that should *not* be teaching is the woman *in each and every one of us*. She is the imaginative factor which accompanies knowledge. This is true with any knowledge. Knowledge represents power, the masculine, the male. The woman represents the receptive, the receiver of the seed, and a helpmate to the male. This is true in all thinking minds, no matter what kind of physical body it dwells in.

"Ever wonder why in scripture, everyone always wanted a son and not a daughter? Think about it. When the scriptures are taught in the literal sense, it is emotional and gives life to *the story* because it deals with human feelings, which is very essential in appreciating what compassion and caring is all about. As a matter of fact, this is a part of what our *first love* is all about, after being born of water before being born of the spirit. *It is* our *necessary food*.

After being born spiritually the male *and* female become *one* knowledge, or *one flesh,* like the scriptures show us in Ephesians chapter 5, verses 31 and 32, which we'll be covering shortly. My goodness, look at the time. Why don't we take a break and get something to eat. I have plenty of leftovers from yesterday and you guys know you're certainly welcome to anything you want."

"Wow!" exclaimed Bob. "Nearly five o'clock already. I didn't even think about food until you mentioned it. I sort of hate to take a break to eat that kind of food after the feast I've been having."

"Really!" Tony said. "But I guess I should eat something, too. I didn't have *anything* for breakfast."

About that time Martie walked into the kitchen and said, "I'd

THE TWO WITNESSES

Chapter 8
The weekend

be more than happy to fix you guys a sandwich if you like. Sounds like you were going stout and heavy there and didn't want to stop."

"Great, Martie," James replied. "That's my buddy, or should I say buddette?"

"Keep it up, James. Flattery will get you your sandwich last. But you know you were going to anyway," Martie joked.

About that time the phone rang; it was Deena for Bob. She wanted to know how long they were going to be studying. She was through for the day and if they were going to be there for a while longer, she would come on out. Since they all agreed they'd probably be at it several hours, they decided Deena should join them.

Deena arrived about the time they finished their sandwiches. Bob and James, and sometimes Tony, highlighted what they had been talking about. Since it clarified a few things about women, she said she was *really* glad she came. She was good-natured about it and saw exactly what they meant.

"When we, male or female, feel carnal about something we're trying to understand," James continued, "we must always question what *our* wife *or* woman has offered us to eat. As I was saying earlier Deena, once *Christ* is formed in our thoughts, the knowledge or the *male* factor *and* the wife, become *one flesh* or *one mind. One truth* **without contradiction**.

The type of *woman* one would have in his or her mind would be determined by the type of man, because the woman *is* taken *from* the man, or you could say, *taken out* of the man. This works with *all* knowledge, no matter what the subject.

For example, suppose you were studying how to repair automobiles. You have learned enough to do small repairs. Let's say your car needs new spark plugs and a rotor. Through knowledge, you know to get a plug wrench and the parts you need.

"Now assume you were given the wrong parts for that particular model and didn't realize it. Now the knowledge you have accumulated needs reinforcement. Here comes the woman, the helpmate. She is going to ***help*** you figure this out. As long as your imagination is in sync with the knowledge you have about what you

THE TWO WITNESSES

Chapter 8
The weekend

are trying to do, there should be no problem.

The two should come to the *same* conclusion that you were given the wrong parts and then the problem can be corrected and the work completed. On the other hand, suppose you were trying to figure out how you could improvise and make the parts fit without having to go to the **trouble of returning them for the *right* ones**. Well if you are true to your knowledge, you are not going to listen to this **other woman** who will get you into a situation in which not only will you ruin the parts you have already purchased, but you will have to *buy the right ones* instead of being able to exchange them like you should have done in the first place.

This woman was not taken from the knowledge you worked for, she belongs to *another man*, and is in the place of an adulteress, who is married to pride, ego -- things that *should not be* present in a pure -- knowledge mind. You've heard it said, 'Let every man have **his own wife**. And let every woman have **her own husband**.' This is an area where you could run into men with men and women with women, but for now we won't get into *that* because it will be explained later and I don't want to hinder you from getting some of this on your own.

"Anyway, the serpent *in* the scriptures, can deceive the imagination and cause the carnal mind or man to eat of the forbidden fruit, which is *the story* or the *image*. This can be related *from* individuals to the masses, which is Babylon, the harlot, the scarlet woman, the imagination of *all* carnal minds as a whole. This is *the* woman who has been doing the teaching of all scripture worldwide for the last two thousand years and was to do so until the time of the end, or the third day, which is now. The time that was prophesied in Isaiah.

Speaking of Isaiah, now is a good time to go ahead and see when *the* kingdom of God was to be established. Does anyone want to take a break before we get started? You know how I am, you have to remind me."

After refreshing their drinks they were ready for James to continue.

THE TWO WITNESSES

Chapter 8
The weekend

"As usual, there are some areas we've touched on before and I'll be bringing them in again. Just bear with the repetition; you'll understand how necessary it is if you don't already. We were going to Isaiah chapter nine and read verses six and seven: 'For unto **us** a child is **born**, unto *us* a son is given: and the government [spiritual] shall be upon his shoulder: and his name shall be called Wonderful, Counsellor, The mighty God, The everlasting Father, The Prince of Peace.... Of the increase of **His** government and peace *there shall be no end,* upon the throne of David, and upon his kingdom, to order *it,* and to establish it with judgment and with justice from **henceforth even forever**. The zeal of the Lord of host will perform this.' Looking at these two verses in the literal sense or as the system has taught it, *this* prophecy was supposedly fulfilled two thousand years ago. 'Jesus' came and set up his kingdom of *peace and judgment*. But *on the contrary*. There has been nothing but wars and rumors of wars *and* chaos. This kingdom of peace *has not* been established **yet**. It said when he came to set *it* up, from that point on, or henceforth, it would *remain forever*. **Where is this kingdom of peace**? As *the story* goes, he had no intention of setting it up two thousand years ago.

Turn to Matthew 10, verses 34 through 36: '**Think not that I am come to send peace on earth: I came not to send peace, but a sword**. For I am come to set a *man* at variance against *his* father, and the daughter against *her* mother, and the daughter **in law** against her mother **in law**. And a *man's* foes *shall be* they of his own household [mind].' What happened? Are *you* following what's going on here in Isaiah and Matthew? Do we have a beautiful cross or what?"

"Man, how plain can you get?" said Bob excitedly. "I never, never in my life saw *that*."

"I know, me either, honey," Deena interrupted. "How can anyone get around that? In one place it says he was giving us a son to set up peace, and in another the son says he didn't come to **do that**. He came to bring confusion and division and a sword. How does that work James, what does He mean?"

"I thought *you'd never* get around to asking, Deena. Well you

129

THE TWO WITNESSES

Chapter 8
The weekend

guys come back tomorrow and I'll explain how to overcome that contradiction."

"Oh, no you don't, James," Bob growled. "I'm not leaving till you explain that! That's a good one, or two, I think. Heck, I don't know what to think, but I know it's going to be wonderful."

"My, my, Bob," James chuckled. "You really do like this kind of thinking don't you? Okay, tell you what -- over in Psalm 78, verse 62 God said, 'He gave *his people* over also unto **the sword**; and was wroth with his inheritance.' Well, he was talking about sending *his Word* or *his Son* to execute judgment upon those who walked after the graven image which we know is carnal law.

"Why don't we start with Isaiah 34, and to avoid getting off on a three- or- four hour tangent, we'll just read verses five and eight. You can read the rest of the chapter at home. Verse five: 'For *my sword* shall be bathed in heaven [or the law]: behold, it shall come down upon Idumea [which means firstborn of Esau, whom God hates], and upon the people of **my curse**, to judgment [only *by* the truth can there be a judgment].' Verse eight: 'For it is the day of the Lord's vengeance, and the year of recompenses for the **controversy** of Zion.' Or the *spiritual church*.

Now to Jeremiah chapter 9, verses 13 through 16: 'And the Lord saith, Because they [men] have forsaken my [truth] which I have set before them, and have not obeyed my [understanding], neither walked therein; But have walked after the ***imagination*** of **their own** heart, and after Baalim [which means *master possessor*], which *their* [traditions] taught them: Therefore thus saith the Lord of host, the God of Israel; Behold, I will feed *them*, even *this people*, with wormwood [bitterness], and give them water of gall [serpent venom] to drink. I will scatter them also among the heathen, [carnal-minded or Goi] whom neither they nor their [doctrines] have known: And **I will send a sword** after them, till I [the Word] have consumed them.'

Now back to Isaiah 55, verse 11: 'So shall *my Word* be that goeth out of my mouth: *it* shall not return unto me void, but *it* shall accomplish that which I please, and *it* shall prosper **in the thing** whereunto I sent *it*.' Jeremiah chapter four and verse ten: 'Then said I,

THE TWO WITNESSES

Chapter 8
The weekend

Ah, Lord God! *Surely* **thou hast greatly deceived this people** *and* Jerusalem [the one in bondage with her children, the religious system], **saying, ye shall have peace**; *whereas* **the sword reacheth unto the soul** ['Think not that I am come to bring peace'..].'
    Deuteronomy 32 and verses 39 through 42: 'See now that I, *even* I, *am* he, and there is no god with me [saith the scriptures]: **I** kill, and **I** make alive; **I** wound, and **I** heal: neither *is there any* that can deliver out of my **hand** [teaching]. For I lift up *my* **hand** to heaven and say, [the Word] live forever.... If I whet my glittering sword, and **mine hand** take hold on judgment [truth]; *I will render vengeance* to mine enemies, and will reward them that hate me [truth].... I will make mine arrows drunk with blood, and *my* sword shall devour **flesh**; *and that* with the blood of the slain and of the captives, from the beginning of the revengers upon the enemy.'
    "Am I going to fast for you? It *is* necessary for now. Hang in there it will come together soon. Just keep in mind what this is about, and that is, to explain *why* the contradiction between the foretelling of a son to come and bring peace, and the Son claiming *he did not*. To fully understand how this comes together takes a compilation of many *relative* scriptures.
    "What we're witnessing at the moment is the relationship between the *letter* which kills and brings spiritual death, *and* the *spiritual word* that brings life. Let's bring *that* scripture in now, then we'll continue where we left off. Turn to Proverbs chapter 8 verses 35 and 36: 'For whoso **findeth** me **findeth** life, and shall obtain favour of the Lord. But he that sinneth against *me* wrongeth his own soul: all they that hate *me* [truth] love death [the image].'
    "Now, God's vengeance is somewhat different than meets the carnal *eye*. Let's look again at Romans 12, verses 19 through 21: 'Dearly beloved [brethren], avenge not yourselves, but *rather* give place unto wrath: for it is written, Vengeance *is* mine: I will repay, saith the Lord. Therefore if thine enemy *hunger*, feed him; if he thirst, give him *drink*: for in so doing thou shalt heap coals of fire on his head. Be not overcome of evil, *but overcome evil with good* [vengeance].'

THE TWO WITNESSES

Chapter 8
The weekend

For the next few minutes I want you to keep these last three verses in the forefront of your mind, as I add a few more. Remember, the carnal minded are enemies **for our** sakes, **but** beloved for the Father's sake. In John 16 it says they [the carnal-minded] will kill you thinking they're doing God's service. This is *how close* Satan's kingdom is. Ignorance and fear is a poisonous venom from the serpent, *which is* as you know by now, the law, the *left hand* of the word. But on the other *hand*, the *right* one, is the antidote. Just like in nature, the antidote for a snake bite is the *same venom* sterilized, with the scripture -- spiritualized.

"Anyone that doesn't agree with *them*, they fear and strike out at. The *spiritual mind* they greatly fear. The spiritual mind has compassion for them because they were *born in sin* also, and have been in *their* shoes somewhat. It *is joyful* for *brethren* to try to show others the spiritual side of the scriptures; they yearn for them to see it so they can be set free by *the understanding* of what they read. The enemy *I try to expose* are the powers that have deceived the carnally-minded, and have them *bound* to this *death*.

Turn to Proverbs 19 and verse 27: 'Cease, my son [those called out, the Church], to hear the instruction **that causeth to err** f<u>rom</u> **the words of** knowledge.' Did you notice those *two* words, 'that causeth,' were italicized in that verse? That's just to emphasize to *the knower* that the instruction that *does* cause us to err, is the same thing as **the sin** that doth so easily beset us, and is *hand* in *hand* with the word of knowledge. In other words, don't listen to the letter or stories, but to the spiritual side of the word. So speaking of God's vengeance toward *them*, what did he mean for us to do but <u>help</u> them? This tells us that God's vengeance is nothing more than the bringing in of the truth. Or the resurrection of His Son. Because God would not tell us to do something that he wouldn't do.

"This **sword** *that came* to bring division and set at variance families and nations and create confusion was *intended to stir up* our *pure conscience* to cause *u s* to seek, that **we should deliver ourselves** from *the contradiction*, or hell. Example: Proverbs 15 and verse 24, 'The way of life is above [spiritual] to the wise, that he may

THE TWO WITNESSES
Chapter 8
The weekend

depart from hell [controversy, carnal-mind] beneath.'
Let's put a couple more with that one. Turn to Psalm 9 and verse 17: 'The [carnal] shall be turned into hell [confusion], *and* all the [religions] that forget [the truth].' Proverbs 23 and verse 14: 'Thou shalt [show him the truth] and shalt deliver his soul from [the lie].'
Now Jude, verse 23: 'And others save with fear, pulling *them* out of the [law]: hating even the [conscience] spotted by the [image].' In essence, what all this is telling us is, the truth *and* the lie is in the *same* word. I'll throw in a few more to substantiate that. Remember in the book of Job where God was asking Satan.., never mind -- let's look at it. Turn to Job chapter one and verse seven: 'And the Lord said unto Satan, Whence comest thou? Then Satan answered the Lord, and said, From going to and fro **in** the *earth*, and from walking ***up and down in it***.' He's definitely not talking about the planet. In chapter two and verse two he asked him the *same question* again. The first *man,* or mind of the human species, is of the earth 'earthy,' the second is the Lord from heaven. *Earth* represents the letter or the law. So add this to second Corinthians chapter 11, verses 14 and 15, and see how *it* fits: 'And no marvel; for [the deceiver] himself is transformed into a [messenger] of light. Therefore *it is* no great thing if his [carnal teachers] also be transformed *as* the ministers of righteousness; whose end shall be according to their works.'

"Believe it or not, it takes all of this, just to explain one little verse; but we're getting close. It will be worth it when you see it start coming together.
Okay, If there's no questions, turn to first Corinthians chapter 3, verses 13 through 15: 'Every **man's** work shall be made manifest: for the *day* [of truth] shall declare it, because it shall be revealed by fire [the Word]; and the [truth] shall try every **man's** work of what sort it is. If any **man's** work [knowledge] abide which **he** hath **built** thereupon, he shall receive a reward. If any **man's** work shall be burned, he shall suffer loss: ***but he himself shall be saved***; yet so as by [the truth].' That which is within him shall be destroyed, *not* him, or her, as the case may be. 'Is not *our* God a consuming fire?' The very God (fire) that destroys us, is the same God (or fire) that saves us, it's

THE TWO WITNESSES

Chapter 8
The weekend

up to you. Although we suffer the loss of our **traditional beliefs** of our religious doctrines, we are saved by the truth, the fire that burns up *the image* in the mind allows us to see spiritually. This is how we die daily.

"The reason for the *sword?* To **bring judgment!** When He said, 'Think not that I am come to bring peace on **earth,** *but a sword*. He brought judgment. The, '*four sore judgments*,' the '*four gospels*,' the sword, the Word. The clue here is, he did not bring peace to the *earth*, that does not mean the planet, that means exactly what it says, '*the earth.*'

"Think about the *first mind* of of the human species, 'Adam,' which is earthly. *This* is the earth the two-edged sword came to judge, *not the second* man, Adam, or the spiritual mind; *he's* at peace. These *four* books have brought division, confusion, verbal and physical wars, and rumors of wars, hate, condemnation, scorn, *divided* families, churches, fathers and sons, mothers and daughters, nations and on and on. All because they taught them *carnally*, not heeding the warnings about the curses *which are contained in the very words* **they _thought_** would save them.

Remember? 'Search the scriptures, for **in them _you think_** you have eternal life, but you would not come to me... [the truth, or the Christ]. Ezekiel, chapter 15, verse 21: 'For thus saith the Lord God; How much more when I send my **four sore judgments** [Matthew, Mark, Luke, and John] upon Jerusalem [the carnal Jerusalem, the one in bondage], the sword, and the famine, and the noisome beast, and the pestilence, to cut off from it *man* and *beast.*'

Get some scratch paper and write down these scriptures that go along with this; you can rejoice in them later. Chapter 15 of Jeremiah, especially verse 4. The word *manasseh* means *that* which causes forgetfulness. Which refers to those who have forgotten their *true* purpose to find or *go back* to God, or the knowledge, from which we fell away, as it says, 'backwards.' Also chapter 49 especially verses 36 and 37. The word 'Elam,' in verse 36 means, 'those that would kill you *thinking* they do God service.' They have been blinded by the **graven image.** Compare Isaiah chapter 42, and note verses 17

Chapter 8
The weekend

THE TWO WITNESSES

through 20.

"Now Jeremiah chapter 50, verses 35 through 38. Here it's talking about the system of soothsayers, witchcraft or magicians who use sleight of **hand** to deceive you into believing the *story* of the graven image. As you know, the graven image means doctrine, carved out of '*the rock*,' or the word. The *Chaldeans* are masters at it, upon whom **The Sword** is. If you *listen*, you can *see* them in operation all over the planet, fulfilling the prophecy as we speak.

"While you're at it, put Zechariah chapter one, verses 16 through 21 with those. This is about the *four* horns. 'Horn' means to proclaim, herald, publish, or teach. These are the four gospels.

"Now turn to Job 19 and verse 29: 'Be ye afraid of the Sword [the fear of the Lord]: for [contradiction] *bringeth* the punishments of the sword, **That ye may know <u>there is a judgment</u>**...' Isn't that beautiful!? The judgment of God is *in* the Word. The revelation of this judgment is in the first resurrection, the morning of the **third day. Now!** Let's compare these next two verses with what we just read. John 6:63; 'It is the spirit that quickeneth; the flesh profiteth nothing: the words that **I** [the Christ] speak unto you, **they** are spirit, and **they** are life.' John 12:48; 'He that rejecteth me, and receiveth not **my** words, hath one that judgeth him: **the word that I have spoken** [spiritual]**, the same shall judge him in the last day** [the third day].

"There are several more I would like to add to this right now, but I think I'd better wait because I'd just have to repeat them here shortly. It looks like you might have a few questions, Bob. But give me a few minutes and I think most of them will answer themselves for you.

"Go ahead and turn to Proverbs chapter 21, and verse 15: '*It is* **joy to the just to do judgment**: but destruction *shall be* to the workers of [the lie]'. Turn to chapter 28 of Proverbs, and verse 5; '[Carnal] *men* understand not judgment: but they that seek the Lord understand all **THINGS**.' Remember *things*? They are the images.

"Jeremiah 25, verses 26, 29, and 31: 'And all the kings [doctrines] of the north [cold, death], far *and* near, one with another,

THE TWO WITNESSES

Chapter 8
The weekend

and *all* the kingdoms of the world, which *are* upon *the face of the earth:* and the king of Sheshach [a mystical name of Babylon, alluding to it's *iron gates or idols*] shall *drink* after *them*.... For, lo, I begin to bring evil on the city which is *called* by my name [See Isaiah chapter four. All religions say God is their Lord], and should ye be utterly unpunished? Ye shall not be unpunished: for I will call for *a Sword* upon *all the inhabitants of the* **earth**, saith the Lord of hosts. A noise shall come *even* to the ends of the *earth*: for the Lord hath **A controversy** with the *nations*, he will plead with all **flesh** [carnal thoughts]; he will give them that are [carnal] to the Sword, saith the Lord.' The *living* Word is *that* which does judgment on all *flesh*. Remember we read about the outer word being *flesh*. And 'the *flesh* profiteth nothing, it is the spirit that giveth life.' First Timothy 4:8 says the same thing; 'For **bodily** [letter] **exercise profiteth little**: but godliness is profitable unto all things.' Once the spiritual interpretation has been revealed, it is called the revelation of Jesus Christ, or, the Word Living. Then the law and the truth become one, and **there is no more earth**. It is the end of the *earth*. The *earth* that he *did not* come to bring peace to. There is no more enemy, or death. No more sin, no more stories. The Father and the Son *are* one. Then, 'the law', shall be fulfilled.

This is what he was talking about in One John, chapter two, verses seven and eight: '**Brethren**, I write no new commandment unto *you*, but an old commandment which *ye had* from the beginning. The old commandment **is the word** which ye have heard from the beginning.' The *old testament* is the letter, the stories, taught from Genesis **through** Revelation. The *New testament* is the *same scripture* taught spiritually, or in his blood, which is the life of *his flesh*, or Word Body.

Verse eight: 'Again, a new commandment I write unto you, which thing is true in [the Word] and you: because the [lie] is past, and the ***true light now*** shineth.' Another parable in St. John goes along with this. It's chapter 9, verse 39: 'And Jesus said, For ***judgment I am come into this world***, that they which see not might see; and that they which see might be made blind.' You cannot take *that* literally. It

Chapter 8
The weekend

THE TWO WITNESSES

is referring to the law, and the spiritual interpretation. What it's saying is, the law feeds the ego and pride, and causes those who do not see it spiritually to **think** they understand or *see* what the scriptures mean. Thereby confirming the scripture in Hebrews where it says; '*The law* maketh *men* high priests.' Because they're saying we know, we can see what the scriptures mean. When in reality all they can see are the images. *They've* been made blind. But on the other *hand*, those who say, 'I don't understand; I try but I just *can't see* what the scriptures mean, there's just too many contradictions in them,' and so on. They are admitting they are blind. *They* are pure in heart. So, when they hear the spiritual interpretation, then they truly *can* see. Confirming the scripture that say's **'I'll be found** of a people that **sought me not**.'

Turn back to chapter three of John and look at verses five and six: 'Jesus answered, Verily, verily, I say unto thee, Except [the carnal mind] be born of [stories, water] **and** *of* the [understanding, spirit] he cannot [see] into the kingdom of [the Word]. That which is born of the *flesh* is *flesh*; and that which is born of the Spirit *is* spirit.' The *Word* was made *flesh* and we eat *Him*.

"What we've been seeing so far, is the Word saying, **in me** is **hidden** all the *mysteries* from the foundation of all **things**. The truth has been here all along, we've just been too *blind* to see past the flesh, or the image. The word is saying, **in me** is your salvation. We must search the scriptures with all our heart soul and mind for *The Christ*, then lift him up above **the earth**. Look at it this way: if we're supposed to work out *our own* salvation, then we are most likely someplace we don't belong. There are only *two* places we *can* be: broad and tormenting, and peace and joy. Of peace and joy, it says, ' *few* there be that **find it**.' It is hidden, we're supposed to search for **It**, and this **it** will save us and deliver us from hell beneath. This *it* is the *key* for converting the scriptures from carnal to spiritual. Above and below is only a state of mind. In space there is no *up* and *down*. To be *above* the *earth* is to be in the spiritual realm. To be on or *in* the *earth* is to be in hell, or confusion.

"I know we've covered *some of this* but I want to bring it up

Chapter 8
The weekend

THE TWO WITNESSES

while we're on the subject. *Earth* means matter, planets, stars, ground, law, word, veil, outer, image, idol, letter, flesh, parables, stories, woman, mother earth, anything *that is made*. Spirit is energy, life, understanding, Christ, invisible, Holy, sanctified, set apart, separated, spiritual interpretation. Pure spiritual understanding and the love for **it** will bring this *dead letter* to life.

"Look at Psalm 78, verses 34 and 35: '**When he *slew them*, *then*** they sought him: and **they returned** [alive and well] and inquired early after God. And they remembered that [the Word] *was* their rock, and the [spiritual Word] their redeemer.' Did you notice he mentioned *two* God's? Never mind now, we'll discuss it later.

"Okay, Hosea, chapter six: verses one and two; 'Come, and let us return unto the [Word]: for he hath torn, and he will heal us [the *two-edged* thing]; he hath smitten, and he will bind us up. After *two* days [two thousand years] will he revive us: **In** the ***third day*** [three thousand years] He will raise *us* **up**, and we shall *live* in his sight.'

"Okay, let's go on, we're almost there. Turn to John chapter 6 and verse 40, then 53 through 58: 'And this is the will of him that sent me, that every one which **seeth the Son** [the Truth], and believeth on him, may have everlasting life: and [understanding] *will raise him up at the last day*].... Then Jesus said unto them, Except *ye eat* the **Flesh** of the Son of *man*, **and** drink his blood, ye have no *life* in you.' Here he refers to himself as the Son of--man. You're right, *the Son of man*, and we'll see how that works, too. That's *another* story.

"Okay, verse 54: 'Whoso **eateth my flesh**, and **drinketh my blood**, hath eternal life; and I will raise him up at the **last day**. For *my* flesh is meat indeed, and *my* blood is drink indeed [this is the spirit of the Word speaking]. He that eateth my flesh, and drinketh my blood, dwelleth *in me*, and I *in* him. As the living Father hath sent me, and I live **by** the Father: so he that **eateth me**, even he shall live **by** me.' [That was not talking about human **flesh**!].... 'This is that bread which came down from heaven: not as *your fathers* [doctrines of *men*] did eat manna, and *are dead*: he that eateth of *this bread* [*hidden* manna] shall live forever.' These are the scriptures where the clergy carved out the holy communion they do in their services,

THE TWO WITNESSES

Chapter 8
The weekend

where they use crackers and grape juice. Here, it is plain and simple. Why eat *that*, when you *can* eat *His* flesh, and drink *His* blood like we were commanded to do? A little pun there. Believe me, it was only to get a point across. I love them, and have a great compassion for them. I remember, I was there once.

"I think by now you can get the picture of what he meant when he said he didn't come to bring peace on *earth*. However, I have about three tangents going at once, so I'll go ahead and finish these, which includes more about the *two-edged* Sword. It's sort of like Excalibur: one side kills, the other heals.

A while back we read in Hosea 12 and 10, where it was saying how the prophets had written the scriptures in parables, et cetera. Keep *that* in mind as we continue. Turn to Luke chapter 1 and verse 70: 'As he spake by the mouth of his *holy* prophets, which have been *since* **the world began** ['**in the beginning** was the Word']....'

Second Timothy chapter one, verses eight through ten: 'Be not thou therefore ashamed [confused] of the testimony of *our* Lord, nor of me his prisoner: but be thou partaker of the **afflictions of the gospel** according to the power of God [which is understanding].... Who hath saved *us*, and called *us* **with** an *holy* [spiritual] calling, not according to our works [the law], but according to his own purpose and grace, which was given us *in* [the Living Word] before the world began, But is now made manifest by the appearing of our Saviour [from the letter] Jesus Christ, who hath abolished **death** [the lie], and hath brought life and immortality to light *through* **the gospel**:'

Now, go to chapter two, one page over, and read verses seven through nine: 'Consider what I say; and the [Word] will give thee *understanding* in *all* **things**....Remember that Jesus Christ of the *seed* of *David* was raised from the dead **according to my gospel**: wherein I suffer trouble, as an evildoer [because he has to write the *stories*, or lie, in order to hide the truth], even unto bonds; but the word of truth [spiritual understanding] *is not* bound.'

"Now listen to *this*, Paul wants us to **put on** *his* **hands** here in verse six: 'Wherefore I put thee in *remembrance* thou stir up the [spirit] of [the Word], **which is in thee** by the **putting on of my**

THE TWO WITNESSES

Chapter 8
The weekend

***hands*.'** How could you do that if you didn't know that **hands** meant his *flesh* or *the gospel?* We find more of the same in Romans 11 and 14: 'If by any means I may provoke to emulation **them which are my flesh**, and might **save** some of them....' And second Thessalonians chapter 3 and verse 17: 'The salutation of Paul with **mine own hand**, which is **the token** [allegory, symbolism] **in *every* epistle....**'

Everything was written to conceal the truth from men, until the *third* day, the beginning of the third millennium. It was sealed with a great stone, which is the stumbling stone that only the angels, or *spiritual messengers* of the Word could roll away. And this is done the morning of the third day -- *now*. Luke 13, verse 32: 'And he said unto them, Go ye, and tell that fox [numerical value of *fox*, is 666], Behold, I cast out devils, and I do cures today and tomorrow, and **the third day I shall be perfected**' Christ *has to be* perfected?

First Corinthians 15, verses 3 and 4: 'For I delivered first of all that which I also received, how that Christ died for our sins **according to the scriptures**; And that he was buried, and that he rose ***again*** the *third day* **according to the scriptures**.' He didn't rise ***again***, until **the *third day*, according to the scriptures**. *Everything is done* **according to the scriptures**.' Here is more. Second Thessalonians chapter 2, verses 10 through 14: 'And with all deceivableness of unrighteousness in *them* that perish [men]: because they received not **the love** for [understanding], that they might be saved [from the **very word** they read]. And for this cause [the Word has sent] them strong delusion, that **they should believe a lie** [the stories].... That they all might be damned who believed not the truth, but had pleasure in [the lies]. But we are bound to give thanks alway to God for you, *Brethren* beloved of the Lord because God hath **from the beginning** chosen [the righteous] to salvation through **sanctification of the Spirit** and belief of the truth: Whereunto He called you **by our gospel**, to the obtaining of the [beauty] of [the **Living Word**].' Romans chapter 2, verse 16: 'In the day when [Truth] shall judge the secrets of *men* by [the Living Word] according to **my** gospel.'

THE TWO WITNESSES

Chapter 8
The weekend

Remember in verse eleven where it said 'God [the Word] shall send them strong delusion?' And remember where it was said that **Satan's kingdom is so close to God's**, that **IF** it were possible, it would 'fool the very elect'? <u>This is</u> the deception, -- **the image -- the lie -- the letter --** and where is *this deceiver?* Of course! Walking to and fro, up and down *in the earth*, the Word, and of course, the mind, the garden of Words.

We should realize that the truth we all search for has always been here in front of our noses, *hidden in The Word* but was crucified **by men** so *they* could retain the power of the priesthood. The teaching of the letter or lie is the contradiction, **or the crucifixion**. It says he is crucified *afresh*, and *that* word means in the *exact same manner as always*.

"Let's examine why the word 'afresh' was used. Turn to John 19 and verse 34: 'But **one** of the soldiers with *a spear* **pierced his side**, and forthwith came there out blood *and* water.' Notice, this is the *only place* in scripture it says that **only <u>one</u> soldier pierced Him**. Now let's see the contradictions.

Look at Zechariah chapter 12 and verse 10: 'And I will pour upon the house of David, and upon the [carnal] of Jerusalem [religions], the spirit of grace and of *supplications*: and **they shall look <u>upon me</u> whom <u>they</u> have pierced**, and **they** shall mourn for [understanding], as one mourneth for *his* only *son*, and shall be in bitterness for [the truth], as one that is in bitterness for *his* firstborn.' Here it says '**they**' pierced him; that's *more* than *one*. Turn to John 19 and verse 37: 'And again another scripture saith, *They* shall **look on him** whom *they* pierced.' Revelation chapter one and verse seven: 'Behold, he cometh with *clouds*; and every *eye* shall see him, **and <u>they also which pierced him</u>**: and all kindreds of the **earth** shall wail because of him. Even so, Amen.' The word '**cloud**' in the Hebrew is '**kaph**,' which means '**hand**.'

Who are '**They**' who pierced him? For the answer turn to Psalms 22 and 16: 'For *dogs* [servants of the carnal - shepherd] have compassed me: *the assembly of the wicked* have enclosed me: **they** pierced my **hands** and my **feet**.' In this sense of the word, anyone

THE TWO WITNESSES

Chapter 8
The weekend

ever teaching or believing the letter has taken part in his crucifixion, including me. He was crucified by **those who sin**. Sinners nailed his *hands* and *feet* to the contradiction, '**afresh**.'

"Roman's 15 and verse 4: 'For whatsoever *things* were written **aforetime** *were* **written** *for* *our learning*, that *we* through patience and **comfort** *of the* **scriptures** might have hope.' Turn to second Timothy chapter 3 verses 16 and 17: 'All scripture is given by the inspiration of God, and is profitable for doctrine, for reproof, for correction, for **instruction in righteousness**.... That the man *of God* may **be perfect**, throughly furnished unto all *good* works.' I think by now we have covered enough ground to see why the scripture would make such a bold contradiction as to say he was sending us peace but he brought a Sword. He **did bring peace**, *but not to men* of the *earth*. Men rejected it, and chose the murderer [Barabbas; son of the teacher], 'the lie,' instead, and crucified the truth and brought about *their own* judgment, which the truth will declare on the -- you got it -- *third day*.

"How beautiful the paradox, how beautiful the mystery, how beautiful is the Word of knowledge! How beautiful is the controversy! The first impression of Jesus Christ, when we read the scripture is the *image* the *letter* sets forth, the one that portrays him *as* a human being. That was in second Corinthians chapter 5 and verse 16. His second coming is when we see how the spirit works in all **things**, and reveals to *us* who the *Living Word* really is, and has *always been*. Remember, '*Jesus Christ, the same today, yesterday and forever, I am God and I change not?* That's true, He is the *god of change*, and He doesn't change from that.

"Jesus returns on the third day under cover of night, or ignorance. He is coming to destroy his enemy, *death*. Under His vengeance, the truth. The truth is now bringing about the resurrection of the *dead*, through the *gospel of truth*. The **revelation** of Jesus Christ: and **who** and **where** he is. We've read it before, but let's add it to this train of thought. It's in Revelation chapter 19 and verse 13: 'And he was clothed with a vesture dipped in blood: and **his name** is called **The Word of God**.' That is with whom we have to deal, and if

THE TWO WITNESSES

Chapter 8
The weekend

you have this Word in you, you don't have to look far."

Scanning his notes, Bob asked meekly. "Why did you say *Israel* was the Son of man? A little while ago you made the remark about *Jesus* being the *son* of man."

"Very observant Bob." James replied. "And a very good question. But I really think we should discuss that when we have more time. It's nearly ten now, and you know how many scriptures we had to go through to see the contradiction of Jesus not bringing peace to earth. Well, *double* that, and that's about how long it would take to grasp the complete concept. We can get an early start tomorrow and have plenty of time to cover it. How-ever, if you want to get into it now, I'm ready."

"My, how time flies when you're having fun!" Deena gleamed. "I am a little tired. I had to work today while you guys floated around in space. I'm kidding. I'm happy for you. Maybe envious -- In a positive way. I'd better shut up before I get in deeper."

They all grinned and said they knew exactly what she meant.

"Okay then, why don't we plan on getting a fresh start in the morning." James suggested. "No need to call, guys, just come on out when ever you're ready. Deena you are coming with them aren't you?"

"I wouldn't miss it for the world."

"Fantastic. See you all then.

On the way to the car, Tony asked Deena if she would like to hear a little more about the *ox*.

"How long will it take,Tony?" she said kiddingly.

"Oh, just a couple of seconds, at least to get the drift. When breaking the word 'ox' down to the spiritual meaning, it represents **Apostle**. The word '**corn**,' means *understanding*. An ox is one that 'treadeth out the corn,' or the truth. So, when you find truth, you find *the Christ*, making you an Apostle. That was the motive for me saying *that* Bob wanted tread *it* out. Looks like you might be one yourself, Deena."

"Thanks, Tony, I think you might be right. And thanks for

THE TWO WITNESSES

Chapter 8
The weekend

remembering to tell me. Have a nice ride home, and we'll see you tomorrow."

"You too, guys. Goodnight."

Bob and Deena chatted for a while, but mostly, as before, just reflecting *within* themselves. The *next day* was all Bob could think about.

'I can't believe this,' he thought. 'I just can't believe I'm understanding where James is coming from. All my life I've wondered if the Bible could have a *different* message than what was perceived by the masses.'

"What are *you* thinking?" he asked Deena.

"Oh, you know, probably the same thing you are. I was just pondering the right-and-left-hand thing. I've noticed it before, many times, and now that I look back, I remember having had just a *prick* of curiosity about the way the words were used. I guess I thought that was just the mysterious way of God's workings. The *assuming* thing. You know?"

"Yeah, I know. Wow, do I know. You're right, I was doing the same thing. I was wondering how I simply overlooked *so much*. But I can understand now. I guess it's like they say, 'hind sight is 20 20'. Are you going to my place or yours?"

"Oh, Bob! I'm glad you asked. I was going to yours since we were *both* going back tomorrow. But I didn't *even* think about a change of clothes. I guess I need to go home. Sorry about that."

"No problem, sugar. I'll have you there in a minute."

As they pulled up and started to walk to her apartment, it dawned on Bob -- "Deena, *what are we thinking?* I had to come by here anyway to bring you home. Why don't you get a change and you can shower at my place."

"Really! Bob, sometimes you simply amaze me. Good idea. I'll be right back!"

After getting to Bob's place, then settling down after taking a quick shower, Bob said, "You know, honey? I'm very, *very* happy you're getting into *this* with me. I can't imagine what our life together would be like if one of us were not searching."

THE TWO WITNESSES

**Chapter 8
The weekend**

"Me too, honey. Everything looks like it is going to work out beautifully. I look forward to going back tomorrow. I really *didn't* think this way when you first started talking about it. But now that I checked it out, I think I'm hooked."

"I definitely know what you mean."

THE TWO WITNESSES
CHAPTER 9
THE NEXT DAY

The next morning they both started moving around about the same time. Deena was the first to say anything.

"Oh Bob! What a night! It seems like I dreamt *all* night long. I think I know what you were talking about, the night you had *your* dreams."

"You too! Wow! Beautiful! What were they about?" Bob asked.

"It seems like I was walking in this field and I wanted to fly up around the top of the trees. I would sort of run a little, and then push downward with my arms folded then I started to lift. After I reached the top of the trees I just glided around. It was beautiful!

Another one was *weird*. I was in this *white* house, maybe 18th-century, somewhere around that period. And somehow, I knew there was an elderly gentleman in the down stairs bedroom who was dying. The strange thing about it was, *no one* seem to be concerned. It was like everything was all right, it was to be *expected*. Weird. And then there were several little ones I can't piece together yet.

Those two were so *real*. I feel like you did: I have to look around to see if I'm really here or not."

"I *know* it!" Bob exclaimed joyfully. "That's exactly the way mine were. Isn't that neat how that works? I was going to tell Tony and James about them, but somehow it slipped my mind. Let's ask them today if we think about it. Oh look, it's nearly eight. Let's flip a coin to see who does breakfast."

"No need to do that," Deena said. "You made it last time. I'd love to do it this time.

"Okay, I'll help; how's that?" offered Bob. "You get it started while I call Tony and tell him what's up, and we'll be leaving right after we eat and that should take about an hour and a half."

After breakfast they grabbed their books and were off.

"How was Tony when you talked to him?"

"About like us. Ready to go. Oh yeah, I asked him to remind me to ask James about dreams, in case it slipped my mind again."

"Good idea," Deena said. "Look! There's Tony turning the corner now!"

THE TWO WITNESSES
CHAPTER 9
THE NEXT DAY

"It sure is! How's that for timing?

After getting out of the car they looked at each other, and Bob said, "Now that's timing."

"What did you do, follow me?" Tony chuckled. I didn't see you till you turned in behind me. Well, let's go in and get ol' James cranked up. I'll bet he's ready!"

"After you," Bob prompted.

After general conversation, Bob remembered to ask about the dreams, and then he and Deena explained theirs.

"Anyway," Bob said, "I feel they have *some* significance to what we've been studying."

"You're right, Bob, they do, and we'll get into those in the course of the day," James said. "But for now it would take a little while to interpret them. We'll finish what we were talking about last night, then I'll see if they can be interpreted for you, Okay?"

"Excellent," they agreed.

"Great!" James said. "Are there any questions now? O   h yeah, Bob had one about Jesus being the Son of God *and* the Son of man."

"Me too, James," Deena said. "I wanted to ask what Paul meant when he was talking about Jesus being raised from the dead *according* to **his** gospel."

"Both good questions," assured James. "Well, Bob, I'm not saying ladies first, but, it will help answer your question if we explore hers, then yours."

"No problem. Whatever's the best way. You know *that's* what I like," Bob smiled.

"Okay, Deena, I think you were talking about second Timothy... yeah here *it* is. Chapter one. There's some in chapter two also. We read verses eight through ten before, but verse ten is the starting point. Let's break that verse down and then we'll look at chapter two.

"In verse ten he's referring to the truth being brought to life **by the appearance** of the Living Word, **out** of the gospel. Okay verse ten: 'But is now made manifest *by the* **appearing** of *our* Saviour Jesus Christ, who hath **abolished death** [Romans ten and

THE TWO WITNESSES
CHAPTER 9
THE NEXT DAY

four: 'For Christ *is* the end of the law [**death**] for righteousness to every one that believeth [spiritually].' and hath brought life and immortality to light **through the gospel**:' Hold that thought, and look at verse eight of chapter two; 'REMEMBER that Jesus Christ of the **seed of** David was raised from *the dead* according **to my** gospel.' When the Word, or scriptures come to *life* for you, they have been **raised** from a **dead letter** to L**iving understanding** without contradiction *to* anything. This is accomplished by the way the *words are written*. They are *written* to hide the truth on *one hand*, and on the *other*, to raise *the truth* from *death*, to *life*, for the *understanding* of *all things*. This is all done **within the scriptures**.

The Jesus of the *son of David*, is *the* Jesus 'whom henceforth we worship no more.' This is the Jesus of the *stories* or the *flesh*, this is the Son of *Man*.

This is the one who ***had to learn*** obedience through the things *he* suffered. This is the Jesus who ***was not perfect***, and when he ***became*** perfect, he ***became*** the author of eternal salvation. This is the one that would not be perfected *until* the - third thousandth year, that is, the 'third day.' *This is* **Israel**, God's **first** born. This *is* the Son he called out of Egypt. Israel, *is* the church, the one, or many in particular, called out of all religions. The section about Jesus's body is coming up shortly. Anyway, this is the Jesus that came in the *likeness* of *sinful flesh*. This *is not* the one that was **made sin** for us, who knew no sin.' He was made sin for us. Remember the same thing was said in Isaiah 43:24: 'Thou hast bought me no sweet cane with money, neither hast thou filled me with the fat of thy sacrifices: but **thou hast made me to serve with thy sins**, thou hast wearied me with **thine iniquities**.' Isn't that beautiful?

This Jesus said in Saint John that *he* must be lifted **up** from the **earth**. Here again, He's not talking about the planet. The Son of man *is* a product of man -- *the image*. The one we've been worshiping for two thousand years. The image of him that we see when the scriptures are read *carnally* is only **an image** of what He does universally in the universal *oneness* of *all* **things**. The *same* today, yesterday, *and forever:* 'I am God and I change not.' Even

THE TWO WITNESSES
CHAPTER 9
THE NEXT DAY

though -- He is the god *of* change, but not the laws.

I may be a little premature in *some of this*, but I trust you'll wait until we cover these areas before you try to draw any conclusions. All of what we were talking about will be thoroughly explained later. So to answer your question, Deena, *the truth* is raised from corruption, the letter, to incorruption, the Spirit. The scriptures were *written* of old by spiritual -- minded brethren, male *and* female, who understood the mind of Knowledge, or God, the operation of energy *in* earth. This means *all* the matter in the universe.

It also means the operation of energy, Spirit, or life, *in* words. It explains the *life force* and *how it works* in *all things* because of 'controversy,' *or friction*, including the cells in our bodies. The way thoughts beget thoughts, and the many that are offspring from *them*, and so on. It's really some beautiful understanding. But this too will come as we are *diligent* with our intent to know and understand for righteousness's sake. Also Bob, this should give you some insight to *your* question."

"Did it ever!" Bob gleamed. "I saw right away. This *is* truly awesome. Truly beautiful. And I can see where it's leading. I just can't find words for it."

"Me too, James," Deena added. "I see what you're saying and I understand it. *It is* beautiful! I don't know any other words for it either."

"Great!" James replied. "Just hang in there. It'll become much clearer as we go. But if you do have any questions you want to talk about, do like you just did. We can always come back to where we left off. Okay, with that said, where *did* we leave off? Tony, do you remember? "

"You had just finished explaining how the truth was brought to light **through** Paul's Gospel and that Jesus's name *is* the word of God. I think you also mentioned that those who *look for him*, will see Him, or the Word of God "

"That's right, Tony," James remembered. "I believe I was going to Hebrews. I was. Turn to chapter 9 and verse 28: 'So Christ was once offered to bear the *sins* [what *is* sin?] of many; [now get

THE TWO WITNESSES
CHAPTER 9
THE NEXT DAY

this] and **unto *them that look for him*** shall he **appear** [from where?] the *second time without sin* unto salvation.' Did you catch what it's saying here?"

"I think I did," Bob said. "Those who seek shall find, right? But I didn't get the part about the '*second time*.'"

"The part about '*them who look for him*,' does mean the same thing, Bob. He said, 'I love them that love *me*.' And if you seek for *that which you love*, **it** will **appear** to you. Whatever you seek for will **appear** to you when you read the scriptures. As we just read; 'He's coming with clouds - hands;' which as it reads in Hebrews 12:1; 'Wherefore seeing we also are compassed about with so great a **cloud of witnesses** [the scriptures, *and now*, math], let us lay aside every weight, and **the sin** [image] which doth so easily beset *us*, and let us run with patience the race that is set before us.' Another reason to keep in check the intent and desires of our hearts.

The *second time* means after your search the ***first*** time. In other words, when we *first* start searching for truth we are entangled with Satan, the deceiver, the lie, the image, the flaming Sword that surrounds the tree of Life. And if our intent and desire is pure, it doesn't take long to realize there seems to be too many contradictions; then we become disenchanted and think we must be off *base*, and we tend to shy away from churches and church people and become a law unto ourselves. That's the operation of Moses. That's where the *spirit of Moses* brings us out from the condemnation and scorn of the task masters through the red sea *into* the wilderness, where we really have nothing to cling to but hope. *In* the wilderness is where we wander around in our hearts, longing for *true understanding*, the Christ. Then, if we don't give up the search and still trust there *has to be* answers somewhere, we will be urged by the Spirit called 'grace' to *continue* searching on our own until we find ***that*** which we long for. A beautiful little story for that, is in Song of Solomon chapter three verses one through four.

When we start to see the scripture has a spiritual interpretation *along with* a carnal one, then we are compelled by our faith to look for '*that city* whose builder and maker *is God*' and not **men**. When the middle wall or partition is broken down, then we see

THE TWO WITNESSES

CHAPTER 9
THE NEXT DAY

clearly that *it is spiritual*, and this will be the *second time* He, the *Son*, will **appear without contradiction**, or 'sin.' This is how He **appears** the *second time* without sin, the lie, unto our salvation from sin. This is when you see Him on the *right* hand, where he sits *with* the Father, this is where the two *are* one. 'Thy **right hand**, O LORD, **is become** glorious in power: thy **right hand**, O LORD, hath dashed in pieces the [carnal].' Exodus 15 and 6. Psalms 20 and 6 '**Now know** I that the LORD saveth **his anointed**; he will hear him from his holy heaven with the **saving strength** [Christ] **of his right hand**.' There are just too many references of this nature to add right now, but do research as many of them as you can. As you can see, this '*right hand*' is the spiritual interpretation of the Word, or you could say, the *Son* of God! Do you follow me so far?"

"I got it! I got it! I understand now!" Bob shouted. "Since we no longer worship Him, the Word, after the *flesh*, we now, the *second time*, worship Him after the Spirit."

"Exactly Bob. That's a plain and simple way of saying it. I want to throw in two more verses to follow that up. Turn to Hebrews chapter 10 verses 19 and 20: 'Having therefore, *brethren*, boldness to enter into the holiest [Spirit] by the *blood* of Jesus [or, life of the Word], by a **new** and **living way**, which he hath consecrated for *us*, *through* the *veil*, [that is to say, **His flesh** or His Word],'. That's how it is found the *second time*. A new and **living way**. Just beautiful!

"Anyway, we're about to cover a lot of this in the next few minutes. Let's continue where we left off. I was about to go to second Thessalonians chapter 1, verses 1 through 14: 'Now we [the messengers in the gospel] beseech you, *brethren*, by the coming of *our* Lord Jesus Christ, and *by* our gathering together unto him, that ye be not soon *shaken in mind*, or be troubled, neither by spirit **nor** by **word**, nor by **letters** from us, as that the day [light] of Christ is at hand [always '*at hand*'].... Let no *man* deceive you by any means: for *that day shall not come*, except there come a falling away first, and that [teacher] of sin be revealed, the son of perdition; Who opposeth and exalteth himself above all that is called God, or that is worshipped; so that he as God sitteth in the temple of God [our

THE TWO WITNESSES
CHAPTER 9
THE NEXT DAY

minds], shewing **himself** that **he** is [the Word].... Remember ye not, that, when I was yet with you, I told you these things? And now ye know what withholdeth that he might be *revealed in his time*. For the **mystery** of [the lie] doth **already** work: only he [those *who know*] who now letteth will *let*, until he be taken out of the way [exposed]. And then shall that wicked be revealed, whom the Lord shall consume with the **spirit** of his **mouth** [Hebrew word for mouth - Peh- means - **two-edged word**], and shall destroy with the *brightness* [truth-light] of his [**appearing**]....*Even him*, whose coming **is after** the work of Satan [even now, **or we wouldn't know** where he is] with all power and signs and **lying** wonders, And with all deceivableness of unrighteousness in them that perish; because they received not the *love of the truth*, that they might be saved [saved from what?]. And for **this cause** [*not* loving truth] God shall send them strong delusion [you know what that is], that **they should believe a lie**: That they all might be damned who *believed not the truth*, but had pleasure in unrighteousness [or the stories].... But we are bound to give thanks alway to God for you, *brethren* beloved of the Lord, because God hath from the beginning [your first endeavor to find truth] chosen you to salvation through **sanctification** of the spirit and belief of the truth: Whereunto he **called you** -- by **our gospel** [that's where you find it, and that includes - whomsoever will] to the obtaining of the glory of *our* Lord Jesus Christ [the **Living** Word].'

Did I interject too much?"

"Not for me, I think I understood. Sounded just fine," Deena said.

"Me too, James. Just beautiful. I loved it. It *all* made perfect sense in the light of what I already know," Bob added.

"Wonderful! I love it when you say that!" James praised. "Well, what I would like to do now is ease into the understanding of the *body* of Christ and see if we can see a *different way* of looking at it. Are you ready? Maybe we should take a break first. This will take a little while to get into."

"Good," Bob agreed. "Why don't we all go to that little restaurant over on Franklin, I'll treat us to lunch and we can get that

THE TWO WITNESSES
CHAPTER 9
THE NEXT DAY

out of the way."

"Wow Bob! Last of the big spenders alive and in person," Tony kidded. "Heck of an idea. I'll leave the tip."

After inviting Martie, they went to eat, and of course, talked about the things they were studying there and back. After returning home they settled down again and James began.

"Okay guys, there is much to say now, and as you know, I tend to get carried away and go a little fast. *Do not* let me go past a point you do not grasp after a matter of minutes. Okay?...Okay. We're still looking at the *things made* to understand the invisible principle. Our human body has seven layers of skin, or flesh, and scripture *is written* after that **pattern**.

You remember *form* means the *image* don't you? This is how the scriptures are written, spoken of in Exodus by God to Moses when he was showing him how to build him a sanctuary to **live in**. Now the scripture says the kingdom of God is *within you,* right? And also, '*ye are* the temple of the living God.' And if God is *the Word,* where do words dwell? In the mind, of course. Anyway, first of all I want to bring in a couple of scriptures from Exodus where Moses is talking to God on the mount. And he's telling Moses what he wants for an offering. All of the things he wants is an *attitude*. Things like oil for *light,* different colors of linen, gold, brass, stones, et cetera. You may not understand what all of these things mean until you break them down, but *they are* really '*attitudes*' he wants us to have so we can understand his Word. Not only that, but Moses's list is a metaphor for the composition of the mind, words that is. This will all come together for you as you do your own research. Anyway, turn to Exodus 25 and we'll read verses 8 and 9: 'And let **them** make **me** a sanctuary [it has to be done by **us**]: *that I may dwell among them.* According to all that I shew thee, after the **pattern** of the tabernacle [dwelling place], and the **pattern** of all the instruments thereof, **even so** shall **ye** [Moses, or *them*] make it.'

Verse 40 refers to it also. This *pattern* is like the same pattern the physicist are seeing in their equations. There is **something that connects everything** in the universe. In scripture there is the same thing. 'In continuance [connections] is it fashioned.' 'Here a little and

THE TWO WITNESSES
CHAPTER 9
THE NEXT DAY

there a little,' which we're about to get into in Psalms. First of all I'll skim over a few things we've already touched upon and that'll lead us there. As we have seen, the *enemy* of truth **is the spirit of error** that is incorporated in the story *pattern*. That's what it's talking about in Ephesians 6:12; 'For we wrestle not against *flesh and blood*, [the living image] but against principalities [the attitudes the living image creates], against powers, against the rulers of the darkness of this world, against **spiritual wickedness** in high *places*.'

There is a god of the earth, or law, and there is a God of the Spirit. We are instructed to worship him in Spirit and in truth that we may have life. To have life is to partake of Christ's spiritual body as it is resurrected from the fleshly body of the Word. The more we understand, the better the resurrection we can have, or the quicker we can see **it**. Remember in Romans seven, verses five and six? It says, 'For when **we** were in the *flesh*, the motions of sins, which were *by the law*, did work in *our* members [mind-body] to bring forth fruit [thoughts] unto *death* [by thinking *the stories* were the *real* message]. But *now* we are delivered from the law, that *being dead* wherein we were held; that we should serve in *newness* [*all things* become new] of spirit, and not *in* the oldness [or tradition] of the letter.'

"I just wanted to bring those two scriptures in again so they would be fresh on our minds. The understanding, or Christ, must be brought forth. It is in the lowest parts of the earth [or words], just as the blood in our body, seven layers of flesh, and then the blood, or life of the flesh.

Seven layers of allegory, and then the total understanding. The *seven* golden candle sticks, the *seven* churches, the *seven* stars, the *seven* seals, et cetera, all in the *right hand*. Another way of saying, '*His* hand [truth] is **stretched out** still.' 'Here a little *and* there a little, line upon line precept upon precept' on *each level* of allegory, of which there are *seven*. Seven heavens.

Truth is written in a *continued fashion*, after a pattern that connects, so that you can *not* look directly at **it**, **it** has to be found by *following* these patterns until we can *see* the understanding, or Christ. Then everything *becomes light*, even *that* which *was*

CHAPTER 9
THE NEXT DAY

THE TWO WITNESSES

darkness or confusing to us before. Then we *can see Him* as He is, the *Spirit* of understanding, the operation of spirit (life) or energy **in** matter *and* words. We'll see how that works in a few minutes when we get into Psalms 139.

Pay close attention to these next two verses. Isaiah 45, verses 3 and 7: 'And I will give thee *the* **treasures of darkness**, and **hidden riches of secret places**, that thou *mayest know* that I, the [Word], which call *thee* by name, *am* the [Father] of Israel. I form the light, and create darkness: I make peace and create evil: I the [Word] do **all these things**.' Christ was *made in secret*, **hidden** throughout all scripture. Remember where it said, 'Then said I, Ah, Lord God! surely **thou hast greatly deceived this people**, and Jerusalem, saying, *Ye shall have peace*; whereas **the sword** [condemnation] reacheth unto the soul'? I think that was Jeremiah four and ten. Well, this is how he creates good and evil: by The Word.

"As Paul says in second Corinthians about *his* epistles -- I think it's verse 16: 'To the one *we are* the savour of death unto death, and to the other the savour of life unto life, and who is sufficient for these things'? What all of this is saying is, one side of the scriptures can kill you, and the other side can save you. It's up to you and the intent and desire of your heart. 'I have set before you good and evil, life and death; therefore **choose** life, that you might have **it** and have it more abundantly, et cetera.

Second Peter chapter 3, verses 15 and 16 talks more about Paul's epistles; let's look at it. 'And account *that* the long suffering of our Lord *is* salvation; even as our beloved brother Paul also according to the wisdom given unto him hath written unto you: As also in **all his epistles**, speaking in them of these things; in which are some things hard to be understood, which they that are unlearned [not spiritual] and unstable wrest, *as* **they do** *also the other scriptures*, **unto their own destruction** [He's not talking about drug addicts and drunks and so forth].... Ever learning [*they know* the stories!] and never able to come to the knowledge of the truth.' *That* was in second Timothy three verse seven.

I want to add six more verses to this, then we can move on.

THE TWO WITNESSES
CHAPTER 9
THE NEXT DAY

They're in Ephesians chapter 6, verses 15 through twenty: 'And your *feet* [faith or foundation] shod with the preparation of the gospel of peace [spiritual interpretation]. Above all, taking the shield of faith, wherewith ye shall be able to quench all the fiery darts of the wicked [the carnal].... And take the helmet of *salvation* [understanding], and the **sword of the spirit**, *which is the word of God* [*that's* our salvation].... Praying [searching] always with all prayer and supplication *in the Spirit*, and watching thereunto with all perseverance and supplication for all saints; And for me, that I may open *my mouth* [epistles] boldly, to make known **the mystery of the gospel**, For which I am an ambassador in bonds [writing the lie]: that *therein* [his epistles] I may speak boldly, **as I ought to speak.**' This is why he wondered who shall 'deliver him from the body of **this death**' in Romans 7 and verse 24.

By putting all of this together, we can see the truth and the lie are *in the same scripture*. The truth, is seven levels down, just as the blood in our human body is seven *layers* down. This follows a pattern. Another pattern that follows the physical plane about our body and the planet is, the planet is two-thirds water and one-third matter. Our body is two-thirds water and one-third matter. By comparing that to our minds and looking at *earth* as matter or words, and water as emptiness or confusion, we can see a pattern there. We already know that we only use one-third of our minds, and that leaves the other two-thirds as water, or space, no cognizance. By following this **pattern**, we can observe there are two-thirds space and one-third matter. We can carry it further and say all scripture, on the surface, is two-thirds water, or confusion, and one third matter, or **earth**, which *strings the stories* together, like it said; 'in continuance is it fashioned [after a pattern].' This will become clear in your studies.

"Let's go back to back to Isaiah 45 and verse 8: 'Drop down ye heavens [new Jerusalem], *from above*, and let the skies [word of the Spirit] pour down righteousness: let the **earth** open [or scriptures be revealed], and let *them* [scriptures] **bring forth** salvation [Christ], and let righteousness spring up together; I the [Word] have created it.

CHAPTER 9
THE NEXT DAY

THE TWO WITNESSES

Psalm 40, verses 7 and 8: 'Then said I, Lo, **I come** [how?]: **in the volume of the book** it is written of **me** [the truth], I delight to do thy will O my God: yea, thy law *is within* my heart.' Okay, just a few more then we'll go to Psalms 139.

"Turn to Hebrews ten, verses seven through eleven: 'Then said I, Lo, I come (**in the *volume* of *the book*** it is *written of me*,) to do thy will, O God. Above when he said, Sacrifice [men's doctrine, as Cain] and offering thou wouldest not and burnt offerings and *offering* for *sin* thou wouldest not, neither had pleasure therein: **which are offered by the law** [which is the *strength* of sin].... Then said he, Lo, I come to do thy will, O God. He taketh away the *first* [the law, the carnal interpretation], that he may establish the *second* [by a new and **living** way, through the veil]. By the which *will* we are sanctified through the offering of **the body** [the **flesh**]of Jesus Christ once *for all*. And every priest standeth daily ministering and offering oftentimes *the same sacrifice* [stories] which can **never take away sins** [the lie].

Speaking of taking away the first to establish the second, look at Ephesians 2, verses 14 through 16: 'For he is our peace, who hath made **both** *one*, and hath broken down the middle wall of partition [or revealed the deceiver] *between us;* having abolished in his *flesh* [or Word] the enmity, **even the law of commandments contained in ordinances** [*the letter*]; for to make *in* himself twain **one new** man [the way the scriptures are written *do this*], so making peace; And that he might reconcile **both** unto God in one body **by the cross**, having slain the enmity [no more contradiction] thereby:

What I've been doing since we came back from lunch is, to lay a little ground work for what we're about to get into. And this will clear the way for us to see his body, not only in the scriptures, but in **all things**. Next we're going to Psalms 139. But before we do, keep in mind the truth is calling out from the *words* we're reading. This is how you will also feel when you see it all spiritually. If you don't grasp it right away, you will shortly, after we move on from Psalms. Now we can go to verse 1, chapter 139. '**O LORD**, thou hast searched me, and known *me*. Thou knowest my *downsitting* and mine *uprising*, thou understandest my thoughts afar off. Thou

THE TWO WITNESSES

**CHAPTER 9
THE NEXT DAY**

compassest my path [continuance] and my lying down ['here a little and there a little'], and art acquainted *with* **all my ways** [how the spirit operates].... For *there is* not a word **in** my tongue [language], *but*, lo, O Lord, thou knowest it **altogether.** Thou hast beset [swaddled, clothed] me behind and before, and laid thine **hand** [again, word or clothing] **upon** *me* [the hidden truth]. *Such knowledge is too wonderful for me; it is high, I cannot attain unto it* [this *is not* David speaking].... Whither shall I go from thy spirit? or whither shall I flee from thy presence [He and his Father are one]? If I ascend up into heaven, thou art there: if I make my bed in **hell, behold,** *thou* **art** <u>there</u> [Remember where he said, 'I am the first, and I am the last?] *If* I take the *wings* [means passage ways] of the morning [truth], and dwell in the uttermost parts of the sea [waters, confusion]; Even there shall thy *hand* lead me, and **thy** <u>**right hand**</u> shall hold me.... If I say, Surely the darkness shall cover me; even the night [or letter] shall be light about me [what we once saw *as* darkness, becomes truth, or light]. Yea, the darkness hideth not from thee; but **the night** shineth **as** the day [we no longer see the stories, even though it's the *same words*]: the darkness *and* the light *are* both alike to *thee*. For thou hast possessed my reins [**water**-distribution]: thou hast covered me in my mother's [we'll see who *his* mother is later] womb'.

These next few verses make it plain it's not talking about David. It's talking about the truth **of** the word. Verse 14; 'I will praise thee: for I am fearfully *and* wonderfully *made* [not born]: marvelous are thy works; and *that* [the works] **my soul knoweth** right well.... My substance was not hide from thee, ***when I was*** <u>**made in secret**</u>, *and* **curiously wrought in the** <u>**lowest parts of the earth**</u> [this is still *not talking* about David]. Thine *eyes* did see my substance [faith], <u>**yet being unperfect**</u> [on the *third day* I shall be perfected]: and *in* <u>*thy book*</u> **all my members** [*words*] **were written, which** <u>**in continuance**</u> **were fashioned** [after a pattern], when *as yet* there was none of them.' They cannot be seen directly, they are hidden.

You look *and* look, and you *eventually* see **it.** It was there all the time, but it was *not yet fashioned* in your mind. Your eyes, which

**CHAPTER 9
THE NEXT DAY**

THE TWO WITNESSES

also means understanding, were not quite adjusted. It just hadn't come together in the *mind's eye*. The same with his body, it's not perfected until you can see **it** come together. You have to be able to see through *seven* layers of flesh or allegory before you can see the blood, or life of the **word body**, which dwells in all of us. Remember, he was **made in secret**, in the **lowest parts of the earth**. Okay let's move on.

"Isaiah 44 and verses 23 through 25 'Sing [prophesy] O ye heavens: for the Lord hath done **it**: shout, ye **lowest parts of the earth**: break forth into *singing*, ye *mountains* [watchers], O forest, and every *tree* therein [those who know the law, spiritually]: for the Lord hath redeemed Jacob and hath glorified himself in Israel [his Son, or his Word].... Thus saith the Lord, thy redeemer, and he that formed thee from the womb, I *am* the Lord that maketh all *things*; that stretcheth forth the heavens alone; that spreadeth abroad *the earth by myself*; That frustrateth the **tokens** [stories] of the **liars** [the teachers of the letter], and maketh diviners mad; that turneth wise **men** backward ['my people have gone away backward'], and maketh **their knowledge** [of the scriptures] foolish.'

"The Saviour, is *hidden* in the lowest parts of the earth. Okay Bob, I see your face; turn to Exodus chapter 4, verses 22 and 23 'And thou shalt say unto Pharaoh, Thus saith the Lord, **Israel is** *my* **Son,** *even* my **first** born: And I say unto thee, Let *my Son* go, that he may serve me: and if thou refuse to let him go, behold, I will slay thy son, *even* thy **first** born.'

Hold on Bob, there's a couple more. Turn to Hosea chapter 11, verse 1: 'When **Israel** *was a child*, then I loved *him*, and called **my Son** out of Egypt.' Genesis 32, verses 28 and 30: 'And He said, Thy name shall be called no more Jacob, but *Israel*: for as a prince hast thou **power** [Christ, understanding] with God and **men**, and *hast prevailed*. And Jacob called the name of the place Peniel: for I have <u>seen</u> God face to face, and my life is preserved.' To see 'God face to face,' certainly implies you *have seen him* **spiritually**. God is spirit and seeketh *such* to worship him. Israel are those who have wrestled with the carnal understanding of the Word *until they have seen* the true understanding. This makes up the body, or the called

THE TWO WITNESSES
CHAPTER 9
THE NEXT DAY

out ones, the ones called out of Egypt bondage. Or out from under the law. They are called the '**church**,' or, the **body** of Christ. *Many members* in particular making up *one* body or organization, counsel, et cetera.

"Through the centuries many have found a little truth, or understanding of the scriptures, and have branched away from the flock they were with. But too often fall right *back* into the letter. Thus the backsliding daughters. The process has repeated itself over and over again with *all* who have searched and sought for *their* truth. That's why we have such a variety of dogmas and doctrines. Israel, is still scattered over the entire planet. They're in **all races**, creeds, colors and religions. And you will recognize them by the fruit they bear, that is, by the way they speak, which is spiritual.

"As truth and understanding start to come forward, *so do the Israelites*. It will be many people in particular, making up one institution or one **body** of people with understanding in their message. The story of Israel in the scriptures, is the story of *all* that have yearned and sought after righteousness, from the beginning of the creation of the *mind* until now. Scientist have quite well documented the evolution of the human body. We're moving into some of that area in the next few minutes.

"Finishing up the tangent of 'the lowest parts of the earth,' we'll tie it into some other tangents that will wrap it up in a simple-to-understand package. Turn to First Peter, chapter four, verses one, two and six: '**FORASMUCH** then as Christ hath suffered for us in the flesh [those also before us who have sought and found], arm yourselves *likewise* with the *same mind*: for **he** that hath suffered in the **flesh** [whomsoever] hath **ceased from sin** [or if you're born **again**, it's impossible to to see the lie].... That he [whomsoever] no longer should live the rest of his time **in the flesh** to the lust of *men*, but to the will of God. For this cause was the gospel preached also to **them that are dead** [or carnal] to the one, we're the savour of death, and to the other, the savour of life, that they might be judged **according to men in the flesh**, but **live according to God in the spirit**.' First Peter, chapter 1, verses 22 through 25: 'Seeing ye have **purified** your souls in obeying the *truth* **through** *the Spirit* unto

THE TWO WITNESSES
CHAPTER 9
THE NEXT DAY

unfeigned love of the brethren, see that ye love one another with a *pure heart* fervently: Being born again, not of *corruptible seed* [the letter], but of incorruptible, by the *word* of God.... For **all *flesh*** [carnal words] is *as* grass, and all the glory of *man* as the flower *of* grass. The grass withereth, and the flower **thereof** falleth away: But the Word of the Lord endureth forever [for *it is* a pattern of all creation itself]. **And this is the word which by the gospel is preached unto you**.' Yes, were reading it now.

First Peter chapter two, verses one through eight: '**WHEREFORE** laying aside all malice, and all guile, and hypocrisies, and envies, and all evil speakings [or the carnal mind].... As *newborn* babes **desire** *the sincere milk of the word*, that ye may grow thereby: If so be ye have ***tasted*** that the *Lord is* gracious.... To whom coming, as unto a *living stone*, **disallowed indeed of men**, but chosen of God, and precious, Ye also, as lively stones, are built up a spiritual house [many members], an holy priesthood, *to offer up* [from the earth] **spiritual sacrifices**, acceptable to God **by** Jesus Christ.... Wherefore it is also contained *in* the scripture, Behold, I lay in Sion [the *good* Word] a chief *corner stone*, elect, **precious** [living stone, sound doctrine]: and he that believeth **on** him shall *not* be confounded.... Unto you therefore which believe he **is** precious: but unto them which be disobedient, the stone which the *builders* [of Babylon, the city of confusion] disallowed, the same is made the head of the corner.... And a stone of stumbling, and a rock of offense, even to them which **stumble at the word** ['to their own destruction'], being disobedient: whereunto also they were appointed [**their intent and desire** appointed them].' Psalms 27, verse 2: 'When the wicked, even mine enemies and my foes came upon me to ***eat up my flesh***, they *stumbled* and *fell*.' By the very *word* they were trying to *eat*. He's that stumbling stone, as we're going to see next.

Romans 9 verses 31 through 33: 'But **Israel**, which *followed after* the law of righteousness, *hath not attained* to the law of righteousness. Wherefore? Because they sought **it** not by faith, **but as it were by the works of the law** [the stories]. For *they* stumbled at *that* stumbling stone [the image!]. As it is written,

THE TWO WITNESSES
CHAPTER 9
THE NEXT DAY

Behold, I lay in Sion a *stumbling stone* and rock of offense: and whosoever believeth on *him* [the stumbling stone] shall not be ashamed [or confounded].'

We'll get back to Romans in just a minute. But at this point I want to bring in first John chapter four, verses one through seven: '**BELOVED**, believe not every spirit, but try the spirits whether they are of God: because many false prophets [because **they** teach the letter] have gone out into the world.... Hereby ye know the spirit of God: Every spirit that confesses that Jesus Christ **is come in the flesh** i*s* of God.... And every spirit that confesseth not that Jesus Christ **is** come *in the* **flesh** is not of God [but *we know* He definitely **is** come in the *living flesh* -- which we are eating as you read this]: and this is that *spirit* of **antichrist** [against spiritual understanding], whereof ye have heard that *it should come*; and even **now** already is **it** [the lie] in the world [because he is also in the word, that's why].... Ye are of God, little children, and have overcome **them** [the liars]: because greater is he that is in you, than he that is in the world [the *spirit* of the liar. 'For we wrestle not against flesh and blood'].... **They** are of the world [the carnal world, *the one* where he said, 'Father *I pray not for the world'*]: therefore speak *they* of the world, and the world heareth *them* [look at the ones who follow the stories!].... We are of God: he that knoweth God *heareth* us; he that is not of God heareth not us.... Hereby know we **the spirit** of truth, **and** *the spirit of error*.... Beloved, let us love one another: for love is of God; and everyone that loveth is born of God, and knoweth God. He that loveth not knoweth not God; for God is love,' When the scriptures are not taught spiritually, they are not taught with the anointing. That comes through the revelation, or resurrection, from the law or letter. Having the *anointing* means you have been *enlightened*, Christened, or illumined. You *have understanding*. In scripture it represents Christ, Power, Wisdom, Spirit, Understanding, Life, Blood, and Son.

"Now if *men* have been trying to teach the scripture for the last six thousand years (six days), and have been doing it *without* the spiritual interpretation, doesn't it seem possible they are anti - understanding, anti - power, anti - anointed, anti - Spirit, anti - Son,

THE TWO WITNESSES

CHAPTER 9
THE NEXT DAY

and of course, **anti - Christ**, full of confusion, fear and guilt? There is no need to tell you how the world could end up without understanding what we are doing to the elements that bid **our** (every ones) desires, whether they are good, or not. The universe only gives. 'It rains on the just and the unjust alike.' And there is not one jot nor tittle out of place. Everything is as it should be, *according* to prophecy. And if we understand the prophecy, we shouldn't be troubled. For a wonderful and marvelous awakening is about to take place in the universe, and **we're all a part of it**. It is time to awaken and rise from our long sleep. This is the time of the resurrection. It has not quite passed yet, as some have determined. Look at second Timothy chapter 2, verses 11 through 18: 'It is a faithful saying: For if we be dead **with** *him* [for the last two days], we shall also live with *him* [in the resurrection].... If **we** suffer [**in** the **flesh**], we shall also reign with *him*: if we deny *him*, he also will deny us [if you don't *search* for him, you can't find him]: If we believe not, *yet* he abideth faithful: he cannot deny himself. Of these things put *them* [the brethren] in *remembrance*, charging *them* before the Lord that they strive not about *words to no profit* [stories], but to the subverting of the hearers.... *Study* to shew *thyself* approved unto God, a workman that needeth not to be ashamed [confused], **rightly dividing** [the carnal from spiritual] the **Word** of *truth*. But shun profane and vain babblings [arguing over the stories]: for they will increase unto more ungodliness [carnal disputations]. And their [mens] word will eat as doth a canker (gangrene): of whom is Hymenaeus and Philetus [*well-meaning*, but caught up in the stories]; Who *concerning the* **truth** *have erred* [sin], *saying that* **the resurrection is past already**; and overthrow the faith of some.' The resurrection *is not over* until the morning of the **third** day. This is taking place now, and **men** cannot see it. This is the time of the *lifting up* of the spirit. Look at John chapter 3, verse 14: 'And as Moses *lifted up* the serpent [of the law] in the *wilderness,* **even so** must the Son of man be *lifted up*.' Skip on to chapter 12 and verses 31 and 32: 'Now is the judgment of *this world* [the carnal mind]: now shall the prince of *this world* [the son of perdition] be cast out [the lies exposed].... And I, *if* I be lifted up from the *earth*, will draw **all men** unto me [Gods

THE TWO WITNESSES
CHAPTER 9
THE NEXT DAY

vengeance].'

"Psalms 28 and verse 9: 'Save thy people [from what? remember?], and bless thine *inheritance*: feed them also, and *lift **them** up* **forever** [this ***them*** is Him. 'Forever' can *only be done* **by the resurrection**].' His *inheritance* is Israel, His son, His *first* born. The Son *of man* -- **the church**. John 8 and verses 28 and 30: 'Then said Jesus unto them, When ye have *lifted up* the Son of man, **then** shall *ye know* that I am he [truth in the word], and that I do nothing of myself; but as my Father [the Word] hath taught me, I speak these things.... And he that sent me **is with me** [He's the *same* word]: the Father hath not left me alone; for I do always those **things** that please him.'

Psalms 10 verse 12: 'Arise, O Lord; O God, ***lift up thine hand*** [Son]; forget not the humble.' Psalms seven and verse six: 'Arise, O Lord, **in** thine anger [which brings *vengeance*, and you know what the Lord's *vengeance* is -- truth], ***lift up thyself*** [from the **earth**] because of the rage of mine enemies [the carnal]: and awake for me *to* **the judgment** *that* thou hast commanded.' Can you see how the resurrection is just now taking place? Anyway let's go on.

Psalms 94, verses 1 through 5: '**O LORD** God, to whom <u>*vengeance* belongeth</u>; **O** God, to whom <u>*vengeance* belongeth</u>, ***shew thyself***. **<u>Lift up thyself</u>**, thou judge *of the earth*: render a reward to the proud. Lord, how long shall the *wicked*, how long shall the wicked [carnal] triumph?... How long shall *they* utter and speak ***hard things*** [confusion, lies]? and all the workers of *iniquity* boast themselves? *They* break in pieces *thy* people [the spiritual], **O** Lord, and afflict *thine heritage*.'

Isaiah 26, verse 11: 'Lord, *when thy **hand** is **lifted up***, they will not see: but *they* shall see, and be *ashamed* [confounded] for their envy at the people; yea, *the fire* of thine enemies shall devour *them*.' The fire of God's enemies *is the enemies'* **own words**! They will be destroyed in ***their own counsel!*** Which *they* wrest to *their own* destruction.

Isaiah 49, verse 26: 'And **I** will feed *them* that oppress thee [the spiritual] with *their own flesh* [words]; and they shall be

THE TWO WITNESSES

CHAPTER 9
THE NEXT DAY

drunken with *their own blood* [guilt], as with sweet *wine*: and *all flesh* shall know that I the Lord am thy Saviour and thy Redeemer, the mighty One of Jacob.' Remember where it was said, 'the *very thing* I thought would *save* me *slew* me'? Isaiah 33, verses 10 through 12: '**Now** will **I rise**, Saith the Lord; **now** will I **be exalted**; **Now** will **I** *lift up myself*.... Ye shall conceive chaff, ye shall bring forth stubble: *your* breath [spirit, attitude] *as fire* shall devour you.... And the people [thoughts] shall be *as* the burnings of lime: as thorns cut up shall they be *burned in* **the** *fire*.' You could say we created *our own* **hell**. The only way to burn a spirit, is always according to **his thinking**. The carnal thought people *in the mind* are the ones to be burned out or up; by the spirit of truth, thereby saving the individual that *it*, the lie, was in. Remember we read that earlier? Also, 'we wrestle not against flesh and blood,' which means the guilt from the stories or the image, but the attitude or spirit of *them*. Again, principalities and powers they're called.

For a more complete understanding of the Son of man and *his being* **lifted up** *from the earth*, and how it relates to the resurrection from **the dead**, we need to break down a few more *stories*. Turn to first Corinthians 15 and verse 21: 'For since *by man* came **death**, *by man* came also the *resurrection of the dead* [by the sweat of his brow].'

Romans 5 verses 12 through 14: 'Wherefore, as by one **man** [carnal attitude] sin entered into the world, and death by sin; so death passed upon **all men**, for that **all have sinned** [the scripture hath concluded *all* under sin]: for until the law sin was in the world: but sin is not imputed when there is no law. Never the less **death** [the law] reigned *from* Adam **to** Moses, *even* over them that *had not* sinned *after* the **similitude** of *Adam's* [not Eve's] transgression, who is the *figure* of him that was to come.' First Corinthians chapter 15, verses 21 through 23: 'For since *by* man *came* **death**, *by* man [Son of man] came also the resurrection of **the dead**.... For as **in** *Adam* all die, even so **in** Christ [the second Adam, the Lord from heaven] shall all be made alive. But every man in *his own* order: Christ the first fruits; afterward they that are Christ'[s] at his coming.' This is when

CHAPTER 9
THE NEXT DAY

THE TWO WITNESSES

the *church* or the *bride* comes forth. This is in the gathering now. The bride *is* making herself ready.

"Paul, said he *dies daily*. If this is the case, he also must be *resurrected daily*. The point here is, until we have pure understanding, we fall back into the *image* and have to over come it with spiritual knowledge, and then we go to another level until Christ is formed **in** us. And as he says, it is done **by the scriptures**.

"Let's go back to the first verse of this chapter, and read one through four; '**MOREOVER**, *brethren*, I declare unto you **the gospel** which **I** preached unto you, which also ye have received, and *wherein* ye stand [in the spirit]; *By which* also *ye are saved*, if ye keep in memory what I have preached unto you, unless ye have believed in vain. For I delivered unto you first of all that which I also received, how that Christ died for our sins **according to the scriptures**; **And** that he was buried [in the earth], **and** that he rose **again** the *third day* **according** to [by-way-of] **the scriptures**.'

"Speaking of 'every *man in his own order*,' which we just read, I want to lay a verse out for you to pigeonhole for now. We're still in first Corinthians chapter 15. Look at verse 19: '**If in this life only** we have hope in Christ, **we are of all men** most miserable.' And also (taken literally) remember where he told us to forgive each other seventy times seventy times seventy, and so on? And on the other hand he says *of himself*, 'It's allotted *unto man* seventy years then cometh the judgment.' He wants *us* to forgive *each other* so many times, *and He* only allows us *once* times seventy to get it right? We'll cover how this works in a few more studies.

For now let's get back to first Corinthians chapter 15, and we'll go to verses 45 through 54: 'And so it is *written*, The first *man Adam* was made a living soul; the last Adam [I am the *first*, and I am the *last*] *was* **made** a quickening spirit.... Howbeit that *was* not first which is spiritual, but that which is natural [there has to be the natural first, then the observer]; and afterward that which is spiritual. The ***first man*** [living **soul**, state of mind -- verse 45] *is of the earth*, **earthy** [remember, **of the ground**]: the second **man** [Adam] *is* the Lord from heaven.... As is the earthy, such *are* they also that are earthy: and *as is* the heavenly, such *are* they also that are

THE TWO WITNESSES

CHAPTER 9
THE NEXT DAY

heavenly. And as we have born the *image* of the earthy, we shall also bear the *image* of the heavenly.... Now this I say **brethren**, that flesh and blood [the **living dead** or image] cannot **inherit** the kingdom [spirit] of [the Word]; neither doth corruption inherit incorruption.... Behold I shew you a mystery; *we* shall not all sleep, but we shall all be changed [remember, he's talking to **brethren**], In a moment, in the twinkling of an eye [*eye* represents *understanding*], at the last trump [trump: to make straight, set in order]: for the trump shall sound, and the *dead* [in Christ] shall be raised incorruptible, and **we** shall be changed [and have a new mind].... For *this corruptible* [mind] must **put on** incorruption, and this mortal must put on immortality. So when this corruptible shall have put on incorruption, **and** *this mortal* shall have **put on** immortality, then shall be brought to pass, the saying *that is* written, **Death** [ignorance] is swallowed up in victory.' Yes, Deena, did you have a question?"

"Well, something you read earlier isn't quite clear. Can you go back to the part where it said death passed on everybody, even the ones that *didn't* do anything to deserve it? Or something like that."

"I think I know what you mean. I believe that was back in Romans 5, verses 12 and 14: 'so death passed upon **all men**, for that **all** [men] have sinned: even over them that **had not** sinned.' It is a *beautiful* contradiction. And very confusing if you don't catch the part about Adam's transgression. Okay, Deena, if you'll look at verse 12 you'll notice that death '*passed*' upon **all** <u>men</u>.' And in verse 14 'death *reigned*' was stated, not *passed* upon. I guess the best way to explain what it means is to look at the situation we have today. It's the same thing. We have those who teach *the lie*, and those who believe it. Thereby, death passes upon *all* of *them* -- **men**. And we have those who are brought up under these teachings that *do not* adhere to them, but the teachings hold sway in the land *anyway*. And for years held control in most all decision-making. So *it* reigned **even** *over them that did not sin* after Adam's transgression. And that was, to **accept** *the lie* from *the woman*. Even at that, it still has some influence over how a person carries him or her self at *this* time.

THE TWO WITNESSES

CHAPTER 9
THE NEXT DAY

This, *one man's* disobedience, was the **second Adam**. For *he knew the law*. Remember [as the story goes] God told **this Adam** what he could and could not do, eat and not eat. He *was* warned. *He* knew better. And as the story goes he will *have to* learn obedience by the things he will have to suffer. We'll cover this when we get to the part about the mystery of Christ and the church. Deena, did, or rather do you follow the parable there?"

"It's coming together now, James, I felt it was simple." Deena giggled.

"We'll see some of this again. but as I said before, *all this* will be necessary for grasping what is to come. Okay, let's go back to first Corinthians, chapter 15 and read the next two verses where we left off, and they were 55 and 56: 'O **death**, where *is* thy sting? O grave, where *is* thy victory? The sting of death *is* sin; and the **strength of sin** *is* the *law*.' **This** *is* what reigns from Adam ['for in Adam, all die'] to Moses. Moses brings us *out from under* this cruel bondage and slavery of the law of sin and spiritual death.

"Turn to Matthew 22 and verse 32: 'I am the God of Abraham, and the God of Isaac, and the God of Jacob.' **'God is *not* the God of the dead** but of the living.' Are these guys alive? Abraham, Isaac and Jacob? *If* they *are* dead, then he is *not* their God. But since he said *he is their God* that must mean they're alive. If they are alive, where are they? I thought I would plant that little seed for later.

"Let's get back to the *two* Adams. I think we should start with the creation of the *creature*. What this entails is the creation of the physical human, the animal, or survival instincts, the mental personality and ego, *and then* the enlightened mind. Have we covered the pattern of water yet? If we have, I still want to insert it again. You know the planet is *two-thirds* water, the human body is *two-thirds* water, we only use one-third of our brain, or mind the other *two-thirds* haven't been found or explored *yet*. What we call space is *two-thirds* space and one third matter. The scriptures are, on the surface, *two-thirds* confusion and one-third truth. There are seven layers of flesh on the human body, there are seven allegorical layers of flesh on the scriptural body. There are **twelve** sons of

CHAPTER 9
THE NEXT DAY

THE TWO WITNESSES

Jacob, there are **twelve** disciples, then there are **twelve** apostles. Ishmael, son of the bond woman, had **twelve** sons or princes. There are the **twelve** tribes of Israel, referred to as sons. Everybody it seems in first Chronicles chapter 25, verses 9 through 31 had **twelve** sons and brethren. There were **twelve** baskets of fish and loaves left over at the sermon on the mount. Mark 5 and 42: 'And straightway the damsel arose, and walked; **for she was *of the age*** of **twelve** years. And they were astonished with a **great astonishment**.' Did you see the reason she walked? **Because** she was of age, **twelve**! Jesus was **twelve** years old when he said he **must be** about his Father's business. Luke 8 and verse 43: 'And a *woman* having an issue of blood **twelve** years....' Revelations **twelve** and one, 'And there appeared a great wonder in heaven; a woman clothed with the sun, and the moon under her feet, and upon her head a crown of **twelve** stars.' And don't forget the **twelve** zodiacal signs. Revelations 21 and 12: 'And had a wall great and high, *and* had **twelve** gates, and at the gates **twelve** angels, and names written thereon, which are *the names* of the **twelve** tribes of the children of Israel.' Revelations 21 and 14: 'And the wall of the city had **twelve** foundations, and in them the names of the **twelve** apostles of the Lamb.' Revelations 21 and 21: 'And the **twelve** gates *were* **twelve** pearls; every several gate was of one pearl: and the street of the city *was* pure gold, as it were transparent glass.' Revelations 22 and 2: 'In the midst of the street of it, and on either side of the river, was *there* the tree of life, which bare **twelve** *manner of* fruits, *and* yielded her fruit every month: and the leaves of the tree *were* for the healing of the nations [religions].' And did you know there are **twelve** faculties of the mind? Or should I say in the house of words, where all of this takes place. By following *the patterns of the things* that are **made**, we can understand the *invisible* principle of, like it says, '*the things* that **aren't**.'

"A couple more verses then we'll get to the *creature*. Turn to Genesis chapter five verses one and two: 'This *is* the book of the generations of **Adam**. In the day that God created **man**, in the **likeness of God** made he him [God *is* Spirit].... Male **and** female created he **them**; and blessed **them**, and called <u>**their name**</u> Adam,

THE TWO WITNESSES
CHAPTER 9
THE NEXT DAY

in the *day* when **they** were created.' Here, it is quite plain. The male *and* female were named **Adam**. And as it said in verse one, **they** were made in the image of God, which is Spirit. *This* Adam, [**they**] are not physical beings! He, they, were made in the **likeness** of God. God, *is not* a physical being! This Adam and this Eve are *in* humans, but they themselves are not human. To top this off, Adam's heirs are not human either! Look at verse three: 'And **Adam** lived an hundred and thirty years, and begat a *son* in ***his own likeness***, after ***his*** [their] image; and called his name Seth:' And so on with the rest of the people of the Bible.

"I see your eyes crossing, Bob. Hang on just a few more minutes and we will discuss some of this, but for now, let's add to what we just read by reading Luke chapter 3 and verse 38: 'Which was the son of Enos, which was the son of Seth, which was the son of **Adam**, <u>**which was the son of God**</u>.' Remember, we have in Exodus, where he called **Israel** his **first** born. Israel had **twelve** sons, Christ had **twelve** disciples. Now we have Adam, whom is, male **and** female, and is also called the Son of God. And *according to the story* the first created of God. Adam, the Son of God, Israel the Son of God. Try to keep this in mind as we go into the *body* of Christ.

Okay, first Timothy chapter 2, verses 11 through 15: 'Let the woman [we now know what **woman** represents] learn in silence with all subjection. But I suffer not a *woman* to teach, nor to usurp authority over the man, but to be in silence. For Adam was first *formed*, then Eve.... And Adam *was not* deceived, but the *woman* being deceived was in the transgression. Notwithstanding, she <u>**shall**</u> be saved *in* child bearing, ***if*** **they** <u>**continue**</u> in faith and charity and **holiness** with sobriety [not drunk on the wine of the *stories*].' Taking this carnally would mean this was written some 4,000 years after their beginning. But *here*, it speaks of *future* tense. The child bearing represents multiplying and replenishing the **earth**. Or you could say, working out your salvation.

"In John, chapter three and verse five it says; '....Except a *man* be born of **water** *and* of the Spirit, he cannot enter into the kingdom of God.' We know that *is* spiritual. The physical would be the same. We are nine months in a womb of water, then out into the

THE TWO WITNESSES
CHAPTER 9
THE NEXT DAY

air. Water and then Spirit, water and then air, a *pattern*. Remember how we follow the *pattern*.

"Okay, turn to Genesis chapter one and we'll see if we can find a pattern. Let's start at verse 20 through 22: 'And God said, Let the **waters** bring forth abundantly the *moving creature* **that hath life** [not the dead ones?], and fowl that may fly above the earth in the open firmament of heaven [birds evolved from the ocean?].... And God created great whales, and **every living creature that moveth** [that includes our physical body], which the **waters brought forth** abundantly, after their kind, *and* every *winged* fowl after *his* kind: [or after his seed] and God saw that it was good. And God blessed them, saying, Be fruitful, and multiply, and fill the **waters** in the seas, and let fowl multiply *in* **the earth.**' This is the record of what **the waters brought forth.**' It would take a book in itself to explain these verses. You will comprehend it later in your research. Verses 24 and 25 are dealing with *instinct*. I don't want to get into *these two* verses just yet. There are some other things to understand first. We will cover it shortly.

"For now, let's look at verses 26 through 28: 'And God said, Let **us** make *man* in **our** image, after **our** *likeness* [spirit, right?]: and let them have dominion over the fish *of the sea*, and over the fowl of the **air**, and over the cattle, and over all the **earth**, and over every creeping thing that creepeth upon the **earth.**'

"Take notice where it said, 'let **us** make man in **our** image...' It is definitely implying more than *one* is going to **make** man in **their** image. Now notice what happens in the next verse. 'So God created man in **his own image**, in the **image of God** created He him; male **and** female created He **them**.' Did you notice anything different about *whose image* they were created in?"

"Wow," Bob said excitedly. "Am I seeing this straight? It did say **they** were going to make man in **their** image. But it didn't work that way. It says God made *them* in **his** image, not **theirs**. Unless he's referring to himself as plural. What's happening, James?"

"Well, let's look at the last part of that verse again, Bob. He's talking about making *man*. It turns out, **this man** that God created is male **and** female. And it is **they** that are created in *his image*.

THE TWO WITNESSES
CHAPTER 9
THE NEXT DAY

Remember, he called **their** name Adam. This *is not* a physical male and female, this is the *observing mind* of the physical species. This is why it was written this way, so we could grasp the duality of our mind. Without Christ that is. If the body of Christ is made up of many members in particular and He and his Father are one, then God is one in His plurality of many members in particular. That'll be cleared up in a little while. Let's continue.

"And God blessed *them* [**man**], and God said unto them, be fruitful, and multiply, and replenish the **earth**, and subdue it: and have dominion over the fish *of the sea*, and over the fowl *of the air*, and over every ***living*** thing that moveth upon the earth [take control of your mind]. And God said, Behold, I have **given you** every herb bearing seed, which is upon the **face** of **all** the **earth** [image], and every **tree**, in the which is the fruit of **a** tree *yielding seed*; **to you** it shall be for **meat** [not food, but **meat**].' Trees represent knowledge. Wood represents knowledge. Jesus's Father is a *carpenter*. The house of God is within you. Trees in the natural sense that bear edibles **also** put out oxygen. Trees in the spiritual sense do the same thing: oxygen would be the spiritual understanding that comes out of the words. The tree or cross, is made out of the *dead* wood of trees. The spiritual cross is *contradiction*, and it is made with *dead* words. The earth represents knowledge. Out of **this** grows things we eat. That's the same physically *and* mentally. What we're seeing is the *emerging* of the mental faculty of the human **creature**, the one that emerged from the waters earlier.

The reason I say that, is because it's talking about the **image of God**, and *that,* is *invisible*. In essence, words represent what is in the mind, where you and *they* live. Using Adam and Eve as metaphors for words, we can understand that *we* have the power to arrange how these words act and interact. *We* are to take control or dominion, over them. We are to be fruitful and multiply, or learn. To subdue the fowl of the air, which is spiritual ignorance. These are **things** in the **waters**, the emotions, fear guilt and so on. And to take dominion over every <u>**living thing**</u> that *moveth* upon **the earth**, or in the mind. Thus the human mind evolves into being. But at this

THE TWO WITNESSES

CHAPTER 9
THE NEXT DAY

point all they have are cave-man - like *instincts*, they are not yet a *living soul*. And the reason I say that is because of what's coming next.

"In Genesis 1 and 26: 'Let *us* make man in *our* image. Then he blessed them. And in chapter two, 'He rest from **all** that He had made, and ended His works.' **But**, in verse five, after He has created male and female (not woman yet, just female) in His image, He says 'there **is not a man to till the ground**,' which implies they do not *yet* know how to *reason*. Proof of this lies in the next few verses. Let's read in chapter two, verses five through nine: 'And every plant of the field [the mind, where the seed is sown] before it was in the earth [or formed], and every herb of the field before it grew: for the LORD God had not caused it to *rain* upon **the earth**, and **there was not a *man* to till the ground**.... But there went **up** a mist *from* the earth [knowledge], and **watered** the whole *face* of the **ground** [which means the mind was starting to comprehend]. And the LORD God **formed** [in chapter one it was *created* or *made*] **man** of the *dust of the ground*, and breathed into his nostrils [animal survival instincts and fear] the breath *of life*; and *man* became a living soul [he was now more of a rational animal].... And the LORD God planted a garden eastward in Eden [in the mind]; and there he put the man [now he is the *good* instinct] whom he had formed. And **out of the ground** made the LORD God to grow **every tree** that is pleasant to the sight, and **good for food**; the tree of life [*intuition* of righteousness] also in the midst of the garden, and the **tree** of knowledge of good and evil.' This is describing the creating of consciousness, and the **ability** to reason. You'll understand the *four* rivers or the **four** elements of the mind in a little while, when we discuss the four gospels.

"Now that we know what earth, ground, sheep and cattle represent, these next few verses should make sense to us. Remember, cattle eat the top of the grass, sheep get to the root. Were going to go through verses 18 to 25 and then we can go back through and break it down, or go to the root if you want to. 'And the LORD God [in this case the process of evolution] said, **It is not good that the man** [the first *man* Adam] **should be alone; I will make**

CHAPTER 9
THE TWO WITNESSES
THE NEXT DAY

him an help meet for him.... And '**out of the ground**' the LORD God formed [the helpmate] every beast of the field [or mind], and every fowl of the air [this is Adams helpmate]; and brought them unto Adam to see what he would call them: and whatsoever Adam called every '**living**' creature [thought], that was the name thereof [exercising intellectual reason].... And Adam gave names to all **cattle**, and to the fowl of the air, and to every *beast of the field* [now notice this next line], <u>**but for Adam**</u> [the *second* man Adam] **there was not found an help meet <u>for him</u>**.... And the LORD God caused a deep sleep to fall upon Adam [the mind], and he slept: and he took one of his ribs, and closed up *the flesh* instead thereof.... And the rib, which the LORD God had taken **from** *man* [male and female], made he a **woman**, and brought her unto **the man**. And *Adam* said, This *is* now bone of my **bones** [substance, or faith], and **flesh of my flesh**: she shall be called Woman, because she was *taken out of* Man [the other one was taken out of the ground]. Therefore shall a man *leave* his **father** and his **mother**, and shall cleave unto his wife: and they shall be **one flesh**.... And they were both naked [innocent], the man and his wife, and were not **ashamed** [not carnal. It was a good mind].' Who *was* Adam's *father* and *mother*, that he should have to *leave* in order to be joined to *his* wife? Think about it. It'll come to you in a little bit. A clue is, the use of *'bride,'* instead of 'wife.' The part of closing up *the flesh* instead thereof, was the sealing of the word or flesh, which was to prevent dictator-type attitude between the two faculties, thereby making them one in intent without conflict: one word, one flesh. Or you could say, neither male or female. This was the *first* innocent state of mind of the human race. Okay, keep in mind about having to leave *your* Father and Mother and turn to Ephesians chapter 5 and verses 30 through 32: 'For **we are members of *his*** body, of ***his* flesh**, and of his **bones** [this is not physical].... For ***this cause*** shall **a man** leave his Father and Mother, and shall be joined unto **his** wife, and they *two* shall be **one flesh** [mind]....***This is a <u>great</u> mystery:*** but I speak concerning **Christ** [the husband] <u>**and the church**</u> [the bride]. This is the *same thing* we read in Genesis about, 'you must leave *your* Father and Mother and be joined unto your wife.' Our Father and

THE TWO WITNESSES

CHAPTER 9
THE NEXT DAY

Mother, spiritually speaking, are the traditional teachings that have been handed down through the centuries. The ones Jesus said we *should hate*. We'll look into that after we check out the part about the wife. Keep in mind, *in truth*, there's **neither male nor female**, but all are *one* in the the spirit. I want to add a couple more verses to these. Look at Romans seven and verse four: 'Wherefore, my brethren, **ye also are become dead to the law** by the body of Christ; that *ye should be married to another*, **even to him** who *is raised* [lifted up] from **the dead** [the earth], that *we* should bring forth *fruit* unto God [as Able].' Second Corinthians 11 and verse 2: 'For I am jealous over you with godly jealousy: for I have **espoused** you to **one husband**, that I may present you as a chaste *virgin* [not lain with **man**] to Christ.' I had to pass over a few verses to finish a tangent about *His* body, but now we need to go back and cover them, so we can tie up some loose ends.

"First, the part about leaving *your* Father and Mother. Let's look at Luke 14 and verse 26: 'If any <u>**man**</u> come to me, **and hate not <u>his</u>** father, and *mother*, and *wife*, and *children*, and **brethren**, and **sisters**, yea, and *his* own life also, he <u>**cannot**</u> be my disciple.' Without understanding *which* father and mother this is talking about, it could create quite a contradiction with what we're about to read. I want to go back to Ephesians to the part about *the wife*. This is very important to tie in the male and female part. And that's in Ephesians chapter 5, verses 22 through 30: '**Wives, submit** yourselves unto *your own* husbands, **as unto the Lord**. For the husband is **the head** of the *wife*, even as Christ is the head of the church: and he is the saviour of the body [the church].... Therefore as the church is subject unto Christ, so let the wives be to their own husbands in **everything**.... Husbands, love your wives, *even* as Christ also *loved* the church, and *gave himself* for *it*; that he might sanctify and cleanse *it* with the **washing of water** [confusion] *by the word* [of truth], that he might present *it* to *himself* a glorious church [body], not having spot, or wrinkle, or any such *thing*; but that **it** should be holy [spiritual] and without blemish [carnality]. So ought *men* to love their wives as **their own bodies**. <u>He that loveth</u>

175

THE TWO WITNESSES
CHAPTER 9
THE NEXT DAY

his wife loveth himself [one flesh].... For no *man* ever yet hated ***his own flesh;*** but nourisheth and cherisheth it, even as the Lord the church: For we are members of his body, of his *flesh*, and of his *bones* [substance].' As you can see, now, this is not talking about *human* flesh.

"A **man's own flesh is his beliefs.** No one ever professed he liked and cared for someone very much, and hated them at the same time. You cannot serve two masters. To love a human wife **as Jesus loves the church** is also quite a contradiction taken carnally. Why love someone *that* much, and then they die and return to dust? And in the resurrection they neither marry nor are given in marriage. In Christ there is neither male *nor* female. And then the commandment to **hate** your wife for *his* sake. Thus we have loving **the illusion** in vain. But love what is in each other, *the good*.

"What *wife are we to love* as Jesus loved the church, or his own body? **The wife** that *we are* to love *that* much is the *wife of our youth*. When we were baptized with **water**. When we had the *emotions of innocence*. It was when we first vowed our lives to *that Jesus* we **first** loved. It is that feeling of compassion and caring for **all**. Having a **pure love** for everyone on the planet and wanting to *save the world*. Having a *great love* in your heart, that **beautiful virgin**, our **first** love.

Proverbs chapter 5, verses 18 and 19: 'Let thy fountain be blessed: and rejoice with the **wife of thy youth**. Let **her** be as the loving hind and pleasant roe; let her **breasts** [milk of the word] satisfy thee at all times; and be thou ravished always with her **love.'** Some I have met still have the veil on their eyes and take that verse carnally!

"Malachi chapter 2, verses 14 through 16: 'Yet ye say, Wherefore? Because the LORD hath been witness between thee and ***the wife*** of thy **youth**, against whom thou hast dealt treacherously: yet *is she* thy companion, and ***the wife of thy covenant***.   And did not he make **one** [they were one flesh]?... Yet had he the residue of the spirit. And wherefore **one**? That he might seek a **godly** seed [the Lord our God is one]. Therefore take heed to *your spirit*, and let none deal treacherously against **the wife of his youth**.... For the LORD,

THE TWO WITNESSES
CHAPTER 9
THE NEXT DAY

the God of **Israel**, saith that he hateth *putting away* [divorce]: for one covereth violence with his **garment** [words], saith the LORD of hosts: therefore take heed to *your spirit*, that ye deal not treacherously [with the wife you **love as much** as Christ loved the church].'

"There is another reminder in Revelation chapter two and verse four: 'Nevertheless, I have *somewhat* against thee, because thou hast left thy **first love**.' Now there *is* such a thing as having a human wife and a human husband. I don't want you to think that I forgot about that, Deena. I saw the *curiosity* in your eyes as I was reading about the wife," James kidded.

"Oh, I'm fine," Deena replied. "I just had to think about it for a minute. I can see it's a totally different kind of love you're talking about. And I can also understand that if you have that kind of love for everyone, your love for your spouse is going to be richer, knowing that we're all in the same boat, if you will.

"By understanding how the *human* love affair works, you can see how the spiritual love works, but on a different level. Like we're supposed to be married unto Christ, then we might stray away to the arms of a different doctrine, which would represent committing adultery with -- man. Well, as human emotions go, if we didn't know how that felt, we couldn't get an idea how it grieves the spirit when we worship the images instead of the truth, or Christ that is. There *is* something else I wanted to ask you and when you can find the appropriate time to get into it, I would like to know what you think about reincarnation. What set me off on that was the scripture you read earlier about, 'if in **this life only** we have hope in Christ we are most miserable.' You know what I mean, don't you, James?"

"Yes I do. And that was a good example of the love situation. We *have to* experience the things that are *made*, or the human experience, to understand the spiritual things of God. And as far as reincarnation, we'll be getting into that subject shortly. You knew it was coming, didn't you?

"For now, looking at what we've seen about Adam and Eve so far, you should have a pretty good idea it's referring to the male

THE TWO WITNESSES
CHAPTER 9
THE NEXT DAY

and female states of mind and their evolution in the beginning of the human species. And as said before, where does that leave *their* offspring, according to the scriptures? Where does that leave Esau and Jacob? Or any other of the descendants of Adam and Eve, if it's not talking about the human race?

"Since Israel *is* the true church, that is, the son of man, the **body** of Christ, or the Son of God. What are all these *so called people* in the scriptures, **since** Adam? The scriptures *look like* they're talking about humans. But researched *that* way, it is nothing but contradiction upon contradiction, and the truth is not supposed to be divided or of contradiction. Taken spiritually there is not even *a hint* of contradiction, in *any* religion or natural science whatsoever, at least none that I have found. All of the sacred scriptures from all of the ancient cultures are written the same way. Once you understand their culture and terminology literally, *the conversion* is the same. All of them are written by the natural, universal and spiritual laws.

"The answers to *all things* are here and have been here *all along*. But there again, it wasn't time. Not until the ***information age***, where, '**that without contradiction**,' the truth, could be proven beyond a shadow of a doubt. This is mentioned in Daniel 9 and 24: 'Seventy weeks are determined upon thy people and upon thy *holy* city, to finish the transgression, and to make an **end of sins** [teaching the lie], and to make *reconciliation for iniquity*, and to **bring in everlasting righteousness**, and to **seal** up the **vision** and prophecy, and to anoint the most Holy.'

Daniel 12, verse 4: 'But thou, O Daniel, **shut up the words** [by using similitudes] and seal the book, ***even to the time of the end***: many shall run to and fro [looking], and ***knowledge shall be increased***.' This rings true when we bring into account the fact that the fall was *from* **knowledge**, as it says, 'my people are destroyed for the **lack of knowledge**,' or God. 'The god of many shall wax cold.'

"There is a movement in the land *now* for knowledge. People are being drawn to study or learn *something*. Some are not sure what they want to get into. They have a feeling to go to *some kind* of trade school, college, or home course. This is the time! Now,

THE TWO WITNESSES

CHAPTER 9
THE NEXT DAY

people are being drawn to look and seek, but without guidance, they don't understand the source of their motivation. However, the time *is* ripe. Those that are searching *will find* whatever they are *yearning* for.

"Deena, in answer to your question about reincarnation, it will probably be about another hour before things lead us into the explanation of how that fits in. Keep in mind until then, 'Deena' was not, and never was created *until this lifetime*. This is *your* soul, but *your spirit* knows all things, even from the beginning.

There are some more things we need to wrap up for now, and I believe it was in Romans where I was going to finish the part about Israel. Then there are a couple more tangents that need to be tied in, then we'll get into how theoretical physics is a most significant counterpart to everything we have talked about thus far.

Also keep in mind the part about God driving *the man* out of the garden, 'to earn his *bread* [knowledge] by the sweat of his *face*.' It never mentioned driving the *woman* out, just the **man**. You know why now. I'll tell you what, that was one of the tangents I wanted to finish anyway. Let's go ahead and finish that one, then we'll go to Romans and Israel *next*.

"Turn back to Genesis chapter 2 and we'll start with verse 19: 'In the sweat of thy face [which represents the personality of our soul] shalt thou eat *bread*, **till thou return** unto the **ground**; for out of *it* wast thou [the mind] taken: for dust thou art, and unto dust shalt thou return [he's talking about the carnal mind].... And Adam called his wife's name Eve; **because** she was the mother of **all living**. Unto Adam also and to his wife did the LORD God make coats of *skins* [opinions], and clothed *them*. And the LORD God said, Behold, the **man** [what about the woman?] is become as **one of us** [plural], **to know good and evil**: and now, lest **he** put forth his **hand**, and take also of the **tree of life**, and *eat*, and live for ever.... Therefore the LORD God sent **him** [male *and* female] forth from the garden of Eden, to till the ground from whence **he** was taken. So he drove out **the man**; and he placed at the east of the garden of Eden Cherubim's, and a **flaming sword** which turned every way, to keep the way of the tree of life.' These cherubims and flaming sword are

THE TWO WITNESSES
CHAPTER 9
THE NEXT DAY

the swaddling clothes or allegories, parables and metaphors *wrapped around* the hidden truth.

The whole point here is, *the man* has become *like* God. He was created 'good.' Now he's like God, he *knows evil*, but they disobeyed and lost the understanding, the Christ. And since they were deceived, the Christ was hidden because of the guilt, until they should deserve it. There's a book I've just finished and it explains the power of the mind. Tony, if you'll reach behind you and hand me that blue paperback book, the one we were looking at a couple weeks ago, I'll read a paragraph to Deena and Bob.

"That's it. Bob if you'll write this information down, I think you'd enjoy adding this to your and Deena's studies. The name of it is *Molecules of the Mind: The Brave New Science of Molecular Psychology*. It says here it's based on the six-part Pulitzer-prize winning series of articles by Jon Franklin and published by Laurel Trade Paperback, Dell Publishing Co., Inc. Here we go. It's on page four of the introduction. Actually, there are *two* paragraph's, the fourth and fifth one. It goes like this: 'This new science's **equivalent** of the atomic bomb has *not yet* exploded, *but the moment rapidly approaches*. And as it does insiders have *begun to recognize* the implications of what is **about to happen** -- and to **tremble at the prospect**.

A thousand years hence, when our descendants look back on *this* time, it will not be the name of Albert Einstein that comes to their lips. For while the forces contained within the nucleus of the atom are *truly powerful*, and though the hydrogen fires may burn hot and bright, **they pale when compared to the energy contained within the human mind**.' Now you can get an idea why the truth of how things work had to be hidden in paradoxes and allegory until the information age. We must know what we are dealing with before we destroy everything. But those days shall be shortened, for the elect's sake.

"As we've seen in several places of scripture, to look at the 'things that are *made* to understand the things that aren't.' Scientists and very few others, have been pursuing this for some time now. What I mean by that is, they have taken nature, the things that are

THE TWO WITNESSES
CHAPTER 9
THE NEXT DAY

made, the ground, and have tried to explore and explain their function as far back as we can recall. On the other hand as far as I can find out, the mass majority of the religious community has not tried to break down the *images*, the things that are made, to see what *their* hidden meanings are. The challenge *to do* this is being brought forth by people like myself, and you, once you have learned to convert them. This is what is meant by we must earn *our bread*, or *lost knowledge*, by going to *the ground*, the *earth*, the *image*. For this is what the mind has recorded and named. In other words, instead of the mind absorbing that which is natural, which is its birthright, it has to work for it. *Man* could not be trusted with this kind of power, he has to earn it. Now is the *judgment* of *his* learning.

"The other thing I wanted to mention was the part where Adam 'called his wife's name Eve, *because* she was the mother of all *living*.' I found a book that explains it as well. I've found it very helpful in cross-referencing some things I was curious about. It's called the *Dictionary Of All Scriptures And Myths* by G.A. Gaskell, published by Avenal, 1981 edition, distributed by Crown Publishers, Inc. It defines Eve as '**A symbol of the emotion-nature united to the mental-nature of the lower mind**.

The mind recognizes the life principle within the soul to be the *emotion*-nature, for it is the originator or former of all qualities that subsist, that is, of all qualities that have in them the germ of the higher life.

Eve is the right magical child, for she is the matrix in which the Love-desire stood in *Adam*. She was Adam's paradisical Rose-garden in peculiar love wherein he **loved himself**.' (J. Boehme, *Mysterium Magnum*, p. 83.) That reminds me where the Bible says, 'no *man* yet hated his own flesh,' I felt this explanation would fit right in with *our* studies.

Another helpful book is the *Metaphysical Bible Dictionary* published by the Unity Church. I have found it very close in its metaphysical interpretations of names and places in scripture. There are several more books that will come up in our studies about theoretical physics that I would like for you to get. I'll give you their names as we come to them."

THE TWO WITNESSES
CHAPTER 9
THE NEXT DAY

"Excuse me, James," Tony asked. "Where's that book you got in a couple of weeks ago? I think it was just before I met Bob. You know, the one we laughed about. But in a good way. It was published by you-know-who."

"Oh, that one," James laughed. "It's still funny, and one of the most beautiful paradoxes going. What Tony's referring to is *The Bible Handbook.*"

"What's so funny about that, James?" Bob couldn't help but ask.

James and Tony both burst into laughter at Bob's genuine curiosity. James still trying to compose himself attempted to answer Bob.

"Tony! I'll get you for this. Let's see.. how to explain to Bob? Here you go, Bob. You and Deena browse through it a minute or two and tell me what you think."

At that, James handed Bob the book and he and Deena thumbed through it. Handing it back to James and in a scratch-your-head manner, Bob said, "I still don't understand. It's full of scripture. And it has a picture of the Bible on the front. Wait a minute! Let me see it again. There's a devil's tail hanging out of the pages of the Bible like a book mark. Is that what's so funny?"

James and Tony were still laughing under their breath. James took the book and opened it to where it showed the publisher information, handed it back to Bob and told him to read who the publisher was.

"Well I'll be darned!" Bob remarked as he showed Deena. "It's published by the *American Atheist Press*. I *still* don't get what's so funny."

"Okay," James said. "Are you familiar with Dr. Madalyn O'Hair? She's referred to as the first Lady of Atheism."

"Oh yeah!" Bob and Deena both nodded. "Who hasn't heard of her, and her sons too? I really have to hand it to her. She has a lotta guts to go up against the religious system the way she does. What's *this* book about? Why is *she* using *scripture* to publish a book?"

"Well, you remember when we read, '**without**

THE TWO WITNESSES
CHAPTER 9
THE NEXT DAY

controversy, great is the *mystery* of godliness'? What they have done in this book is compile just *about all* of the controversy, or contradictions for us. And they have done a great work. This book is extremely helpful in breaking down the conflict. This is what the spiritual-minded student can use for their research without spending hours upon hours of trying to locate the contradictions throughout the Bible. And yes, Tony, this *is* one I was going to recommend also.

    I guess you could say, in a way, that Dr. O' Hair is a disciple of John the Baptist and doesn't know it. She sees *the danger* of teaching the scriptures literally, and knows quite well the wars and turmoil they have caused when taught the wrong way. She, like John, doesn't have the answers, but knows there has to be something better than the teachings of prejudice, scorn, and condemnation. She has seen the 'anti-Christ' at work personally, which has created in her a hatred for those who teach the lie. But I think she'll be one of the first to see what the scriptures really mean when applied to the physics aspect of the natural sciences. And how they fit hand-in-glove *without* a contradiction.

    "Anyway, for me, her contribution is deeply appreciated. And to answer your question, Bob, the funny thing about this book is that it was created to destroy or eliminate the teachings of the scriptures, but ends up supporting their true message. It's just a beautiful, beautiful paradox, and joyfully pleasurable. It's the paradox that makes it laughable."

    "I get! I get it!" Bob leaped. "It is beautiful. That's just great, absolutely wonderful. There is just no way to tear down *the truth* is there?"

    "No wonder you two were laughing like that," Deena remarked, almost with tears in her eyes. "I agree, that is a beautiful paradox. Who would have believed it? Boy, will she be surprised when she sees what you've said about that book. I can see now that she really does have a good heart, and cares for people more than the general public could ever comprehend."

    "You're right, Deena," James answered. "She made a stand for what she believes in without trying to get rich off of it. Much

THE TWO WITNESSES
CHAPTER 9
THE NEXT DAY

more than I can say for those who are doing it for profit only. And some of them *will tell you* that. After all there's billions of tax free dollars floating around. They could care less if there is a God or not. That's not their concern. All they know is that good-hearted people will swallow anything you throw at them if you present it with enough emotion and invoke enough fear. You could even take over a country without firing a shot if you knew how to get in on their religious grandstand. Whoops, getting ahead of myself. Okay, let's get back to Romans, and Israel.

"Let's see...we were looking at Israel, the son of God, the *first* born, the letter, the body, the flesh. Turn to Romans chapter 11. We'll start with verse one and probably go through the complete chapter. Okay, verse one: "I say then, **Hath God cast away his people**? God forbid. For I *also* am an Israelite, of the seed of Abraham, of the tribe of Benjamin [son of the *right* hand].... God hath not cast away his people which he foreknew. Wot ye not what the scripture saith of Elias? how he maketh intercession to God *against* Israel, saying, Lord, they have killed thy prophets [by teaching scripture carnally], and digged down thine altars; and I am left alone, and they seek my life.... But what saith the answer of God unto him? I have reserved to myself *seven* thousand men [hidden meanings], who have not bowed the knee to the **image** of Baal. Even so then at this present time also there is a remnant according to the election of grace. And if by grace, then is it no more of works: otherwise grace is no more grace. But if it be of works, then is it no more grace: otherwise work is no more work [grace spurs you on to seek until you find].... What then? Israel hath not obtained that which **he** seeketh for; but **the election hath obtained it**, and the rest were blinded (according as it is *written*, God hath given them the spirit of slumber, eyes that they *should not see*, and ears that they should not hear;) unto this day [*even unto this* day they cannot hear it spiritually].... And David saith, Let their **table** be made a snare, and a trap, and a **stumblingblock**, and a recompence unto them: Let their *eyes* be darkened, that they may not see, and bow down their back alway. I say then, Have they *stumbled* that they should fall? God forbid: but rather through *their fall* salvation is come unto the Gentiles, for to

THE TWO WITNESSES
CHAPTER 9
THE NEXT DAY

provoke them to jealousy.... Now if the fall of them [the carnal] be the riches of the world, and the diminishing of them the riches of the Gentiles; how much more *their* fullness? [when they behold the truth] For I speak to you Gentiles, inasmuch as I am the apostle of the Gentiles, I magnify mine office.... If by any means I may provoke to emulation them which are **my flesh** [think like I do], and might save some of them. For if the casting away of them be the reconciling of the world, what shall the receiving of them be, but **life from the dead** [and all Israel shall be saved]? For if the firstfruit be holy [the necessary food], the lump is also holy: and if the root be holy, so are the branches.... And if some of the branches be broken off, and thou, being a wild olive [truth] tree, wert graffed in among them, and with them partakest of the root and fatness [anointing] of the olive tree; Boast not against the branches. But if thou boast, thou bearest not the root, but the root thee.... Thou wilt say then, The branches were broken off, that I might be graffed in. Well; *because of unbelief they were broken off,* and thou standest by faith. Be not highminded, but fear: For if God spared not the natural branches [His son Israel], take heed lest he also spare not thee [Romans 8 and 32: 'He that **spared not his own Son**, but delivered him up for us all, how shall he not with him also freely give us all things?'].... Behold therefore the goodness and severity of God: on them which fell, severity; but toward thee, goodness, **if thou continue** in his goodness [or 'be careful how *ye* stand, lest ye fall']: otherwise thou also shalt be cut off. And they also, if they abide not still in unbelief, shall be graffed in: for God is able to graff them in **again**.... For if thou wert cut out of the olive tree [scripture] which is wild by nature, and wert graffed contrary to nature into a good olive tree: how much more shall these [the pure in heart], which be the natural branches, be graffed into their own olive tree [with understanding]? For I would not, brethren, that ye should be ignorant of *this mystery*, lest ye should be wise in your own conceits; that blindness in part is happened to Israel [the son of man], until the fullness of the Gentiles be come in.... And so **all Israel shall be saved**: as it is written, There shall come out of Sion the Deliverer, and shall turn away ungodliness [carnality] from *Jacob*: For this is my covenant unto

THE TWO WITNESSES
CHAPTER 9
THE NEXT DAY

them, when I shall take away their sins [images]. **As concerning** *the gospel*, **they are enemies for your sakes** [because they teach it carnally]: but as touching the election, they are beloved for the fathers' sakes ['Father forgive *them* for they know not what they do...'].... For the gifts and calling of God are without repentance. For as ye in times past have not believed God, yet have now obtained mercy through *their* unbelief [which caused **us** to search further].... Even so have these also now not believed, that through *your* [the spiritual] mercy they also may obtain mercy [by God's vengeance].... For [the scriptures] **hath concluded them all in unbelief**, that he might have mercy upon all. O the depth of the riches both of the wisdom and knowledge of God! how unsearchable are his judgments, and his ways past finding out [to the unenlightened]!.... For who hath known the mind of the Lord? or who hath been his counsellor? Or who hath first given to him, and it shall be recompensed unto him again? For of him, and through him, and to him, are *all things*: to whom be glory for ever. Amen.'

"If you remember, Israelites are those in the global religious community that are truly searching for answers without contradictions. They are not the wolves in sheep's clothing. They are the ones getting to the root and will not follow a doctrine that does not satisfy their hunger and thirst for righteousness. As it says, 'They are not all in the system either.' Some have strayed into many different pastures or teachings. '..For they are not all **Israel**, which are of **Israel**.'

Let's look at chapter ten just a moment. Verse one through eight: '**Brethren**, my heart's desire and prayer to God for Israel is, that they might be saved. For I bear them record that **they have a zeal of God, but not according to knowledge**. For they being ignorant of God's righteousness [Christ], and going about to establish their own righteousness [understanding], have not submitted themselves unto the righteousness of [the Word].... For Christ *is* the **end of the law** for righteousness to every one that believeth.... For Moses describeth the righteousness which is of **the law**, That the **man** which doeth **those things** shall live by them [trying to follow the letter].... But the righteousness which is of faith

THE TWO WITNESSES

**CHAPTER 9
THE NEXT DAY**

speaketh on this wise, Say not in thine heart, Who shall ascend into heaven? (that is, to bring Christ *down from above*:).... Or, Who shall descend into the deep? (that is, to bring up Christ **again from the dead**.) But what saith it? **The word is nigh thee, even in thy mouth, and in thy heart: that is, <u>the word of faith, which we preach</u>**;' It's been here all along. It, the truth, is hidden **in** you *and* **hidden** *in* the word. You must find **it**. 'The kingdom of God is **within you**.' *Healing* is always from **the inside out**. Not the opposite.

I have to bring in these next few verses to cap off what we've been talking about. Keep in mind what we read in Psalms, where Jesus, or the truth was made in secret. Let's go to Isaiah chapter 49, verses 1 through 4: 'Listen, O isles [religions of the world], unto me; and hearken, **ye people, from far** [that can't see spiritually]; The LORD hath called **me from the womb**; from the bowels of my mother hath he made mention of my name. And he hath made **my mouth like a sharp sword**; **in the shadow of his hand** [word] **hath he <u>hid me</u>**, and made *me* a polished shaft; in his quiver hath he **<u>hid me</u>**; And said unto **<u>me, Thou art my servant,</u> O Israel**, *in whom* I will be glorified.' How plain can it be, after knowing what *we've* seen? This mind, *Adam*, Israel the Son of God, this *truth hidden* in the **word**, and those that find it and bring it forth are many members in particular, the Son of God. Let's add verses five and six: 'And now, saith the LORD that formed **me** from the womb *to be his servant*, to bring Jacob **again** to **him**, Though Israel be not gathered [in process now], yet shall **I** be glorious in the eyes of the LORD, and my God shall be my strength.... And he said, It is a light thing that thou shouldest be my servant to **raise up** the tribes of Jacob [sons of God], and to restore the preserved of Israel: I will also **give thee for a light to the Gentiles**, that thou mayest be my salvation unto the end of the **earth**.' To the end of the earth simply means until the end of *the law*. And only truth can do that. These scriptures are definitely presenting the fact that *this* Israel **is** Jesus **in the Word**, His flesh.

Isaiah chapter 42, verses 1 through 8: '**Behold my servant, whom I uphold; mine elect**, in whom my soul delighteth; I have

THE TWO WITNESSES
CHAPTER 9
THE NEXT DAY

put my spirit upon **him**: **he shall bring forth judgment to the Gentiles**. He shall not cry, nor lift up, nor cause his voice to be heard in the street [streets of religion]. A bruised reed shall he not break, and the *smoking flax* [the wick - the power of the word that supports the fire or flame] shall he not **quench: he shall bring forth judgment unto truth**. He shall not fail nor be discouraged, **till he have set judgment in the earth**: and the *isles* [branches] shall wait for **his law**.' The isles, you could say, are the whole creature that's waiting.., well, we have a minute, let's read it. Turn to Romans 8 and 22, *and then*, Romans 8 and 19: 'For **we** know that the whole creation groaneth and travaileth in pain together until now.... For the earnest expectation of the creature **waiteth** for the manifestation of the sons of God [or Jesus].' Back to verse 5, Isaiah 42: 'Thus saith God the LORD, he that created the heavens, and **stretched** them out; he that **spread** forth the *earth*, and that which cometh out of **it** [truth, in continuance is He fashioned]; he that giveth breath unto the people upon it [the law], and spirit to them that walk there **in** [the spirit].... I the LORD have called thee in righteousness, and will *hold thine* **hand**, and will keep thee, **and give thee for a covenant of the people, for a light of the Gentiles; To open the blind eyes, to bring out the prisoners from the prison, and them that sit in darkness out of the prison house**. Six: 'I am the LORD: that is my name: **and my glory will I not give to another** [remember this], neither my praise to **graven images** [or the worshipers of *them*].' One more in Genesis about the prophecy of the messiah. It's in chapter 49, verse 24: 'But his bow abode in strength, and the **arms of his hands** were made strong **by the hands of the mighty** God of **Jacob**; **(from thence** [Adam, Jacob, Israel, Jesus] **is the shepherd, the stone of Israel**:)'

"Well, now we can see that Christ has been in the scriptures all along as the 'stone of Israel' standing at the door knocking trying to communicate with the observer, or, the reader that is, let me show you something you're going to love. Turn to Acts chapter 13, verses 46 and 47: 'Then Paul and Barnabas waxed bold, and said, It was necessary that the word of God should first have been spoken to you: but seeing ye put it from you, and judge yourselves unworthy

THE TWO WITNESSES
CHAPTER 9
THE NEXT DAY

of everlasting life [truth], lo, **we** turn to the Gentiles.... For so hath the Lord commanded **us**, saying, I have set **thee** to be a light of the Gentiles, that **thou** shouldest be for salvation unto the *ends* of **the earth [carnal doctrines]**.'

And, Acts 26, verses 14 through 18: 'And when we were all fallen to the **earth**, I heard a voice speaking unto me, and saying in the Hebrew tongue, Saul, Saul, why persecutest thou me? it is hard for thee to kick against the pricks. And I said, Who art thou, Lord? And he said, I am Jesus whom thou persecutest.... But rise, and stand upon **thy feet** [meaning faith]: for I have **appeared** unto thee for this purpose, to make *thee a minister* and a witness both of these things which thou hast seen, and of those things in the which I will **appear** unto thee; Delivering thee *from* the people, and from the **Gentiles, unto whom now I send thee**.... **To open their eyes, and to turn them from darkness to light**, and from the power of Satan [the image] unto God, that they may receive forgiveness of **sins**, and inheritance among them which are **sanctified** by faith that is *in* me.' Now scan on down to verse 23: 'That Christ should suffer, **and that He should be the first** that should rise from the dead, **and should shew light unto the Gentiles**.'

"What happed to Paul? I thought he was supposed to give light unto the Gentiles? And to top this off let's turn to Luke 2, verses 30 through 32, where the child Jesus was brought to Simeon and *he* said, 'For mine eyes have seen thy salvation.... Which *thou* hast prepared before the face of all people.... **A light to lighten the Gentiles, and the glory of thy people Israel**.' I'm going to let you find the answers to why Paul and Jesus are the same **one** to give light to the Gentiles. One clue: Death **and** salvation was **according to Paul's gospel**, and God had just said He would not give His glory to another."

"Bummer!" Bob moaned. "I want *you* to do all the work for me. No, I'm kidding. I know it will be great when *that's* revealed. I have a pretty good idea what's happening. But I *will* search until it all comes together for me, you can bet on that."

"Yeah, me too," said Deena. "I guess if it said the Lord our God is one, then I guess you could say that the word our Word is

THE TWO WITNESSES
CHAPTER 9
THE NEXT DAY

one. In other words, all scripture is of the same author, no matter what names they go under. Does that make sense, James?"

"Very much so. Each name of these authors has a special meaning and you're very close to seeing the message behind all the stories. Okay, I think we'll break for questions and wrap it up for this evening. We'll continue tomorrow. You still have tomorrow off don't you, Bob?"

"You bet. I'll be here. I think Deena has to work, though."

"Well, not really. We're fairly well caught up on things at the office, I could take off without any problem. As a matter of fact, I think I will. I don't want to miss the end of what we've studied the last couple of days."

"Say, Deena," Tony suggested, "did you want James to explain the dreams you and Bob were talking about earlier this morning?"

"Oh yes, thanks, Tony. That is if you don't mind James?"

"Of course not, if I can. Run through them for me."

After explaining the dreams James endeavored to interpret them for her.

"Okay. The first thing you remember is walking in a *field*. Now we know the word 'field' represents where the *seed* is sown: in the womb of the mind. Next you had a feeling of wanting to fly around the *top* of the trees you saw in *this field*. We've already covered the area of trees meaning knowledge. Then you were halfway running, not walking anymore. And by using the *strength* of your *folded arms* you started to *lift up* off the *earth*. And by the way you described the dream there was no fear of flight. Well, by evaluating how you're doing in your desire for knowledge, with no fear of height, I feel the dreams were a witness to what you've been experiencing mentally and spiritually.

In other words, with regards to your spiritual self, you've left your old way of thinking for a higher one, by using your mental strength to manipulate your thoughts against their carnal nature.

And the second part of your dream seems to verify that. You said you were in an eighteenth century white house. And *white* houses, in dreams, are usually wood houses. There again, *wood*

CHAPTER 9
THE NEXT DAY

THE TWO WITNESSES

means, knowledge. And in this, apparently, **two-story** house, an *old man* was dying *below* you, and you felt no one else there thought it was any big deal. As you probably suspect, this two story house is a place in your mind. Your knowledge-house pertains to the newly acquired knowledge you are developing with your studies. The *white* wood house represents the good word, the good knowledge. This old man dying is the traditional way you had of looking at the former knowledge you'd acquired in life about religious matters. These kind of dreams are usually present when you've made a connection with your spiritual or higher self."

"Wow, that made perfect sense," said Deena, "I had chills as you were interpreting them. I mean, I just can't tell you how all of this is affecting me. It's sort of like I've felt this way inside before, and it's like an old friend came home. Do you know what I mean?"

"We sure do, Deena," James replied. "That's the witness inside us that seems to let us know we're on the right track. Sort of like a comforter, if you know what I mean?"

"That hit home for me too, James," Bob added. "My dreams were similar enough to translate them while you were doing Deena's. And I too feel like her. Looking at the scriptures spiritually has been a most enlightening experience. You know, James, it *is* like a puzzle. It keeps you *wanting* to put all of the pieces together. Much more when you see the picture coming into focus. And of course I guess you'd have to like puzzles."

"Yes it is," James agreed. "Especially when you have the <u>box top</u>. *That*, has been the difficulty for thousands of years. The box top's been missing and everyone's been arguing over what piece of the puzzle goes where. But now, there should be a little more tolerance because everybody who has *a* piece can figure out where it goes, *without* disagreement. If I write another book, I think I'll call it 'The Box Top.'

"Okay, then, I guess I'll see your smiling faces in the morning. I'm really glad you've had the opportunity this weekend to come over. It's so refreshing to find people sincere enough to take time to find out what's going on in our universe. Outside of scientists, that is. And there are others *like us*."

THE TWO WITNESSES

CHAPTER 9
THE NEXT DAY

"Where's Martie? Tell her we said goodnight and we'll see her tomorrow. I'm taking Deena home so we can get on with our dreaming," Bob chuckled.

"Sounds good to me, honey, I'm ready. Goodnight, James, I thoroughly enjoyed it, as usual, and we'll see you in the morning. Goodnight to you too, Tony, you're a great guy -- for an *ox*, that is," Deena kidded.

THE TWO WITNESSES

Chapter 10
The Levels

    The next morning they both started to move around about the same time. *Realizing* they were waking they turned to each other and *at the same time* smiled. *And* at the *same time* asked each other if they had a dreamt or not.
    "No...," Deena said in a half - whisper.
    "Shucks, me either. Oh well. Maybe we wanted to dream, and that desire prevented it. I don't know. But I do think it'll happen again. Don't you?" Bob asked.
    "Yeah! I definitely feel I'll dream again. Don't know when, but I just *feel* it. No big deal though, you know? I've really got a good feeling about a lot of things lately. I'm glad we met Tony and James, they really do a good job of making you think. I like that, it's something I'd *almost* forgotten. So much going on in life, it seems nobody has time to reflect on things of this nature anymore. People *in general* I mean.
    Another thing. I understood the way he interpreted my dreams. True or not, they *fit the pattern* spiritually. Didn't it seem like it to you?"
    "Not *really,* Deena. Just kidding, honey! You bet! I saw the significance right away. And as far as I'm concerned, it was on the money. Say, flip you for the shower first. Unless you just want to be first?"
    "No, let's flip. That sounds like fun. Where's a coin? You know you don't have a chance, Bob. Do you want to give up now?"
    "No, thank *you*. Here's a quarter, *I'll* flip it. Which do you want, heads or tails? Okay, tails you say...Ha ha, you lose."
    "Wait a minute! Let me see that! Bob! You tried to cheat me!"
    They both laughed and Deena was off to the shower. After breakfast, as they discussed some of the things James had talked about, the subject of *eating flesh* came up. And Deena said, "I wonder what it means when you're not supposed to eat pigs? Surely *that* has to be spiritual or something. Why don't we look it up?"
    "Sounds like a good idea," Bob said. "But I don't think the

THE TWO WITNESSES

Chapter 10
The Levels

word 'pig' is what we're after. Let's look up *swine's* flesh. I think that's what the scripture calls it."

After running references on *it* they came up with no conclusive interpretation, and decided to wait and ask James about it. It was almost time to leave anyway. And, *at that time* the phone rang. It was Tony letting them know he couldn't take off work *but* he would talk to them later. So off to James's. After arriving and getting past general conversation, Deena told James what she and Bob were trying to find out about *swine's flesh*. James said, "Well, as you probably found, there's not much to go on in the text alone. What you do in a case such as this is to convert the physical aspect of it by looking at what the nutritionists have to say about it and how it affects the human digestive system. Some people should not eat it at all. There are many health reasons for this, the high salt content being one of them.

By using this reality as a parable, we can see that it's harmful to swallow something that's hard to believe. There are many people who interpret these things literally, *or carnally*, who will not eat pork to *this day* because of the reference to it in the scripture. And because of certain passages in Mark and James, some people will risk their lives to prove their devoutness to their righteousness by literally swallowing poison and handling poisonous snakes or serpents as they would call them. I believe that's in Mark chapter 16 and verse 18, if you want to look it up."

"Sure, let's do it," Deena said.

"Alright. Turn to it and let's read, 'They shall take up *serpents*; and if they drink any **deadly thing**, it shall not hurt them; they shall lay **hands** on the sick and they shall recover.' Now James three and verse 8: 'But the tongue can **no man** tame; **It** is an unruly evil, full of **deadly** poison.' First we should look at the inference where God gives unto us the intent and desires of our hearts. Psalms 81 and verse 12: 'So I gave them up unto their own hearts' lust: and they walked in **their own counsels** [doctrine].' And Psalm 78 and 29: 'So they did eat, and were filled [mentally]: for he gave them **their own desire**.' This *deadly drink* is the words

Chapter 10
The Levels

THE TWO WITNESSES

of **men's** mouths and it comes from the *tongue*. The Hebrew word for tongue is *Lashon*. And it simply means *language*. Unknown *tongue*, unknown *language*. And like a serpent, the scripture is written with a split *tongue*, or **two** *languages*.

"Thus we have the *two edged-sword*, or word. And if we break down the word **edge**, it means **mouth**. Thus we have the **'two-mouthed word,'** the **left hand**, and the **right hand**, since *hand* means ministry or gospel. Now, if the intent and desire of our heart in searching for God or truth is pure, *in* righteousness, then we will find the spiritual understanding for interpreting the words.

"If there's a spot or wrinkle in our desire, then we'll receive the poison of the serpent. You wouldn't think *swine's flesh* got us off on all this would you? Anyway, if the intent and desire is pure it will not want to eat the letter, or the image. It will be very hard to digest. And if one forces himself to eat or *drink* this *deadly language*, then he gets sick, or grieved and confused. Which is *greatly disheartening* to one truly searching.

"If in your studies a serpent bit you on **the right hand**, you could shake it off in the fire, as it were, knowing *the fire* is the carnal interpretation, then *the image* that bit you by way of the story would not affect you in any way, thereby not killing you, because you are full of the antidote, Christ'. So if you did drink anything deadly you would not die, spiritually of course. I wouldn't suggest handling real snakes *or* drinking strychnine, because you're dealing with chance.

By following the pattern of the body we can see how the mind accepts and rejects things. In other words, if you hunger for answers, the intent and desire behind this hunger will bring *to you* answers that feed *that* intent and desire. Let's say for example you were hungry for a hot dog. You have millions of dollars in the bank and can buy any kind of food in the world you wanted, but your taste buds wanted a *hot dog* and you *would not be satisfied* until you had one, no matter *what you ate*. The *analogy* here is; the millions of dollars represent your ability to *choose*. You are free to *choose anything* your mind hungers for. Your taste buds *in this*

THE TWO WITNESSES

Chapter 10
The Levels

case would represent your intent and desire. If your intent and desire are to *know the truth with all your heart mind and soul*, and you are diligent in your search, your taste buds will not be satisfied, until they have acquired truth. If you were to pick up a book and read it, and there was some deadly poison in it and you read or drank it accidentally, don't worry -- you wouldn't swallow it. This is why it's so important to know the intent and desire of our search. What are our motives, why and what do we want to know? As long as they're pure there is nothing to fear. There again, 'man know thyself.'

That leads us to one of the tangents I wanted to finish. And *that* was about the pure *in* mind consciousness. Some of this I know we've touched upon several times, but now I want to bring it together. We'll start with Hebrews chapter six, verses one through six: '**Therefore leaving the principles of the doctrine of Christ, let us go on unto perfection**, not laying again the foundation of repentance from **dead** works [carnal interpretation], and of faith toward God, **Of the doctrine of baptisms**, and of laying on of **hands**, and of resurrection of **the dead**, and of eternal judgment. And this will we do, if God permit. For **it is impossible** for those who were **once enlightened**, and have **tasted** [eaten], of the heavenly gift [spiritual understanding], and were made partakers of the Holy Ghost, And have *tasted* **the good word of God**, and the powers of **the world** to come, If they shall fall away, to renew them **again** unto repentance [or take the scriptures carnally]; seeing they **crucify** to **themselves** the Son of God **afresh**, and put [Truth] to an **open** [confusion]'. I think we discussed the word *afresh*, how it means the same as before. Romans 12 and verse 2: 'And be not conformed to this [carnal-mind] **world**: but be ye transformed [born again] by the **renewing of your mind** that ye may **prove** what is that *good*, and acceptable, and **perfect**, will of [the Word].' Second Timothy chapter 3, verse 17: 'That the *man* of [knowledge] **may be perfect**, throughly furnished unto all *good* works.' Ephesians 4 and verse 13: 'Till **we all** come in the **unity** of the faith, and of the knowledge

THE TWO WITNESSES

Chapter 10
The Levels

of the [Truth], unto a **perfect** [mind], unto the measure of the stature of the fullness of [understanding]' First Peter five and verse ten: 'But the God of all grace, who hath called **us** unto his eternal glory by *Christ Jesus*, after that ye have **suffered** a while [in the **flesh**], **make** you **perfect**, stablish, strengthen, settle you.'

Who makes *us perfect?* It just said, **Christ Jesus** - the **living Word!** And where is he? **Hidden <u>in you</u> and the <u>Word</u>**, that *you may do **it**.* James chapter one verse four; 'But let patience have her *perfect work*, that **ye may be perfect** and entire, <u>**wanting nothing**</u>.' When can this happen? Any time <u>**you're**</u> ready! Colossians chapter 1, verse 28: '<u>Whom</u> we preach, **warning** every **man**, and teaching every man in all wisdom; that we may present **every man <u>perfect</u> in <u>Christ Jesus</u>** [by my gospel]:' Matthew chapter 5 verse 48: **'Be ye therefore perfect, even as your Father which is in heaven is perfect.'** Luke 6 and verse 40: 'The disciple is not above his master: but every one that **is perfect** shall be **<u>as</u>** his master.' Phillipians 3 and verse 15: 'Let us therefore, **<u>as many as be perfect</u>**, be thus minded: and if in anything ye be other wise minded, [the Word shall *reveal* even this unto you.'

There are too many scriptures in the Bible that confirm we are *without excuse* for not having the mind of [understanding]. It would take hours going through and breaking them down. But *you* can run reference in your studies later.

"We've been taught through the ages that we *can't* be perfect, that we can only strive for perfection, which is a *direct contradiction* of what we have *just read*, and that was not the *half* of it. The negative teaching, 'you **can't be perfect**,' was written for **man**, the *unenlightened*. This **man** has never seen God, nor *can he ever*. As long as *this* man was understood to mean the *human* race, there was, for the most part, *no hope*. This attitude was handed down from generation to generation. Each generation **looking to the future** for a savior, *when he has been <u>here</u> all along*. 'He came among his own [those searching, *supposedly*], but his own received him not.' The scriptures read, **'My people** are destroyed for the

THE TWO WITNESSES

Chapter 10
The Levels

lack of knowledge.' 'My people have gone away **backwards.**' **They** have asked amiss, because of the image. They have gone from the spiritual to the carnal. There are numerous references to that effect. John 5, verses 39 and 40: '**Search the scriptures**; for *in them* ye think [the imagination thing again] **ye** have eternal life: <u>**and they are they which testify of me**</u>. [those that profess to serve God] And ye will not come to me, [the *spirit of the Word*] that **ye might have <u>life</u>**.' There again, we are without excuse. To be perfect, is to worship His Word in *spirit* and *truth*. There is nothing hard or *mysterious* about it.

"Remember, it is the **intent and desire** that is judged, and a just man will fall *seven* times, one for each level of allegory. As for everyday living in the *human* experience, there are going to be many trials and tribulations trying to balance the contradiction, or cross, of one's perfection. Just as ascribed to Jesus in Hebrew's chapter five, verses eight and nine: '**Though he were a Son** [*the* church], *yet* **learned he obedience** by the things which he suffered; **And** [after three days] **being <u>made</u> perfect**, he **became** the author of eternal salvation unto all them that **obey him**.' He has to *become* perfect.

"Second Thessalonians chapter one verses four and five; 'So that we ourselves glory in you in the <u>churches</u> of God for your patience and faith in all your persecutions and tribulations **that ye endure: Which is a manifest token of the righteous judgment of God** [in scripture], **that ye may be counted worthy of the kingdom of God, for which ye <u>also</u> suffer**:' The *letter* is to the righteous, a chastisement, a school master to bring us **unto perfection**, or the mind of Christ. But not studied lawfully, it will destroy us. As it says in second Timothy chapter two verse five, 'And if a *man* also strive for masteries, *yet* is he not crowned, except he **strive lawfully**.' And Romans 7, verse 14: '**For <u>we know</u> that the law is spiritual**; but I am carnal, sold under sin.' And to take it *carnally* would be to embrace all the curses *written therein*. Look at our planet today, you can plainly see the results. *But* necessary to the universal development of *all* things. We're more or less at a

Chapter 10
The Levels

THE TWO WITNESSES

breaking point, if you have any questions, now would be a good time to discuss them."

"Well," Deena said, "if I'm not getting ahead of you, I would like to know more about what you said yesterday, about my never having *lived before*. That is if you want to get into *that* at this time?"

"Sure we can," James assured. "Now would be a *very* good time. It's a very important subject, and one I was going to cover anyway. This will take a lot of scripture to unfold a *clear conception* of how it all works, if you're ready, let's go.

"I guess the best place to start would be where Jesus's disciples asked him about the *end time*, and what it would be like [as the *story* goes]. If you'll notice, He keeps telling **them** *what* to watch out for. He keeps telling **them** what's going to happen to **them** at the end of time. It's really an eye opener when you see it all come together. We can start in Matthew chapter 24 and 3: 'And as he sat upon the mount of Olives [olive means truth], **the disciples came unto him** privately, **saying, Tell us,** when shall these things be? And what shall be the *sign of thy coming*, and of the **end of the world**? And Jesus answered and said unto **them**, Take heed that no *man* deceive **you**.... For many shall come in my name, saying, I am Christ [or *this is the truth*]; and shall deceive many. Then shall *they* [carnal teachers] deliver **you** up to be afflicted, and shall kill **you**: and **ye** shall be hated of all nations [religions] for my name's sake [the truth].... And **this** gospel of the kingdom shall be preached in all the world for **a witness** [*which has to be the spiritual understanding*] unto all nations; and *then* shall the end come [*after* the truth does]. When **ye** therefore shall see the abomination of *desolation* [the lies and images], spoken of by Daniel the prophet, stand in the holy [spiritual] place, (whoso readeth, let *him* **understand:**).... Wherefore if they shall say unto **you**, Behold, he is in the desert; go not forth: behold, he is in the *secret* chambers; believe it not. Watch therefore: for **ye** know not what hour **your** Lord doth come.' I skipped a few verses, you can read them later. The point *here* is what he told **his** disciples to do and watch out for

THE TWO WITNESSES

Chapter 10
The Levels

at the end, as **though they were going to be <u>here</u>**. Interesting! Now keep these clues in mind while I add a few more to fill in the gaps.

We understand being *carnally minded* is **death**. And *being spiritually* minded *is* life, and peace. What we're about to look *at* are statements of this nature. Let's go to Psalms chapter 6 verses 4 and 5: '**Return**, O LORD, deliver my soul: oh save me for thy mercy's sake. **For in death** [or carnal understanding] **there is <u>no</u> <u>remembrance</u> of thee**: in the grave [carnal bondage] who shall give thee thanks?' If you're carnal, you can't know Him. He is not a God of the **dead**. But of the **living, or spiritual-minded**.

Ecclesiastes chapter 1, verses 9 through 11: 'The *thing* that **hath been**, it is that **which shall be**; and that which **is done** is that **which shall be done**; and there is no *new thing* under the sun [or, in the light of truth]. Is there anything whereof it may be said, See, *this* is new? It hath been *already* of old time [tradition], which was before us [sort of like, reaping what you sow or karma].... **There is no remembrance of former things** [because of no understanding, Christ], neither shall there be any **remembrance** of things that are to come with **those that shall come after**.' Ecclesiastes chapter 3 verse 15: '**That which hath been <u>is now</u>**; and **<u>that which is to be hath already been</u>**; and God [creation] *requireth* **that <u>which</u> is <u>past</u>**.'

"In other words we *definitely* reap what **we** sow. A true saying; your past *will* catch up with you. But in **death** there is **no remembrance of former things**. Only in Christ, or spiritual understanding can we *see* the past or path that we must have taken to bring us to where we are now, and that there is *nothing new* because we understand. It has been created in the past, and we are *now* reaping it as we create our future, which will make **this** the past, once we're *there*. You could say, *is this the future* of a past that is gone? Or, is *this the past* of a future *yet* to come along? Either way it all stands for **now. Now** is the day or *enlightened* era for salvation, which is understanding. It is always **now**. What we **think** now is what we'll **be** then. 'If **in this life <u>only</u>** we have hope

THE TWO WITNESSES

Chapter 10
The Levels

in [understanding], we are of all *men* most miserable.'

Okay, back to Isaiah 26 and verse 8: 'Yea, in the way of thy **judgments**, O LORD, have we waited for thee; the desire of our soul is to thy **name**, and to the **remembrance of thee**.' Isaiah 43 and 26: '**Put me in remembrance**: let us plead together: declare thou, that thou mayest be justified.'

Malachi 3 and 16: 'Then they that feared [feared lying about the Word] the LORD spake often one to another: and the LORD hearkened, and heard it, and a **book of remembrance was written** before him for them that feared the LORD [Word], and that thought upon his name.' The book of **remembrance** is recorded in atoms, or sub-atomic particles, the ether, the Lambs book of life, the akasa records and simply, in the air we breath.' Not to mention the *words* that have been written.

"John 14 and 26: 'But the comforter, which is the Holy Ghost, whom the Father will send in my name [the Word], he shall teach you all things, and **bring all things to your remembrance**, whatsoever I have said unto you.' *Once* you receive spiritual understanding. John 16 and 4: 'But these things have I told you, that when the time shall come, **ye may *remember*** that I told you of them. And these things I said not unto you at the beginning, because I was with you.'

"Ezekiel 29 and 16: 'It shall be no more the confidence of the *house of Israel*, which bringeth their iniquity [lies] to **remembrance**, when they shall look after them: but they shall know that I am the Lord GOD.'

"Psalms 22 and 27: 'All the ends of the world **shall *remember*** and turn *unto* the LORD: and all the kindreds [like minded] of the nations [all that had believed the lie] shall worship before thee.' And as it said, 'all *Israel* shall be saved.'

"Revelation 16 and 19: 'And the great city [Babylon] was divided into three parts [carnal, valley of decision, and *hearing*), and the cities [hub] of the nations [religion] fell: **and great Babylon** [those which teach confusion] **came in remembrance** before God, to give unto her the cup of the wine of the fierceness of

THE TWO WITNESSES

Chapter 10
The Levels

his wrath [truth].'

Revelation 18, verses 3 through 8: 'For all nations [world doctrines] have **drunk of the wine** of the wrath of **her fornication**, and the kings [world-renowned religions] of the *earth* have committed fornication [sex before **marriage**] **with her**, and the merchants **of the earth** are waxed *rich* [intellect, pride and ego, let alone material wealth] through the abundance of *her* [religious system] delicacies. And I heard another voice from heaven, saying, **Come out of her, my people**, that ye be not partakers of her **sins** [the lie], and that ye receive not of her plagues. For her [lies] have reached unto heaven, and God hath **remembered** her iniquities. Reward her even as she rewarded you, and double unto her double according to *her works*: In the cup which she hath filled fill to her double.... How much she hath glorified herself, and lived deliciously, so much torment and sorrow give her: for she saith in her heart, I sit a queen, and am no widow [*Christ is not her husband*], and shall see no sorrow [who can destroy the **carnal teachings** of the world? Only Christ].... Therefore shall her plagues come in one day [era of light], *death*, and mourning, and famine; and she shall be utterly burned with **fire**; for strong *is* the Lord God who judgeth her.' And as we saw, His judgment is *truth*, that's all. You'll be in awe, with what the entire Bible has to say about Babylon.

Anyway, our point for now is about coming into *remembrance*. If *we* **have to** *come into remembrance, then there* **must have been** *something* **we've done** *to remember.* Right? Since *we 'reap only what we have sown* and no one else,'*how can we remember something* we've done, if **we haven't lived before**?

Bob, Deena, Tony, Martie, myself, and everybody else who was born **in this lifetime** could not have lived before, *as a personality* that is. Before we're born as a human being our cells and DNA begin receiving in-put from the time the sperm fertilizes the egg. This is done by way of genetic vibration of ether DNA frequencies. These are *much* more finite than human - made air wave frequencies.

THE TWO WITNESSES

Chapter 10
The Levels

"Anyway, every sound, every impression and emotion felt by the mother, by whatever way she receives them *during* pregnancy, is passed on down the chain of *the life force* to the fetus. By the time we are *12* years old we have pretty much developed all the basic instincts *for the foundation* of *this life's* experience. And, as the story goes, we must be about *our Father's* business. *The business of building.* The physical ability to build would be the age of puberty.

And being the sons of a carpenter, as we *all* are, we're off to to build *our house, that is,* our personality. And this house as you know is made of wood, which also means knowledge. Our personality is the **face** of our **soul** *which is* the accumulation of **all the input** since the sperm and egg marriage. It is **that**, which we put forth to others.

"A persons soul is *most often* in conflict with his or her *own* personality, which *was* created **around** *their soul* (swaddling clothes), to survive in everyday life with *other* personalities. The personality is also like the word or letter. Unless the soul and the personality *are one*, the personality has to be seen **through** to see the *human* self the soul.

"You've heard it said, 'man know thyself,' or 'to thine own self be true.' These *are* true statements that should prompt us to do just *that*. Remember the 'brush strokes'? Well, let's compare *them* with *all* of the experiences we've had in *this* life, whether we remember them or not. All of these strokes or experiences, *paint the picture of our real self,* but we mostly put forth a *different* picture for *others* to see. Sometimes we show *them* a picture we think *they* want to see. You, Bob, probably have a different personality *around me* than you do around others. All of us have been there one way or another. The personality, in this case, is made up of paradoxes, contradictions and half-truths. This is the *same pattern* of the way the scriptures are laid out. And until we make the *two* one, we're going to have conflict with ourselves, and with others also, this would be *our* cross. It follows a *pattern*. Unless *all* that is on the surface or personality becomes one with the inner-soul, all of life's

THE TWO WITNESSES

Chapter 10
The Levels

equations will *pull and push* us in directions to cause us to *want to* find peace, or truth. If you've ever longed for *your soul mate*, this *is* the *one* you've been looking for. And because of *tradition*, we've always looked for it *somewhere else*, or *in someone else*.

"There again *with* the scriptures. We've always been looking for *someone else* to save us. In Phillipians chapter 2 and verse 12 it says, 'work out **your own** salvation with fear [of the lie] and trembling [considering consequences, or karma].' And in second Timothy chapter 2 and verse 15: 'Study to **shew thyself** approved unto God...' **Our birth right is** <u>**to know**</u> **and** <u>**to be perfect**</u>.

"The scriptures, just as *the personality*, will present *the personality* that **you** want *it* to have, and *this is* what we'll get if *our* heart or intentions are *not* pure. Remember it says, 'I rain on the just and the unjust alike'? And, 'I will give unto every *man* the intent and desire of **his** heart.' 'I am unto all *men* all things...' The *scriptures* say this! But if the intent *is pure*, then we find *the Christ*, then the two *scripture personalities*, **and** the truth become *one*, and there is no more conflict, or contradiction.

"Back to our point. A person with *no* spiritual understanding, is *man*, the *soul* in conjunction with *his* personality. Now there *is* a *third* party, and it is called *the spirit*. This spirit **has lived before.** And *this* spirit knows *all things*. It is silent to those who do not seek it. And it is the one that stands at the door of the *righteous* or *seeking* **soul**, and knocks. Revelation 3 and 20: 'Behold, I **stand at the door** [of the soul], and knock: if any **man** <u>hear</u> **my** *voice*, and open *the door*, I will come in to him, and will sup **with him**, and **he with me.**'

"Remember where it said in Colossians chapter 1 and verse 27, 'To whom God would make known what *is* the riches of the glory of **this mystery** among the Gentiles; *which is* <u>**Christ in you**</u>, the hope of glory'? First Peter three and verse four: 'But let it be the **hidden** man of the heart, in that which **is not corruptible**, even the ornament of a **meek and quiet spirit**, which is in the sight of God of great price.' As the truth, *hidden* in scripture, wants to be

THE TWO WITNESSES

Chapter 10
The Levels

lifted up and brought forth, so does the truth, or Christ **in** us -- everything wants to grow *toward* the light. And He *dwells* hidden in the *righteousness* of *our* conscience, in the lowest parts of *our earth*, or word *body*. Keep in mind, we're trying to *see* who *has* lived *before* and who *hasn't*. So far, we've seen that *this lifetime's* soul *could not* have lived before, because it was not created *until* this life experience.

"*Without* wisdom and understanding a person is born to *survive* in a world of confusion and strife. And this is how their *personality* is formed. *Survival!* The *soul wants* laughter, peace, joy, and *above all*, love. But because of the lack of truth, the *personality* has to take the lead, and become what *it has to* in order to survive under the conditions necessary to find jobs, food housing, companionship, and *try* to protect its soul.

"At this point, I need to bring in a couple more tangents, or *brush strokes*. Then what we've just discussed will become more clear. Turn to Psalms 63 and verse 1; 'O God, thou *art* my God; early will I *seek* thee: my **soul** thirsteth for thee, my **flesh** [personality] longeth for thee in a dry and thirsty *land* [knowledge], **where no *water*** is [the wilderness].' Here it divides his *soul* from his *flesh*, and says his *soul* thirsteth, and his *flesh* longeth. We know this can't mean *human* flesh. We *can* see *now*, it represents the **outer body**, the word *body*, the *personality*. In this case the soul *and* personality are in agreement. They **both** *want* the Christ *within* to make them **three in one** -- complete. Job 14 and 22: 'But his *flesh* [personality] **upon** him [outer body] shall have pain, and his **soul** within *him* [true self] shall mourn.' Matthew 10 and 28: 'And fear not **them which kill the body** [condemnation of *the person*, or personality], but are *not able* to kill the soul [the inner you]: but rather fear him [the Word, and *its* curses] which *is* able to destroy both soul *and* body [not human body] in hell [total confusion].' As it implies in this next verse, Psalms 17 and 13, 'Arise, O LORD, disappoint **him**, cast **him** down: deliver my *soul* from the wicked, **which is thy [s]word** [lies, confusion, the stories, **hell**]; Acts 2 and 27: 'Because thou **wilt not leave my *soul in hell***,

THE TWO WITNESSES

Chapter 10
The Levels

neither wilt thou suffer thine Holy One [pure in heart] to see corruption.'

This was said in Psalms 16 and 10: 'For thou wilt not **leave** my *soul in hell*; neither wilt thou suffer thine Holy One [Christ] to see corruption.' **Acts** 2 and 31: 'He, seeing *this before*, spake of the *resurrection* of Christ, that *His* **soul** was not <u>*left in hell*</u>, **neither his flesh** did see corruption.' He just *came* in the **likeness** of *sinful flesh*. Remember, he had to *learn obedience*, by the things *He* suffered, and *had to become* perfect. This next verse ties the *three* in together.

First Thessalonians 5 and 23: 'And the very God of peace sanctify you *wholly*; and I pray God, your *whole* **spirit** *and* **soul** *and* **body** [not human body] be **preserved** blameless, unto the coming of **our** Lord Jesus Christ.' To make **these three one**, is to *have* the *mind* of Christ, the **perfect** being: **Our** birthright! Let's examine first John, chapter five, verses seven and eight: 'For there are **three** that bear **record** in heaven, the **Father** [all creation], **the Word** [knowledge or mind], and the **Holy Ghost** [spiritual understanding]: and <u>***these three* are one**</u>. And there are **three** that bear **witness** *in* <u>**earth**</u>, the Spirit [life, energy], and **the water**, and **the blood**: and **these three** [which are the stories, water and blood] *agree* [it looks like the truth] **in one**.'

Let's add a few more then we'll return to these two verses. Remember where it said in Exodus, 'And God said unto Moses, I AM **THAT** I AM: and he said, Thus shalt thou say unto the *children of Israel*, **I AM** hath sent me unto you'? That was in Exodus 3 and 14. The point here is, he didn't say to tell them God sent you, or Jehovah, or any other title, He sometimes ascribed to himself, but here he said, 'I am that I am.'

"I've heard it said that *we are* 'star stuff', which means the results of the big bang. And as a *matter of fact* we are. Imagine for a moment if you will, walking outside on a clear night when the stars and moon are shining, and look to the heavens. And as you gaze around at the majesty of it all, then ask yourself, 'am **I** <u>that</u>, am I?' *Then* if you know *you are* **that** (a part of the whole), you can

THE TWO WITNESSES

Chapter 10
The Levels

reverse the question and make it a *statement*. Thus, 'I am **That**, I am.' This *is* what it's telling us. 'I am *that* I am,' simply means the all, or everything that is in creation. The word *God* is referred to as *creator*. And the creator is said to be *omnipotent, omnipresent* and *omniscient*. The word 'omnipotent' means, 'almighty; *not limited* in authority *or* power.' The word 'omnipresent' means, 'the quality of being **everywhere present** -- *at the same time*.' The word 'omniscient' means, 'knowing **all things**. All knowing. **Infinite** knowledge.' Knowledge means *words*. Words are born of *that* which is *observed* and named. And **if** before the arc or the big bang, there was **nothing** to observe, then there *could not* have been a mind, and there would not have been *a thinker* because there could not have been any thoughts. There was no word, or God if you will.

"Like the 'waka-paka' thing I talked about before. If there is **nothing created**, then there is **nothing** to be named. Or no one to name *the nothing*, nothing. But, as the scriptures impress, *all things are one*, **the creator and the created are one**. Thomas Troward puts it nicely in his book, *Bible Mystery And Bible Meaning*. It's published by Dodd, Mead and Company, New York, 1913. This is another book I *highly* recommend. As a matter of fact, *all of his works* are a great witness. About 95 percent of his works, to me, are right on the money. And at *the time*, I'm not sure if he was familiar with the big bang theory or not. Some of his other books are with different publishers. I want to read you a couple pages of what he says. It starts in chapter 7, page 173, second paragraph: 'The new *personality* thus generated may be considered as the child of the individual soul which gives birth to it; and since there is only ONE Spirit **anywhere and every where**, it can be only *another mode* to the original ONE --- consequently the "Son" who is thus born to David "the beloved," is *Himself* "the Everlasting Father," and thus the answer to the sacred puzzle is that the man, who has really learned the inner meaning of the words "know thyself," discovers that the true **I AM** in himself is one with the universal **I AM**, which is the root of all individualized being.

It is in the light of these sublime truths, that the Name of

THE TWO WITNESSES

Chapter 10
The Levels

"the Son" is equally with that of "the Father" the Sacred Name, in the true knowledge of which salvation is alone to be found. For what do we mean by "Salvation"? "That we might be saved from the **hand** of all them that hate **us**," is the answer; that is, from the power of everything that in any way militates against our enjoyment of the fullest life. That we might attain to continually increasing degrees of Life was the declared object of the Master's mission, and therefore, salvation means the power to ask and receive that our joy may be full; and the only way this power can ever come to us is by the recognition of our own possibilities as being each of as the image and likeness of God. Therefore it is written, "To them gave he power to become the sons of God, even to them that believe in His Name;" and the word rendered "power" may also be rendered as "right," so that this passage assures us both of our power and right to take possession of our inheritance as sons and daughters of the Almighty [our birth right]. Now, mark well that this promise is not held forth as a reward for the acceptance of some theological speculation, which conveys no real meaning to us, and which by its very terms must be incapable of proof; but it is the natural and logical outcome of the initial proposition with which the Bible opens, that Spirit is the ONE and Only source, Origin, and Substance of all things, a self evident truth the contrary of which it is impossible to conceive. What I here call "Spirit" you may, if you please, call "the Unknowable," or x, or denote it by a single stroke; the name or symbol we use is quite immaterial, so long as we grasp the fact that the initial originating Power must of necessity reproduce itself all the way down the scale, no matter how different the forms under which it does so. In whatever way we may denote it, it is always the Great Expressor; and **all that is**, we ourselves included is its Expression of itself; so that the whole teaching of Truth may be summed up in the words, "**The Expressor and the Expressed are ONE**."

Work out the problem in any way you will and you **will never arrive at any other final result than this**; and so we always come back to that fundamental axiom which Jesus

THE TWO WITNESSES

Chapter 10
The Levels

announced as the supreme statement of the LAW. This is the great truth enshrined in every form of the Sacred Name; and therefore, it is that every form of the Great Name, when rightly understood, is found to be "**the Word of Power** [Christ]." (brackets and darkened emphasis, are mine)

Listen to these verses carefully. Deuteronomy six and four: 'Hear, O **Israel**: The LORD our God **is one** LORD:' Mark 12 and 29: 'And Jesus answered him, **The first of all the commandments** is, **Hear, O Israel**; The Lord **our God is one** Lord:' Galatians 3 and 20: 'Now a mediator is not a *mediator* of one, **but God is one**.' Christ, the **power** of God, and the **wisdom** of God, it's *all* **in the Word**!

Which brings us back to the *three* that bear record in heaven. Before the big bang, there was an **infinity** of *nothing*. And as inferred by research in the scripture, out of **necessity** and by **occasion** in the vastness of this infinite nothingness *there was* a **heaviness,** which in an *innumerable* amount of eons, this, as the Bible calls it, *'tiny chamber'* (smaller than an atom), began to shift ever so slightly, at first. This is known as the *invisible* father-mother, because at this point, the differentiation *principle* is two.

It took billions of years for it to move even a thousandth of an inch. Anyway, regardless of the time, it did move, or in this case, sag, because of its '**heaviness**.' Speaking of time, this *was* the beginning of *time*; because at that point of differentiation, there became **something** to *measure* -- energy and antimatter. And from these *two* principles, visible matter with its energy field *was* created out of the arc, thus the big bang. At this point there was nothing but *matter* and *energy* heaved out *in all conceivable directions* **at once**, blowing up the balloon, or universe, which is forever traveling, expanding *and* contracting **in** this infinity of *nothing*, which was, and is, *its* womb.

This is the **Father**-Mother of **all things**, but yet *they're* one; as Adam and Eve were one. We now have *total chaos*, and the *forerunner* of what is considered the Word or **God**, which came from chaos, or Teman, as the *scriptures* record it. And this chaos

THE TWO WITNESSES

Chapter 10
The Levels

and confusion had to *learn obedience* through the things it encountered, suffered, or allowed. Which was the universe coming into *some kind of order*, and thereby establishing the law and order of the operation of orbiting and traveling, without banging into everything at random. This took much time.

I know you remember when we had the barbecue we discussed the Hebrew meanings for God. Let's look up the meaning for *father*. The Hebrew *root* letter for it is 'A,' which means 'timber,' or **wood**. This is where we get the materials to build *our house*, it's the carpenter again. The Hebrew *word* is 'AB,' and it means 'Father,' 'principle,' and chief.' Also 'desire,' 'clay,' 'cloud,' 'thick *beam*,' 'thick cloud,' and 'thicket.' Thus we have creation in the making, or *building*.

Has anybody forgotten we're still unraveling the subject of, who has lived before, and who hasn't? Well hang in there, we still need to explain **these three** -- the *Father*, the *Word*, and the *Holy Ghost* -- first. Okay, at this point we have the *Father*, which is energy **and** matter: two. And we have the **images**, the heaved up things, that will eventually *become words* in someone's mind, but there is *no observer* to receive these images and *name* them yet. This comes in the *process* of time which *is* differentiation, *a form* of dividing and multiplying of mathematical *or* biological law, or any laws, and is of *necessity* the building blocks of *evolution*.

This takes us to the next word of **the three**, and that is, '**Word**.' The Father, one; the **Word**, two and the Holy Ghost, three.

I'll need to bring in some more scriptures for a foundation, for this is where we come into the *second* father part. Yes, Bob there are *two*. The one we've just been discussing, the *invisible* father-mother (nothingness and heaviness) which brought into being the *visible* Father-Mother-creation, or universe, and now the father as in the Father-God, the operation of energy in matter. I'll try to explain.

Turn to Ephesians chapter 5 and verse 20: 'Giving thanks always for **all things** unto God [2] **and** the Father [1] in the **name of** our Lord Jesus Christ [3].' Colossians 3 and verse 17: 'And

Chapter 10
The Levels

THE TWO WITNESSES

whatsoever ye do in word or deed, *do* all in the name of the Lord Jesus, giving thanks to God **and** the Father **by him**.' First Thessalonians chapter 3 verse 11" 'Now <u>God himself</u> **and** <u>our Father</u>, **and** <u>our Lord Jesus Christ</u>,' direct our way unto you.' Colossians two and two: 'That their hearts might be comforted, being knit together in love, and unto all riches of the full assurance **of understanding**, to the **acknowledgement of the mystery of God** [2], **and** of the *Father* [1], **and** of *Christ* [3].' These are also called 'God the Father,' 'God the Word,' and 'God the Son.' One, two, three, and *these three* **are one**.

Has anyone thought who the observer might be yet? If you thought it was the Son, you're *half* right. Because the **observer and the observed**, *are* one. This will become clear a little later. I just thought I'd throw that in as a double whammy for when all this does sink in. You'll appreciate it when it happens.

While I'm at it I might as well throw *this one* in too, it's *also* coming up later. It's the part where **we have made God serve with our sins**. That's Isaiah 43 and verse 24: 'Thou hast bought me no sweet cane [joy] with money [knowledge], neither hast thou filled me with the fat [anointing] of *thy* sacrifices [rituals]: **but thou hast made me to serve with thy sins**, thou hast wearied me with *thine* iniquities [images].' How's that for a kicker? How is it possible? How can anyone *make* God sin? This is the most beautiful thing I can imagine. *Finding these contradictions* and then seeing the understanding. What a joy! There I go again. It may seem like I'm evading your question, Deena, but bear with me. I need to explain how it all came together so you can *comprehend* how reincarnation works. It'll be a little while yet.

Anyway, at this point, let's discuss how verbal communication started developing. And I'm not sure just when that was, but all indications put it way before what we now know as the cave man era. And no, Deena, we truly did not, in a sense, evolve from apes. Remember, 'seed *after* **it's own** *kind*.,' even though *we all* came from the big bang. As our species evolved *mentally*, they desired to do more and be more, physically. These *changing* desires

THE TWO WITNESSES

Chapter 10
The Levels

were the *creating factor* to our presently evolved physique because the mind governs our biological make-up. The apes on the otherhand do not have the mental capacity to go beyond where they are now. The Father doesn't actually create, the Son does, **by way of** the Father.

"Turn to Colossians 1 and verse 16: 'For **by him** [the Son] were all things **created** [but not without the Father], that are in heaven, and that are **in earth**, **visible and <u>invisible</u>**, whether they *be* thrones, or dominions, or principalities, or powers: all things were created **by him, and for him**.' In the beginning of our species, with its *infancy* of the mind, and *its* wonderment *of it all*, had no impressions of right or wrong, they were free. Free to think and receive impressions from creation that would feed and satisfy their desire and curiosity, they were in harmony. They learned and shared with those of the same interest. They realized *they themselves* in their *totality* were in fact **one** *with* the whole, the **I Am**. And with this unadulterated pure logic and understanding, they loved *the revelations* from the knowledge they beheld. They saw the sun and how it made one feel warm, and caused things to come forth from the *earth* and *things for food* and associated that with the mind. It lit the path for their feet to ponder. Above all, it showed them the *image* of things they could not see *in darkness*. They saw that the moon was the lesser light, actually, a *reflection* of *the truth*. And the stars (which means guides, teachers or evangelist), how they guided one's course upon *the waters*. They also understood you had to plant something if you wanted to *eat*. And as time would have it they realized *we are all* a unique part of the Father, *and* God *and* the Son.

"They also knew the *power* of *this* knowledge when in unison with the universal energies, *or Father*, and how *it* could *create* and *shape* others beliefs and attitudes. And *with it* you could not harbor envy, hate, or condemnation for *anyone*. They *understood reciprocity* and were **pure**. *This was love*. Not love for some*thing*. But love *of* and for love itself. She *was* and *is* **wisdom**. And these *that could* receive *according to their* desires, received

THE TWO WITNESSES
Chapter 10
The Levels

pure knowledge, and this pure knowledge became The Word, or God (knowledge) *of the Father*. And with this *love* was *understanding* and wisdom. Now their mind and the universe were one. They, now were one with God, Emmanuel, God **with** us.

"Their thoughts could enter into the *energies* of things *made,* and create new designs, new patterns, different colors of flowers and plants. They (male and female) were the *eyes* ears and *hands* of the Father-Mother, they *were* in their totality, the *Sons of God in humans*. As it says in John 10, 35, 'He called *them* **gods, unto whom the word of God came,** and **the scripture cannot be broken**.' These we're the Sons Of God that went in unto the *daughters* of *men*. Adam and Eve partaking of the forbidden fruit.

"Thus the prophecies were written -- by *Holy* men of old, as the understanding of the Father-God had been revealed to them. Second Peter chapter 1, verse 21: 'For **the prophecy** *came not* in old time *by the will of man*: but **holy** *men* [spiritual minds] **of** *God* spake *as they were moved by the Holy Ghost*.' Or you could say, the prophecy came not by the *carnal* investigation, but by the spiritual as it was revealed to **them** by the *one* they were enamored with: pure **understanding**, or Christ. Stay with me, Deena, I'm working on it.

"Glance up to the previous verse -- 20: 'Knowing this *first,* that *no prophecy* of the scripture is of any **private** interpretation....' This Means that prophecy *cannot be divided*. **If** *it is* truth, then *all can see* and understand. And don't forget, it's supposed to be *simple*. Remember where it said, 'the *simplicity* in Christ'? If *you* can see the truth, then it must be seen in **all things**, and **by all**, and *that* could not make it *yours*. Or mine, as far as that goes.

"Look down to chapter two and verse one of second Peter: 'But there were false prophets *also* among the people [just as they are *among the stories in the scriptures*], even as there shall be false teachers among you, who *privily* shall bring in damnable *heresies,* even denying *the Lord* that bought them, and bring upon themselves swift destruction.' You should recognize *them* by now. They are **in** the scripture; and *they* know *their* own. Here is what

THE TWO WITNESSES

Chapter 10
The Levels

Revelation chapter 19 and verse ten says about prophecy: 'And I fell at his feet to worship him. And he said unto me, See *thou do it not*: I am thy fellow servant, and *of* thy **brethren that have the testimony** of Jesus: worship *God*: for the **testimony of Jesus is the spirit of prophecy**.' Knowledge came *from observing* the operation of what came from the big bang: energy and matter, which scripture refers to as the image of Words, *and* God. And to worship God, is to worship the Father **also**. To have the Son, is to have God *and the* Father, and *knowing* who *they* are. You cannot know ***this*** without *understanding*.

As it says in John one, verses one and two, '**In** the **beginning** was **the Word**, and the Word **was with** God, and the **Word was God. The same** was in the beginning **with** God.' You **cannot** have one ***without the other***. **But -** you can have the **word** *without* understanding. But then all you would have are **images** of *darkness*. And since He is two-fold He is still the God of all. Because He said He rains on the just and the unjust alike. And those *without* Christ are *those* who are 'ever learning, and never able to come to the knowledge of the truth.' And, 'wrest to their own destruction.'

Having just the word without Christ and teaching it carnally is to make God *sin* with *your* doings. You have also **taken** the name of the Lord in vain, meaning you have said the Word saith this the Word saith that, when *it* or *He* did not. That is cursing, with *the curse*. And you are accursed for hanging on *that* tree of knowledge. Galatians 3:13; 'Christ hath redeemed us from the curse of the law, being made a curse for us: for it is written, Cursed *is* every one **that hangeth on a tree**:'

"James, I need to ask you something about *that*, before you go too much further-- If it's Okay?" Bob asked.

"No problem, Bob. What is it?"

"It was the 'two-fold' part you just mentioned, you know, when you said God was two-fold. What about the trinity? Before, you said they were *three* in one. Doesn't that make a contradiction?"

THE TWO WITNESSES

Chapter 10
The Levels

"Okay, I'll bring in two scriptures that should clarify it for you. Turn to Daniel chapter two verse seven: 'The king answered unto Daniel, and said, Of a truth *it is*, that *your God* is a God of gods, and a Lord of kings, **and a revealer of** *secrets*, seeing thou couldest reveal this secret.' And Matthew 11 and verse 27: 'All things are delivered unto me of **my** Father: and **no man** knoweth the Son, **but** the Father; neither knoweth **any man** the Father, save the Son, and **he** to **whomsoever** the Son *will* **reveal** *him*.'

"Now *that's* a beautiful paradox. As we know, the Word has the truth hidden *in it*. And that *it is veiled* to keep the **secret**. And remember, no **man** can see the truth, never has been able to, never will. Here, where the truth **in the Word** is saying 'All things are delivered unto me of my Father,' means the more *understanding* you have, the more knowledge is revealed to you or the more you are a son to him the more of a Father He will be to you. *'He who does the will of my Father.'*

"It's that 'you shall never hunger and thirst' thing. And if you are a **man**, you *cannot* know the Son *or* the Truth. Only the Father relates or gives *life* to the Son. Neither does any **man** *know* the Father or the good Word, **except** he in *particular* is *a* Son, *or* has seen the spiritual Christ *in* the Father Word. Thus; 'If you've seen me [the spiritual understanding], you would **had to have** seen my Father [the Word], **also**.' It boils down to this: you can't have *truth* without the *Word* from which it came. And you can't get it from the *Word* if you're carnal-minded. *These* parables are just more confirmation to what we've been studying.

Now to answer your question, Bob. You have, first of all, the Father; second, the Word: and third, the trinity, which is the understanding, or the spirit, or the Christ, or the holy ghost, or the truth, or the life, or the son or the blood, or the living Word, or the bread, and on and on. Nevertheless, these three *are one*. Which takes us back to the verse, 'There are *three* that bear record in heaven, the *Father*, the *Word*, and the *Holy Ghost*.' And now we know *where* they dwell: **in all things**, including **us**, but all have crucified or killed the Christ. He has to be raised from the dead,

THE TWO WITNESSES

Chapter 10
The Levels

then making the three one.

"The verse that follows that one says, *'these three* **agree** in one.' Not *one* but *agree* in one. It was talking about the stories of the word. For the sake of avoiding another long tangent, you can study *that one* on your own, I believe you can understand it okay now that you know what the other verse means.

"Deena, would you believe it's taking all these scriptures just to answer your simple question? I could have answered you straight up, but that wouldn't have been as good as having it *revealed* to you by the scriptures. Do you understand why I'm reading the ones I'm reading?"

"Yes, I think so. What I've seen so far seems to be showing me the *oneness* of *all things* and how they live off *pure energy* and how it is tied *in* or connected *in* patterns. I think you called these connections DNA type patterns. And we all know you can't destroy perpetual energy, especially when the eternal expansion and contraction of the universe with its propelling velocity throughout infinity keeps supplying it with renewed life, which I think you said is derived from the *friction* of all this movement. Now this explains to me that we can *never* cease to to exist. I guess that's what the Bible means when it says we have eternal life. But I'm still trying to piece together what happens to us when we leave our body."

"Goodness, you have been paying attention. Very good!" bragged James. "Well, we're right on the edge of seeing *that* now, Deena. Leaving your body is sort of like when we believed *the scriptures* carnally, and now we don't. They *were* alive to us *that way* once, but *now* they're dead. They haven't gone anywhere, they've been changed, you might say, 'born again.' We no longer see them in the flesh, but in the spirit. They're no longer the head, but the tail, the root, so to speak, which means we're no longer going *away backwards* with our understanding. We're still the *same*, but we have a much more beautiful understanding of how things work -- without fear, guilt, confusion, or spiritual death

When I was 'first born,' or started going to church, I had changed my way of living, without religion, and turned my life

THE TWO WITNESSES

Chapter 10
The Levels

around. This changed my personality, but I was still the *same person*, I had only changed some of my habits. When I was 'born *again*,' this time by understanding, or Christ, *I was* and still am the *same person*, but this time more complete, with full proof of what I've seen. The inner and the outer are becoming more and more one.

"A movie actor, male or female, can play many different roles, but when the filming is done they are still the *same person*. And out of all the roles or characters they might have played, I'm sure they retained something from all of them, and incorporated, or grafted in, if you will, only the part of those characters that were *relevant* to their *soul nature*. The reason I say *soul nature* is because none of the characters he or she has played changed their everyday personality; he or she was still his or her *own person* with the same personality. However, there must have been *periods of adjustment* to where it could take a lifetime for some actors to shake the characters they've played. Shakespeare put it well when he said, 'the world *is a stage* and we *all play a part*.' Our personality has to play the game of survival in society, and this could take the assumption of many roles. Some may never shake their roles.

"What this is leading to is a discussion of the many different lifetimes or *characters* we've played, and how that works. Yes, Deena, this is all relevant, I'm still painting. Remember we talked about how everything grows toward the light? Well, that *is a law*, in nature, and *in* the Word. When we were in the carnal mind, we yearned for more understanding, or light, thereby being drawn by the light.

"There are many places in the physical universe that we can go to for learning and betterment, until we finally surrender and search for the light, or creator. Before I venture off into *this*, I want to bring in about three verses that will help us understand.

Turn to John 14 and verse 2: 'In my **Father's house** [universe and mind] are **many mansions** [dwelling places]: if *it were* not *so*, I would have told you. I go to prepare a place for you [as he is now preparing our next life, according to *our* doings]'. Acts

THE TWO WITNESSES

Chapter 10
The Levels

7 and verse 49: 'Heaven [universe] is my throne, and *earth* [matter] is my footstool: what house will ye **build me** [only in *our own minds*]? saith the Lord: or what *is* the place of my rest [within us]?' Ecclesiastes five and verse eight: 'If thou seest the oppression of the **poor** [very little, if any, knowledge], and violent perverting of judgment and justice [*heavy* teaching of the law] in a province, marvel not at the matter: for **He *that is higher* than the highest** regardeth; ***and*** there be **higher than they**.' Did you notice how it referred to **He** that was higher than the highest as **they**? And to top that off, there are those that are higher than them, and so on. If the laws of the universe or universes, dimensionally speaking, are just, then you cannot be punished for something you didn't know. As the verse say's, 'Father forgive them for they *know not* what they do.' That is a law, and it is for all. Until we know the truth or until truth presents itself for everyone to behold, they cannot be held accountable. On the contrary, truth *has* been here all along, hidden in scripture but not to be revealed until the third day, and *then* we are judged by the **revelation** of Jesus Christ, that is, the Living Word.

First Corinthians six and two: 'Do ye not know that the **saints** shall judge the world? and if the world shall be **judged by you**, are ye unworthy to judge the smallest matters?' Romans 2 and verse 16: 'In the day when **God** [the Word] **shall judge** the secrets of men **by** Jesus Christ [the truth] according to ***my*** gospel' Who's doing the judging here? It says that **those who know the truth**. And it says it will be done according to Paul's gospel, because it is hidden there.

What is going to do the judging? John 6 and verse 63: 'It is the **spirit** that quickeneth; the *flesh* profiteth nothing: **the words** that **I** speak unto you, ***they are spirit***, and ***they are life'***. Second Timothy four and one: 'I charge *thee* therefore before God, **and** the Lord Jesus Christ, **<u>who shall judge</u>** the quick [righteous] and the dead [carnal] **at his *appearing*** and his kingdom.' How does He **appear**; It says from His Father: **The Word**. Second Timothy four and verse eight: 'Henceforth there is laid up for me a crown of

Chapter 10
The Levels

THE TWO WITNESSES

righteousness, which the Lord [Word], **the righteous judge**, shall give me at that day [the third]: and not to me only, but unto **all them also that love his appearing**.'

"Hebrews 9 and 28: 'So Christ was once offered to bear the sins of many; and unto *them that look for him* shall he **appear** the <u>second time</u> [after we're first born] *without sin* unto salvation.' Here we go again: where do we *look* for Him? Of course, in the gospels! But, what about all the people who have left the planet who never had a chance to see or hear the truth and be judged? Well, some are here and some are coming. There will be approximately one thousand years for everyone to make it through. If **in this lifetime only** we have hope in finding the Christ, we are of all the unknowing, or unlearned, *most miserable.* If we think we only have *one lifetime* to work out our salvation we would be *very* miserable. We *actually have forever* to work it out, but who wants to remain in hell that long? We must deliver *ourselves from hell,* it says. And *we can* do that by *recognizing* what *hell* is, and delivering ourselves from *it*.

Let's look at it again. First Corinthians 15 and verse 56: 'The **sting of death** *is* **sin**; and the **strength of sin** *is* **the law**.' Isaiah 28 and verse 15: 'Because *ye have said*, We have made a covenant **with death** [the law, or letter], and **with hell** [the cross, or controversy] are **we** [the carnal] at agreement; when the overflowing scourge [truth] shall pass through, it shall not come unto us: for **we have made lies** [the stories] **our refuge**, and **under falsehood have we hid ourselves**' How plain can it be? Now that we understand what sin is. In order to deliver ourselves from death and hell we must **find** the truth, the Christ. There are some who desire to remain. But as is said of *them*, 'Let the *dead* bury **their** *dead*; come follow the truth.' Or, 'What is that to thee, come, follow thou me,' says understanding. If you're content with where you are, truth does not compel you to search for it. You must **want** it more than anything in *this* life.

"Since we reap what we sow and sow what we shall reap, then it should be obvious where we are going to be in our next life.

THE TWO WITNESSES

Chapter 10
The Levels

If we are prejudiced in this life we will face prejudice in the next one, which is only just. And creation, or our Father-Mother, wants us to get it right. As we read, 'God requireth **that which is past**.' If we are to return to this planet, or schoolmaster, for further lessons, the circumstances are **now** being created for us to incarnate. A body **is being prepared** for us. Remember, the universe, or God, **must** give you the intent and desire of your heart. God does not lie. If we are prejudiced in *this life, we must face it* in the next. After all, with the help of the universe, *we created it*. That was what it meant in Isaiah where he was talking about the past and wanting to know if we could tell the future from it.

"Let's look at a few of these relative verses right quick. Turn to Isaiah 41, verses 22 and 23: 'Let them bring *them* forth, and shew us what **shall happen**: let them shew the **former things** [the past], what they *be*, that we may consider *them*, **and know** the *latter end* [future] of them; or **declare us things for to come....Shew the things that are to come hereafter**, that we may know that ye *are* gods: yea, do good, or do evil, that we may be dismayed, and behold *it* together.' Our past has put us where we are, and where we are will place us in the future. We are creating it.

"Look at John 10 and 34: 'Jesus answered them, Is it not written in *your law*, I said, **Ye are gods** [meaning they are doing their own creating for themselves]?' He was referring to Psalms 82 verses five, six and seven: 'They [carnal] know not, neither will *they* understand; *they* walk on *in darkness*: all the foundations of the **earth** [teaching of scripture] are out of course.... I have said, **Ye are gods**; and **all of you** [carnal and spiritual] *are* children of the most High. But ye shall die **like men**, and fall like **one** of the princes [the prince of darkness].' And for *this* to happen *would* keep us in darkness, or death *and* hell, and there **is always** eternal life, whether in hell *or* in freedom. We are definitely predestined by *our own* doings. "Okay, remember in Romans seven and verse six where Paul is talking about the law holding us in *death? It* says; 'But now we are delivered from *the law*, that **being dead wherein we were held**; that we should serve in newness of spirit, and not *in*

THE TWO WITNESSES

Chapter 10
The Levels

the oldness [tradition] of the letter.'

And when Christ sets us free from 'the law of sin and death,' we are free indeed, never seeing it *carnally* again. Now, since we were held by the law, or you could say the flesh, we were **dead** to the spirit of understanding, or life. So, when we leave this body of human flesh, which is the *similitude* of the law, and we've been saved **from** death we don't have to enter into death or the human flesh again. Like it says, 'the last enemy to overcome *is death*, living in a human body is *living* under the law -- the living dead. Then to live in a human body, and to have a *carnal mind* is what is called 'twice dead and plucked up by the roots,' meaning you have no **earth** whatsoever. Having no **earth** is the same thing as having no **Word** or knowledge. Then if you have no *Word* then you have no God, for God is the Word; you would be what is called 'the **ungodly**.' And He is *not the God of the dead*, but of the living.

"Now, many *have* the word in unrighteousness, and they are ever learning, but never able to come to the knowledge of the Christ. These are those who see it carnally. I've been there many times when I was ***first*** born. They are called sinners. The question in first Peter chapter 4 and verse 18 reads, 'And if the righteous *scarcely* be **saved**, where shall the **ungodly** *and* the **sinner** appear?' Now, that we know what the word **ungodly** and **sinner** mean, the answer is obvious, they **must remain** in *death and hell*, which means living without Christ. And this is where they **must return**. The laws of creation are just *and* righteous, and according to what we've sown we shall also reap, this is the karma of *all* things; all *things* return to *their* creator.

"If we've allowed Satan, the spirit and power of the image, to create the way we think and live, then it's obvious *again*; you cannot leave death and hell without Christ, and this is done in the resurrection. Those who do leave the schoolmaster will have many other schools of learning forever; like it says; 'in my Father's house are many mansions,' and in these many places of abode, they shall never hunger and never thirst -- or the ultimate free lunch. They can *now* live with all creation and learn and create forever, never

THE TWO WITNESSES

Chapter 10
The Levels

having to *die* anymore; they have Christ always.

"What I'm trying to do, Deena, is paint enough pictures for you so you can see how the law works and in doing so you can see the revelation of your question. Do you follow me?"

"Beautifully!" Deena replied. "A little while ago It started coming together enough that I could understand how it works; but to explain it, forget it! I'm sure that'll come with studying. It is so exciting to see what little I have seen, but I *know now* I can see all that I set my heart to know. I really know *it is* a law, and understand that *it* works, which creates a strong desire for more and I just love it!"

"I know what you mean; I certainly got the picture!" seconded Bob. "It helps me to understand the *seven level* idea; it takes a thousand words to paint that picture. The pictures of each level of allegory are nearly *all alike* with the exception of slight variations. I'm starting to notice how *that* works now."

"I've noticed so *many scriptures* say the same thing, that is, they have the *same* point but with slight variations in their delivery, so you can see it on *all levels* until it becomes three-dimensional. And I might add, this *is* awesome, James!

"I'm so excited I just want to run and tell everybody, but I realize I can't. They would have me under psychiatric evaluation in no time. That's probably what was meant when Jesus said, 'See that you tell *no man*.' You can't! They *can't hear* you! That's a beautiful witness. "

"You bet!" James agreed. "And that's *exactly* what it meant when He said, 'see that you tell *no man*.' They *would* think you were mad. In Corinthians Paul was talking about that. Turn to first Corinthians 14 and 23: 'If therefore the whole church [spiritual] be come together into *one* place, and all speak with tongues, and there come in *those that are* unlearned, or unbelievers, will they not say that ye are *mad?*' If someone walked in and heard us, I know they would say it. It happened to Tony and me one day when some guys came to my door wanting me to join their church. I invited them in and during the discussion they became frightened and said 'y'all

Chapter 10
The Levels

THE TWO WITNESSES

are crazy!' and left immediately. Tony and I just shook our heads and said, 'oh well.' But what *can* you do? They didn't want to hear anything that had to do with the cross, or contradiction, that is.

That reminds me, did you ever notice how *the story* of Dracula portrays the exact *same principles* as the scripture? Well, a virgin is one that has not lain *with man*, right? And who does Dracula look for to suck the life or blood from? The *virgin*. Once *they* have mingled blood they become alike, looking for others. The light, or truth, will kill them. They have to work in darkness, and when there *is* light they reman in their graves. Spiritually it would be sepulcher. Another way to kill them is with the wooden stake through the heart. And we know wood represents knowledge. Also, when you come at a vampire with a cross, they panic! Really! It's the same as when carnal people are full of fear; they panic when you bring out the contradiction, or cross, of the scriptures. Soon they will be free."

"Well, I'll be darned!" said Bob. "It *is* the same thing. Who would've thought it? I wonder if the people who came up with the story of Dracula realized that? It certainly would be interesting to know. The more I think about it, they would have to have known, it's too perfect; the whole *idea* fits hand-in-glove."

"It sure seems like it, doesn't it, Bob?" replied James. "Of course there are *many* more stories and movies that relate to the good *and* evil principle. One that really impressed me was 'Dark Crystal,' an animated movie. It fits the prophecy to a tee. I thought it was well done, in general. Anyway, where were we? Oh yeah, I was wrapping up the preliminary ground work for Deena's question. It will all clarify itself pretty soon, Deena."

"Oh no problem, James. I know it will, I can see the handwriting on the wall now."

"I can see it, too," Bob said. "I know a lot of things will be answered, or revealed, as we study on our own. But there was one question I would like to ask, if we have time?"

"Sure," James replied.

"Well, you've said, more or less, that *all* is involution and

THE TWO WITNESSES

Chapter 10
The Levels

evolution. If this is the case, how did you mean we didn't *actually* come from apes? I thought the whole idea of evolution was that *we* came from apes?

"Well, if we take into account that *all* seed is after its own kind, we can see that the *individual* original seed, of *all* things has evolved into what *it is* today, which shows me, at least, what the original seed *must have been*. At the *very* nano second when the big bang arcked, it was pure absolute energy cast out in all *conceivable* directions in the invisible configuration of the numeral eight. The intensity of *this* absolute *perpetual* energy at the instant of the arc, emblazoned the very essence of all things that came into existence. If the scientists in Texas could have finished the super collider conductor, I feel they would have discovered *this eight* somewhere in their efforts. Anyway, the point here *is* the *degree* of the *intensity* of the energy as the universe was *heaved* out from the arc. The ape *species* quite assuredly had the same creator we did, with the exception of the energy factor. The energy in our genetic makeup is a degree or so higher than that of our *physical* look a-likes, and being thus, allowed our species to receive energy input and subliminal communicative intercourse with that higher power.

And as everything is drawn toward the light, or energy in this case, we had a strong desire to come forward more than any other living thing. The end result was mutational development, mentally and physically, above the ape, because we had intent and desire for *more,* over and above all things. *Their* instincts and mind have developed into what they are today, because that was and is *their* seed. Because it flows from the initial arc energy, our seed has allowed us to become what *we* have *desired*, and this was because of our mental energy connection with the Father-Mother-God. Physically we both started out very similar. But the apes could only go so far. *We* retain the power to progress or digress by using creation, or God, as our fashioning tool.

"It's all in the mind, dear Watson, as Sherlock would put it. Did you understand the mental implementation congruous to the operation of energy in matter, in mind, and in words. Was that the

THE TWO WITNESSES

Chapter 10
The Levels

explanation you were looking for?"

"Duh, do what? What happened? Who, me?" Bob scrambled. "Oh sure! No problem. I feel I could write a book on the subject now, I mean, since you put it that way. Wow! Man, that really hit home. It's still coming in James, I'll have to report to you later on that. All kidding aside though, I do get the picture, overall that is. I figured it was something close to what you said, I just couldn't make the right connections. But in time with a little more understanding, I know it will become clear, I have no doubt about it, really."

"There is a lot more I could bring in to clarify the specifics, but time wouldn't allow it for now. The best way, I know of, as you said, is to have it revealed to you in your personal studies as you're advanced enough to receive it.

At this time I would like to bring in a little more about the scriptures and how they relate to the universal laws and clear up some things I discussed earlier. Thomas Troward, in another book of his called *The Law and the Word*, published by 'DEVORSS Publications 1993', copyrighted in 1917, elaborates concisely about the the law of truth and liberty, in the Word. It's just about a page and a half, let's read it. It's in chapter 7, pages 135 and 136:

'What is wanted is the realization of a greater Word than that which we form from the current experience of the race. The race has formed it's Word on the basis of the lower principles of our being, and if we are to advance beyond this, the Law of the subject clearly indicates that it can only be by adopting a more fundamental Word, or idea, than that which we have hitherto thought to include the entire range of possibilities.

The Law of our further Evolution demands a Word not formed from past experiences but based upon the eternal principle of the All Originating Life itself. And this is in strict accord with scientific method. If we had always allowed ourselves to be ruled by past experiences we should still be primitive savages; and it is only by gradual perception of underlying principles that we have attained the degree of civilization we have reached today; so what

THE TWO WITNESSES

Chapter 10
The Levels

the Bible puts before us is simply the application to the life in ourselves of the maxim that 'Principle is not limited to Precedent.'

Now the Bible Promises serve to put us on the track of this Principle; they suggest lines of enquiry. And the enquiry leads to the conclusion that the **two ultimate factors** are the Law and the Word. What we have missed hitherto is the conception of the limitless possibilities of the Law and the limitless **power** [Christ] of the Word. On one occasion the Master said to the Jews, 'Ye know not the Scriptures neither the **power** of God (Matt. 22:29), and the same is the case with ourselves.

The true 'Scripture' is the *scriptura rerum*, of **the Law indelibly written in the nature of things** and the written Scriptures are true only because they contain the statement of the Principle of the Law. Therefore until **we see** the Principle of the Law, we 'know not the Scriptures.' On the other hand, until we see the Principle of the operation of the Word **through** the Law, we do not know 'the Power of God;' and it is only as we come to **perceive the interaction** of the Law and the Word that we see the beginning of the way that leads to **life and liberty** (brackets and darkened emphasis, are mine).'

Mister Troward saw exactly what the scriptures were doing within themselves, for themselves, and by themselves. It is a world within a world, on paper, interacting with the universal laws of the operation of energy and matter from the micro to the macro, and vice versa. It is a true saying, 'the Lord our God, is one.'

While I'm at it let's throw in a page from Jeff Love on allegory, which is relative to what we've been reading. His book, if you want to jot it down, is called *The Quantum Gods*: 'The Origin and Nature of *Matter and Consciousness*.' First American paperback edition 1979 by Samuel Weiser, Inc. We'll look at the section entitled *'The Allegorical Level,"* Chapter 3, pages 55 and 56:

'The allegorical level of the Bible is a hidden description of a step by step process of personal spiritual evolution. To paraphrase Sam's (Samuel Bousky) statements, he say's that the whole allegorical story of the Bible is the development from Adam to

THE TWO WITNESSES

Chapter 10
The Levels

Christ of each individual human being. Adam is prototype Man, the animal nature. Christ is the God-Man, the divine nature. The Bible is a detailed story of that growth, its pitfalls, the direction it takes, and the guidance needed when taking the journey. **All the names in the Bible, especially those of the Old Testament, are codified personal names representing stages of consciousness.** All the **places in the Bible are conditions under which these states of consciousness exist**.

These states and conditions of consciousness refer to stages that each individual human being goes through in his or her personal growth. The Bible actually states that there is allegory in it. Paul says: 'For it is written that Abraham had two sons, one by a slave, one by a freed woman. He who was of the slave was born after the flesh. He of the free woman was by promise. **These things are an allegory**, for **these** are the two covenants, one from Mt. Sinai and one from Jerusalem (Galatians, 4.22-4).'

Let us see, then, what the allegory of Abraham and his two son's might also be saying: Abraham means **the state of faith or the beginning of spiritual growth**; Sarah, the name of the free woman indicates the state of bringing forth divine consciousness; Hagar, the slave woman, means consciousness of the material world or the façade of the personality; Sarah gives birth to Isaac which means the joyous dawning of the divine consciousness while Hagar gives birth to Ishmael which is the state of listening **inattentively**; Sinai refers to some moral code or law enforced on an individual **from the outside** while Jerusalem, a contraction of two Hebrew words - *yara*, which means outward flow, and *shalom* which means peace and harmony - indicates a natural out-flowing of a morality which comes from inner harmony. By introducing the allegorical meanings, we can see what Paul was probably saying: If you place all your faith in the façade of your materially oriented [or letter] personality you will only attain a limited awareness, one which requires a moral code to prevent you from being too destructive. If, however, you invest your faith in the bringing forth of your divine nature, you will experience a joyous

THE TWO WITNESSES

Chapter 10
The Levels

dawning of divine consciousness within you, one that requires no outside moral code, since you will be **in harmony with the universe**.'

"If you remember, we discussed this very scripture earlier. I forgot to add another verse to it; now would be a good time. Turn to Ezekiel chapter 33 and verse 23; 'Son of man, they that inhabit those wastes of the *land of Israel* [the carnal-minded], speak, saying, Abraham *was one*, and **he** inherited the [promise] land: **but we** [Abraham] **are many**; the land is given *us* for inheritance.' This tells us quite clearly, Abraham is made up of *many members* in particular, constituting one group or *body*.

"Before I found Christ in the scripture this was *one cross* to bear. What I mean is, it was *one beautiful contradiction*, the ***two*** Abrahams that is. The first Abraham of the letter *looks like* the scripture was talking about a human being called Abraham; the spiritual interpretation was saying Abraham was *anyone* who had faith in something greater than the law. Abraham looked for a city whose *builder* and maker is God.

Abraham was the father of *the faith* in the stories, which was of the flesh, *his* offspring was Ishmael, *one side* of the covenant, which is the letter. The other side of the covenant was Isaac, in whom was the seed of Christ, which is the New Testament in his blood, or the life of the truth; *these two* represent the Old *and* New Testament. Evidence for this is in John chapter eight if you would like to see it? It might take a few minutes."

"I'd love to see it," Deena remarked.

"Okay, turn to John chapter eight and we'll start with verse 31 and wind our way down to verse 56. 'Then said Jesus to *those* Jews which believed on him, If ye continue in **my** word, *then* are ye my disciples indeed; And ye shall know the truth, and the truth shall make you free.... They answered him, **We be Abraham's seed**, and were never in bondage to any man: how sayest thou, Ye shall be made free? Jesus answered them, Verily, verily, I say unto you, Whosoever committeth *sin* is the servant of sin [the Law]. And the servant abideth not in the house for ever: *but* the Son abideth

THE TWO WITNESSES

Chapter 10
The Levels

ever.... If the Son therefore shall make you free, ye shall be free [from the law] indeed. **I know that ye are Abraham's seed** [*remember* this statement]; but ye seek to kill me, because **my** word hath no place in you. I speak that which I have seen with my Father: and ye do that which ye have seen with **your father**.... They answered and said unto him, **Abraham *is our father*.** Jesus saith unto them, If ye were Abraham's children, ye would do the works of Abraham [He just said they were Abraham's *seed*]. But now ye seek to kill me, a man that hath told you the truth, which I have heard of God: this did not Abraham. Ye do the deeds of your father. Then said they to him, We be not born of fornication; we have one Father, *even* God.... Jesus said unto them, If God were your Father, ye would love me: for I proceeded forth and came from God; neither came I of myself, but he sent me.

Why do ye not understand my speech? *even* because ye cannot hear **my** word. ***Ye are of your father the devil***, and the lusts of ***your father*** ye will do. He was a murderer from the beginning, and *abode not* in the truth, because there is no truth in him. When he speaketh a lie, he speaketh of his own: for he is a liar, and the father of it [He's talking about the Jews He just called Abraham's seed].... And because I tell *you* the truth, ye believe me not. Which of you convinceth me of sin? And if I say the truth, why do ye not believe me? He that is of God heareth God's words: ye therefore hear *them* not, because ye are not of God. Then answered the Jews, and said unto him, Say we not well that thou art a Samaritan, and hast a devil?... Jesus answered, I have not a devil; but I honour my Father, and ye do dishonour me. And I seek not mine own glory: there is one that seeketh and judgeth. Verily, verily, I say unto you, If a **man** keep my saying, he shall never see death [the law]. Then said the Jews unto him, Now we know that thou hast a devil. Abraham is dead, and the prophets; and thou sayest, If a man keep my saying, he shall never **taste** of death.... Art thou greater than ***our father Abraham*, *which is dead*** [God is not the god of the dead]? and the prophets are dead: whom makest thou thyself? Jesus answered, If I honour myself, my honour is

THE TWO WITNESSES
Chapter 10
The Levels

nothing: it is my Father that honoureth me; of whom ye say, that he is your God: Yet ye have not known him; but I know him: and if I should say, I know him not, I shall be *a liar like unto you*: but I know him, and keep his saying. <u>**Your father**</u> Abraham rejoiced to see my day [the father of lies?]: and he saw *it*, and was glad.'

That was very plain! He called *their* Father Abraham. And back in verse 44 He said **their Father was the devil**. Beautiful! All through the conversation *it was* the **two** Abrahams that were being discussed. The one of the letter, which is dead or of the law, and the one of the spirit which is alive.

Let me throw in just a few more to highlight the issue. Keep in mind, the *two sons* are the *two covenants*. Look at Romans 4 and verse 13: 'For the promise, that he should be the heir of the world, ***was not*** to Abraham, ***or to his seed, through the law***, [which is dead] but through the righteousness of faith [in Christ].' Galatians 3 and verse 29; 'And **if ye be Christ's** [not of the law], ***then*** are ye Abraham's seed, and heirs according to the promise.' Romans nine verses seven and eight: 'Neither, because they are the seed of Abraham, *are they* all children: but, In Isaac [not Ishmael, the Law] shall thy seed be called. That is, **They which are the children of the flesh, these *are* not the children of God**: but the children of the promise [the Spirit] **are counted for the seed**.' Romans four and verse one: 'What shall we say then that Abraham our father, **as pertaining to *the flesh***, hath found?' I'm going to leave that question for you to play with; even though I believe you understand it by now."

"You know, James," said Deena, "this place we live in, *really is* just a school - master, and eventually all *who try* will make it, won't they?"

"Yes, Deena, all who try," James assured. "That reminds me of a story I copied from another book which would be appropriate right now. Let me read it for you. It's called Why: an Allegory, It's anonymous, so I really don't know where it came from, but I thought it was *food for thought*. Anyway it goes like this:

'I leaned from the low-hung crescent moon and grasping

THE TWO WITNESSES

Chapter 10
The Levels

the west pointing horn of it, looked down. Against the other horn reclined, motionless, a Shining One, and looked at me, and I was unafraid. Below me the hills and valleys were thick with humans, and the moon swung low that I might see what they did.

"Who are they?" I asked the Shining One. For I was unafraid. And the Shining One made answer: "They are the Sons of God and the Daughters of God." I looked again, and saw that they beat and trampled each other. Sometime they seemed not to know that the fellow - creature they pushed from their path fell under their feet. But sometimes they looked as he fell and kicked him brutally.

And I said to the Shining One: "Are they ALL the Sons and Daughters of God?"
And the Shining One said: "ALL."

As I leaned and watched them, it grew clear to me that each was frantically seeking something, and it was because they sought what they sought with such singleness of purpose that they were so inhuman to all who hindered them.

And I said to the Shining One: "What do they seek?"
And the Shining One made answer: "Happiness."
"Are they all seeking Happiness?"
"ALL."
"Have any of them found it?"
"None of *those* have found it."
"Do they ever think they have found it?"
"Sometimes they think they have found it."

My eyes filled, for at that moment I caught a glimpse of a woman with a babe at her breast, and I saw the babe torn from her and the woman cast into a deep pit by a man with his eyes fixed on a shining lump that he believed to be (or perchance to contain, I know not) Happiness.

And I turned to the Shining One, my eyes blinded.
"Will they ever find it?"
And he said: "They will find it."
"All of them?"

THE TWO WITNESSES

Chapter 10
The Levels

"All of them."
"Those who are trampled?"
"Those who are trampled."
"And those who trample?"
"And those who trample."

I looked again, a long time, at what they were doing on the hills and the valleys, and again my eyes went blind with tears, and I sobbed out to the Shining One:

"Is it God's will, or the work of the Devil, that *men* seek Happiness?"

"It's God's will."

"And it looks so like the work of the Devil!" The Shining One smiled inscrutably.

"It does look like the work of the Devil."

When I had looked a little longer, I cried out, protesting: Why has he put them down there to seek Happiness and to cause each other such immeasurable misery?"

Again the Shining One smiled inscrutably: "They are learning."

"What are they learning?"

"They are learning life. And they are learning love."

I said nothing. One man in the herd below held me breathless, fascinated. He walked proudly, and others ran and laid the bound, struggling bodies of living men before him that he might tread upon them and never touch foot to earth. But suddenly a whirlwind seized him and tore his purple from him and set him down, naked among strangers. And they fell upon him and maltreated him sorely.

I clapped my hands.

"Good! Good!" I cried, exultantly. "He got what he deserved."

Then I looked up suddenly, and saw again the inscrutable smile of the Shining One.

And the Shining One spoke quietly.

"They all get what they deserve."

THE TWO WITNESSES

Chapter 10
The Levels

"And no worse?"

"And no worse."

"And no better?"

"**How can there be any better?** They each deserve whatever shall teach them the true way to Happiness."

I was silenced.

And still the people went on seeking, and trampling each other in their eagerness to find. And I perceived what I had not fully grasped before, that the whirlwind caught them up from time to time and set them down elsewhere to continue the Search.

And I said to the Shining One: "Does the whirlwind always set them down again on these hills and in these valleys?"

And the Shining One made answer: "Not always on these hills and in these valleys."

"Where then?"

"Look above you."

And I looked up. Above me stretched the Milky Way and gleamed the stars.

And I breathed "Oh" and fell silent, awed by what was given to me to comprehend.

Below me they still trampled each other.

And I asked the Shining One.

" But no matter where the whirlwind sets them down, they go on seeking Happiness?"

"They go on seeking Happiness."

"And the whirlwind makes no mistakes?"

"The whirlwind makes no mistakes."

"It's puts them sooner or later, where they will get what they deserve?"

"It puts them sooner or later where they will get what they deserve."

Then the load crushing my heart lightened, and I found I could look at the brutal cruelties that went on below me with pity for the cruel. And the longer I looked the stronger the compassion grew.

THE TWO WITNESSES

Chapter 10
The Levels

And I said to the Shining One:
"They act like men goaded."
"They are goaded."
"What goads them?"
"The name of the goad is desire."

Then, when I had looked a little longer, I cried out passionately: "**Desire is an evil thing**."

But the face of the Shining One grew stern and his voice rang out, dismaying me.

"**Desire is not an evil thing.**"

I trembled, and thought withdrew herself into the innermost chamber of my heart. Till at last I said: "It is desire that nerves men on to learn the lessons that God has set."

"It is desire that nerves them."
"The lessons of life and love?"
"The lessons of life and love!"

Then I could no longer see that they were cruel. I could only see that they were learning. I watched them with deep love and compassion, as one by one the whirlwind carried them out of sight.'

"That's just perfect! That's exactly the feelings I had before you read it!" Deena said joyfully. "That's *really* what it's all about. We're *all* trying to find *our* happiness, and in this case, happiness would be the truth; we just lost the direction for a while."

"Really, Deena," said James. "We lost our direction for sure. But as they say, that was *then*, this is *now*. Actually, it is always now. Before I forget I want to give you the names of a few more books you might want to read after you've studied and researched the things *we've* talked about. It would take us months, the way we're doing it, just to read excerpts from all the books that will witness to you the *physics side* of the scriptures. But after you fully comprehend all the things we've discussed, then you can read these books and understand that the Bible and theoretical physics are saying the same thing.

I guess the first one is Looking Glass Universe: *The Emerging Science of Wholeness*, by John P. Briggs, Ph.D. and F

THE TWO WITNESSES

Chapter 10
The Levels

David Peat, Ph.D. [Published by, Cornerstone Library - Simon & Shuster, Inc. New York. Copyright 1984.] And second would be *God And The New Physics*, by Paul Davies, [a Touchstone Book published by Simon & Shuster, Inc. New York. Copyright 1983 by Paul Davies.] The one after that is *The Mind of God* by the same author and publisher.

Fourth is *Beyond The Quantum*, by Michael Talbot, [a Bantam Book / published by arrangement with Macmillan publishing company. Copyright 1986 by Michael Talbot.]

Number five would be *The Great Pyramid Decoded* by Peter Lemesurier. [Published by Avon Books, a division of The Hearst Corporation, by arrangement with St. Martin's Press. Copyright 1977 by Peter Lemesurier.]

And let's not forget the father of philosophy, Pythagoras. The book's title is, *The Life of Pythagoras, with his Symbols and Golden Verses*. [First printed in London, 1707. This facsimile reproduction of the 1707 edition published in 1981 by Samuel Weiser, Inc.]

Some real treasures are in the *Apocrypha's*. I have volumes one and two by Edgar Hennecke and edited by Wilhelm Schneemelcher. [English translation edited by R. McL. Wilson. First published in Great Britain 1963 by The West minister Press. Copyright 1959 J.C.B.Mohr (Paul Siebeck), Tübingen. English translation copyright 1963 Lutterworth Press.]

Now, top those off with *The Nag Hammadi Library* , James M Robinson, General Editor. [Published in San Francisco by Harper & Row, Publishers.]

Well, that should be enough for now. I have about a hundred more when you're through with those. However these are quite ample enough for you to see the transfigurations of all you read to come forth in *one* understanding. All things will be revealed to you if you remain with *grace*."

"What do you mean, 'remain with grace'?" Deena questioned.

"Haven't we covered grace yet? I get off on so many

THE TWO WITNESSES

Chapter 10
The Levels

tangents, I sometimes forget *what* we've covered," James replied. "Grace is that part, or I should say attitude, that is interwoven in the Word which causes us to keep going. It's sort of like a cattle prod. It spiritually eggs you on to find answers to your questions. It is a *positive aggravation*; it won't let you rest until you find *that which you seek*. And when you have found *it*, you found *it* because of *grace*. Hence, you are saved by grace. I'm sure you can relate to that; I'm a witness; I see it working in all of us, that's why we're together doing what we're doing.

You are now on the path, you are now in the arms of eternal life. Never having to die *or* to be carnal-minded again; once saved always saved. Which brings me to the part that I must now tell each of you. I see now, its time for us to move on. Your creator, and mine, has brought us to a place in our lives where we must go out into the world and share with others the revelations that have been given to us."

"I don't think I'm quite ready for *that* just yet, James," said Bob. It will be a while before I'm ready to explain what I've seen."

"Bob, just sharing and explaining how you've come to understand what you *do see* is all you need to start with, the rest comes as you learn. Just never let your imagination get involved with the proven facts, this is called the 'fear of the Lord. And as it says in Acts three and verse six, 'Then Peter said, Silver and gold have I none; but **such as I have** give I thee.' That's *all* that's required: such *as* we have. And as we give, we receive. That goes for all. That's what our creator wants us to do; go to the hearts of men, and try to find reason and take away the fear of the cross that they all may come to the cross and see the image is no longer there, and that he **is** lifted up from the *earth*. And you, Deena, you have a precious little heart, and I can see your love for righteousness. You will attract the mental DNA of all those like-minded. You, Bob, Tony, Cindy, Martie, and I, have just begun. For, as in the scriptures, 'we are just people in this book.' We will live and have our being in the hearts of those who study it. May we all have a beautiful and wonderful experience. And truly, if the world *could*

THE TWO WITNESSES

Chapter 10
The Levels

see what we have seen, it would become one people in love. A new heaven and a new earth, in truth and in righteousness. The *new* Jerusalem, the planet of brotherhood, peace and joy, meet for the master's - *hand*.